Using Flash 5

Other Computer Titles

by

Robert Penfold

BP450 How to Expand and Upgrade Your PC
BP467 How to Interface PCs
BP470 Linux for Windows users
BP479 How to Build Your Own PC
BP484 Easy PC Troubleshooting
BP495 Easy Windows Troubleshooting
BP503 Using Dreamweaver 4

Other Titles of Interest

BP433 Your Own Web Site on the Internet
BP483 Fun Web Pages with JavaScript
BP494 Basic Internet Skills
BP490 Web Pages Using Microsoft Office 2000
BP404 How to Create Pages for the Web Using HTML
BP501 XHTML and CSS Explained
BP453 How to Search the World Wide Web Efficiently
BP403 The Internet and World Wide Web Explained
BP464 E-Mail and News with Outlook Express
BP420 E-Mail on the Internet
BP477 Using Microsoft FrontPage 2000
BP461 Using FrontPage 98
BP488 Internet Explorer 5 Explained
BP460 Using Microsoft Explorer 4 on the Internet
BP507 Easy Internet Troubleshooting

Using Flash 5

R. A. Penfold

Bernard Babani (publishing) Ltd
The Grampians
Shepherds Bush Road
London W6 7NF
England
www.babanibooks.com

Please note

Although every care has been taken with the production of this book to ensure that any projects, designs, modifications, and/or programs, etc., contained herewith, operate in a correct and safe manner and also that any components specified are normally available in Great Britain, the Publisher and Author do not accept responsibility in any way for the failure (including fault in design) of any projects, design, modification, or program to work correctly or to cause damage to any equipment that it may be connected to or used in conjunction with, or in respect of any other damage or injury that may be caused, nor do the Publishers accept responsibility in any way for the failure to obtain specified components.

Notice is also given that if any equipment that is still under warranty is modified in any way or used or connected with home-built equipment then that warranty may be void.

First Published - June 2001

British Library Cataloguing in Publication Data

A catalogue record for this book is available from the British Library

ISBN 0 85934 504 1

Cover Design by Gregor Arthur

Printed and bound in Great Britain by Cox & Wyman

Preface

Flash is a program that has rapidly grown in popularity in recent years and Flash graphics are now a standard part of the Internet. You do not have to surf the Internet for too long in order to encounter some sites that feature animated text, characters, or whatever, produced using Flash. I wish I could say that with Flash it is possible to produce highly sophisticated Web pages having animated graphics and interactivity, with no artistic talent and little learning required. In truth, both artistic talent and a considerable amount of learning time are required in order to exploit Flash's capabilities to the full.

However, this is not to say that Flash is only suitable for accomplished artists who have the time and ability to learn all the "in and outs" of the program. Learning to produce animated text and simple interactivity is relatively quick and painless. Although you do not have to be an artistic genius in order to produce the artwork for Flash animations, it would certainly be an advantage. Fortunately, there is no shortage of clipart available free or at low cost, and this provides an easy way of producing professional looking results for those who are "artistically challenged". Also, although Flash is not primarily designed for use with bitmaps, it can import them. This enables digital photographs to be imported and used as a backgrounds for animations. You can even get Flash to trace bitmaps and turn them into vector graphics so that they can be animated in exactly the same way as objects drawn using Flash.

Flash is available in a Windows PC version and for Macintosh computers. The PC version was used in the production of this book, but in use there is very little difference between the two. The differences are mainly brought about by the use of different conventions in the way the two types of computer are used, and by differences in the nomenclature used in menus. Provided you are reasonably fluent in the use of a Macintosh computer you should have little difficulty following the methods described in this book. Even if you use the PC version you will still need to know the fundamentals of using the computer, but with either version you do not need to be a computer expert. No previous experience with Flash, graphics software, or of web design is required to use this book. It seems reasonable to assume that anyone learning to use Flash is familiar with using web sites and knows a few Internet basics. This book can be used on its own to learn about Flash, but it is strongly recommended that it is used in conjunction with the program itself. The only way to learn about any creative software is to try it out, follow a few examples, and then try some ideas of your own. PC and Macintosh demonstration programs can be downloaded from the Macromedia web site (www.macromedia.com), and these are fully operational for 30 days. About an hour or so per day for half that period should be sufficient to become reasonably skilled in using Flash.

Robert Penfold

Trademarks

Contents

1

Getting started 1

2

Menus 21

4

Editing and panels 121

5

Layers and tweening 181

1

Getting started

Fundamentals

In many ways Flash is like an ordinary drawing program such as Corel Draw! or Adobe Illustrator. Anyone who has used one of these illustration style drawing programs should have little difficulty in getting to grips with producing basic pictures using Flash. Of course, Flash differs from these other programs in that it is designed specifically for the production of animations for use in web sites. Actually, it produces animations that can be used for other purposes, such as educational material supplied on CD-ROM. The current version can also be used to produce complete web sites. Here we will concentrate on its use as a web design tool. Whatever the final method of delivery, the methods used to make the animations are much the same. A less well known aspect of Flash is that it can add interactivity to a web site, and this ability is no less useful than its animation capabilities.

Such is the popularity of Flash these days that you have probably encountered many web sites that utilize its capabilities in one way or another, but you may not always have been aware that Flash was being used. Sometimes it is obvious because two versions of the site are provided. These are the so-called "Flashed" and "Non-Flashed" versions. The one that makes extensive use of Flash is generally slower in operation, but is livelier due to its use of Flash animations, etc. In other cases there is only one version of the site with more limited use of Flash, and you may be unaware of its presence. The easiest way to check out some well designed Flash sites is to go to the Macromedia web site and follow the links to model Flash sites. These will give a good idea of the types of thing that can be achieved using this program.

If you visit some Flashed web sites you should notice that the sites download quite quickly. Yes, they take longer than an equivalent text-only site or one using a few simple images, but considering the facilities provided the download times are remarkably short. The animations should also be quite smooth, with no huge jumps from one frame to another or the picture breaking up. Whether you use a large window for

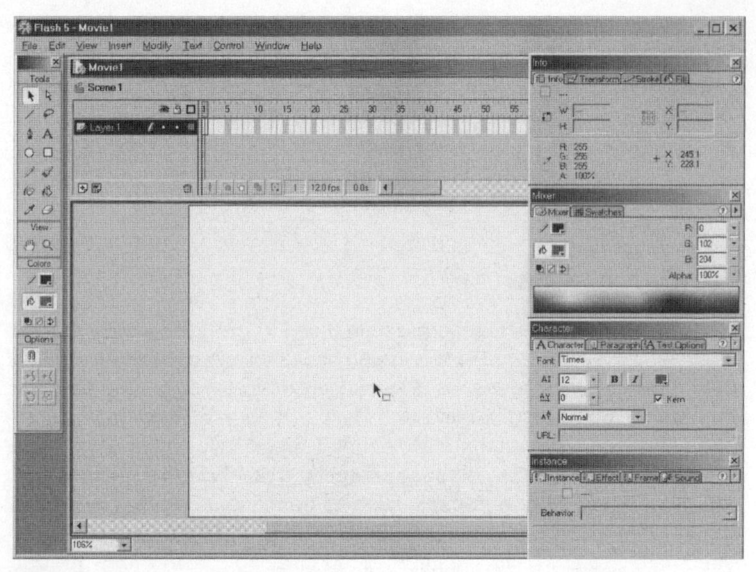

Fig.1.1 A number of windows are open when Flash is first run

the browser or a small one, the animations should still look good. It would be stretching the truth to say that none of this could be achieved via other means such as JavaScript, but it can be accomplished more easily using Flash and the final result should operate very reliably.

First steps

Ideally you would start by learning about the Flash user interface and some background information about the program and the techniques it uses. Being realistic about matters, most people are eager to go "in at the deep end" and try out a simple animation straight away. Accordingly, we will do a couple of simple demonstrations to get things underway, but it is only fair to point out that it will then be necessary to go back and do some further work before really getting to grips with the possibilities provided by Flash. It is assumed here that you have Flash installed and running on your computer.

Note that you do not have to buy the program in order to try it out. A demonstration version is available from the Macromedia web site, and although at over 19 megabytes it will take some time to download using a 56k modem, it is well worth the effort. The demonstration version of the program is also to be found occasionally on the cover discs of computer magazines. The demonstration version is fully operational incidentally, and any work you produce using it can be saved to disc. The demonstration program will only work for 30 days after installation, but this is more than adequate to learn how to use the program and to decide whether or not it suits your requirements.

Once the program is up and running you should have a screen that looks like Figure 1.1. For the moment we are not concerned with the various windows down the right-hand side of the screen. You can close these by left clicking on the crosses in the top right-hand corners of the windows so as to maximise the screen space for the windows we will be using, but this is by no means essential. A small screen area is sufficient for some simple demonstrations and experiments.

The lower middle section of the screen is the drawing area where the animations, etc., are drawn. This drawing area is also known as the "stage" in Flash terminology. The toolbox to the left of the stage provides the means of drawing the objects to be animated, drawing backgrounds, and adding text. There are also some editing tools here. Many of these tools will look familiar to anyone conversant with drawing programs, but we will not assume any previous experience of graphics software here.

Fig.1.2 Most Flash buttons can produce hints

In order to do a very basic animation you must add at least one graphics object to the main drawing area. The tool represented by a diagonal line icon in the toolbox is, as one would expect, for drawing lines. To draw a line, first left-click on this icon to select the Line tool. Then, with the pointer in the drawing area, hold down the left mouse button and drag a line of the desired length in

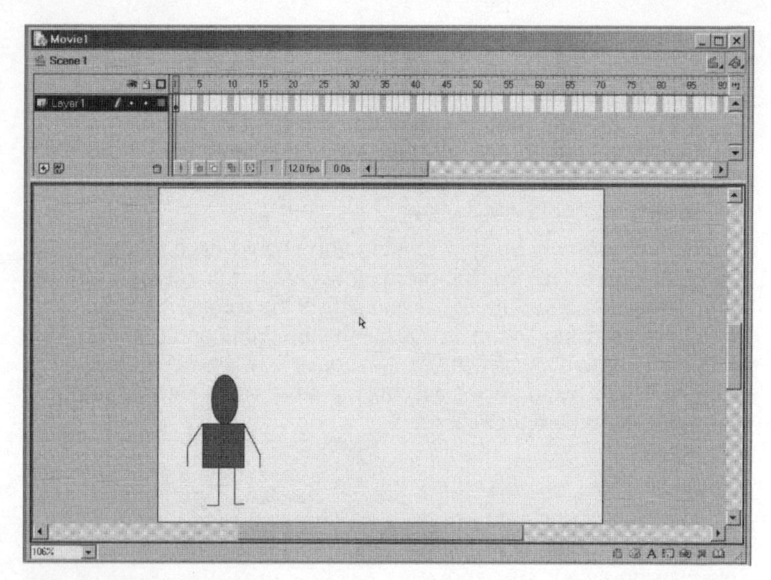

Fig.1.3 The simple figure used for the motion tweening demonstration

the required direction. Having produced the line, release the mouse button and the line will be placed on the screen. By default a snap-grid will be in action, and this limit the resolution with which lines can be drawn. On the other hand, it makes it easy to draw lines that are precisely horizontal or vertical.

The same dragging method can be used to draw circles and ellipses using the tool having the "O" shaped icon, and to draw rectangles or squares using the tool having the square icon. If you place the cursor over one of the icons a hint (a label) showing its function will pop up (Figure 1.2). The letter in parentheses indicates the key of the keyboard that provides a shortcut to selecting the tool. A single object is sufficient to try the most basic of animations, but I would suggest adding a few objects to make it more interesting. I used the very basic figure representation of Figure 1.3. Since we are not using the editing tools at this stage there is probably no point in trying to do anything very artistic unless you are an expert in minimalism. The usual Undo option is available under the Edit menu, so it is easy to remove the last object placed on the screen if it is definitely not what you required.

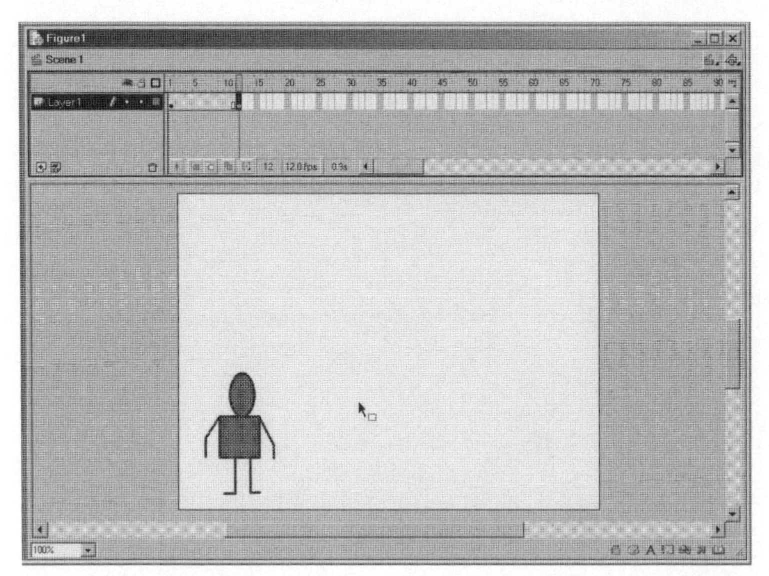

Fig.1.4 The appearance of objects changes when they are selected

Timeline

In the top part of the screen below the menu there is a window that contains the Timeline. Towards the top of this window there are small rectangles with every fifth one shaded in and numbered. These represent the frames of the animation, and are used to select the required frame. A black dot is placed in frames that contain something, and so far only one frame (the first one) does actually contain anything. Only a limited number of frames can be shown on the visible section of the Timeline, but the horizontal scrollbar at the bottom of the window can be used to scroll it in order to bring the required frame into view. This will not be necessary with the simple examples used in this chapter, but you may like to try scrolling the Timeline backwards and forwards anyway.

Here we will settle for an animation of about one second in duration, and the default frame rate is 12 per second, as shown on the status bar at the bottom of the Timeline window. Left-click on frame 12 and then select Keyframe from the Insert menu, or press function key F6 to insert the keyframe. The objects you added are still present, but they have a slightly different appearance because they are selected. Any filled objects will have a hatched appearance for example (Figure 1.4). Select the

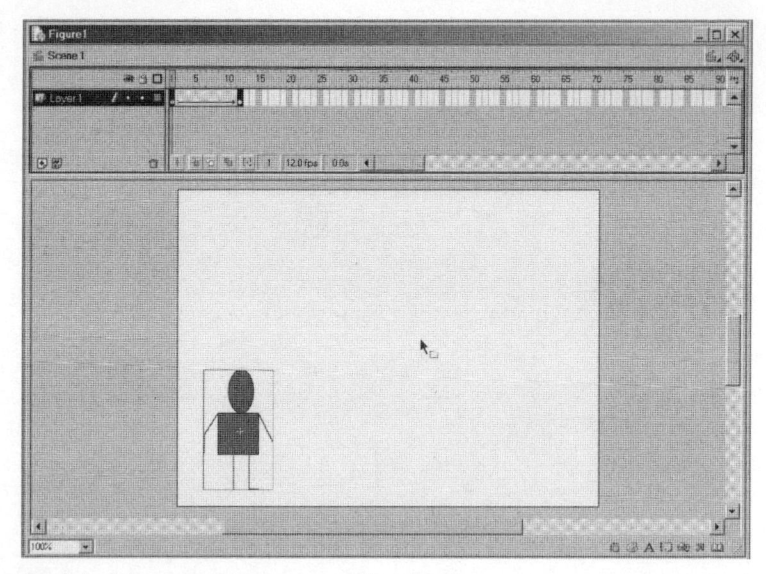

Fig.1.5 A frame appears around the objects

Arrow tool (the one in the top left-hand corner of the toolbox) and then drag the objects to a new position on the screen. You will notice that there is a red marker mixed in with the calibration numbers of the Timeline. This is called the "play head", and it can be dragged to any of the frames in our 12-frame sequence. If you try this you will find that the objects stay in their original positions until frame 12 when they jump to the new position. In other words, the objects have not just been copied into frame 12, but they have been copied into the frames between 1 and 12 as well. However, they have only been moved in frame 12.

Motion tweening

In order to do a very basic form of animation it is not necessary to manually change frames 2 to 11. Flash can work out the in-between frames for you. First select the frames to be used by left clicking on frame 1 in the Timeline, followed by left clicking on frame 12 while holding down the Shift key. From the Insert menu select the Create Motion Tween option. The section of the Timeline for frames 1 to 12 will then change to a blue-violet colour, and an arrow is drawn through these frames. A frame is also drawn around the objects that you placed on the screen

Figs.1.6(a) and 1.6(b) The first two frames of the simple animation

Figs. 1.6(c) and 1.6(d) Frames 3 and 4 of the simple animation

(Figure 1.5), which have been grouped. In order to run your animation either select Play from the Control menu or press the Enter (Return) key. The objects on the screen should then move from their original positions to the positions used in frame 12. To run the animation again just press Enter again or select Play from the Control menu.

With a frame rate of 12 per second and a lot of movement from one frame to the next the animation will be less than convincing. However, it will clearly show how the animation process functions with the objects being steadily moved across the screen frame by frame. Figures 1.6(a) to 1.6(d) show the first four frames of the test animation I produced, and the change from one frame to the next is fairly obvious. Try moving the objects in frame 12 to give smaller and greater offsets from the starting position, running the animation a few times after each change. The smaller the offset used the more convincing the animation should be.

The general process of giving the computer the first and last frames and getting it to work out what goes in between is known as tweening. In

Fig.1.7 The Save As dialogue box offers the standard features

our simple example there is no change from one frame to the next other than objects changing position. This is called motion tweening. This method obviously has its limitations. For example, in this simple example the figure moves across the screen, but there is no movement of the arms or legs. Instead, the figure simply glides across the screen. This simple method of animation can still be very useful though, and it can be quite effective in the right context.

Shape tweening

Flash supports another type of tweening known as shape tweening. As its name suggests, this changes one shape into another shape, rather like morphing. In order to try shape tweening start with a new movie. If you wish to save your first efforts select Save or Save As from the File menu to bring up the usual file browser (Figure 1.7). Either way you will actually get the Save As version since the movie has no name as yet. By default the animations you produce will be named Movie1, Movie2, etc., but the File Name field can be edited to give them more appropriate names. The buttons at the top of the window provide the usual facilities to move to the required directory and create a new one if necessary. Having selected the required name and directory, operate the Save button and the file will then be saved to disc with a “fla” extension.

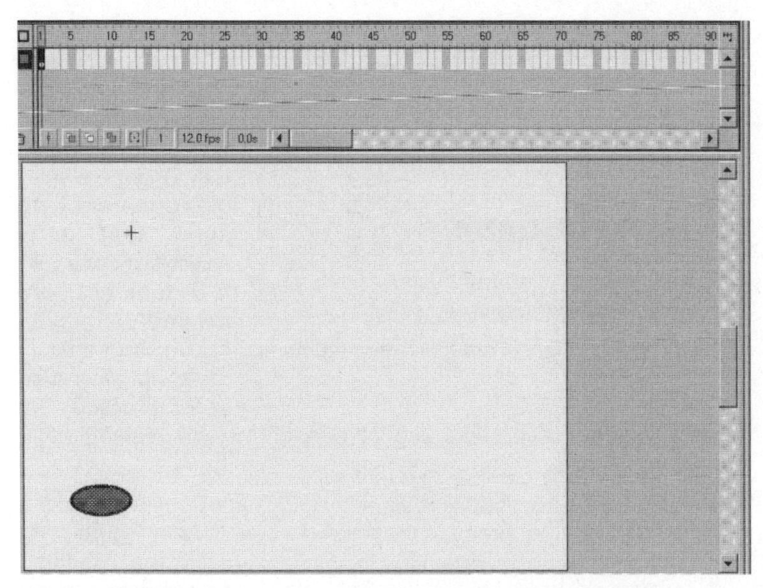

Fig.1.8 The beginnings of the animation using shape tweening

Note that there are two types of Flash file. The ones having the "fla" extension are the ones that can be loaded into Flash and edited. Files with a "swf" extension are the ones that are generated for use in web sites, etc. Next select the Close option from File menu to clear away the first movie. If necessary, choose New from the File menu to bring up a new drawing area, etc., and you are then ready to start on the new animation.

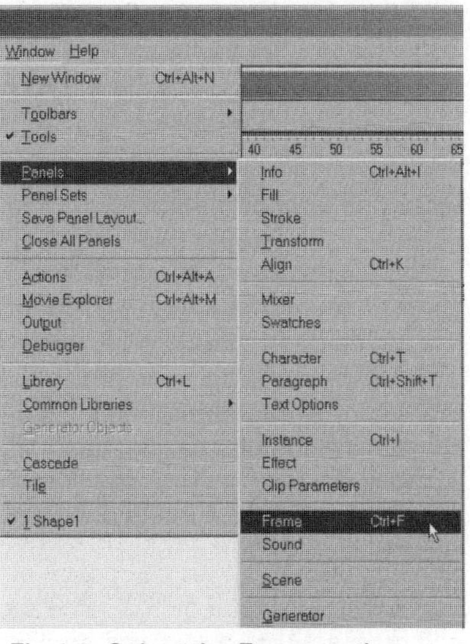

Fig.1.9 Select the Frame option from the submenu

First we need to create our starting object, and I placed a horizontal ellipse near the bottom left-hand corner of the screen. Having created the

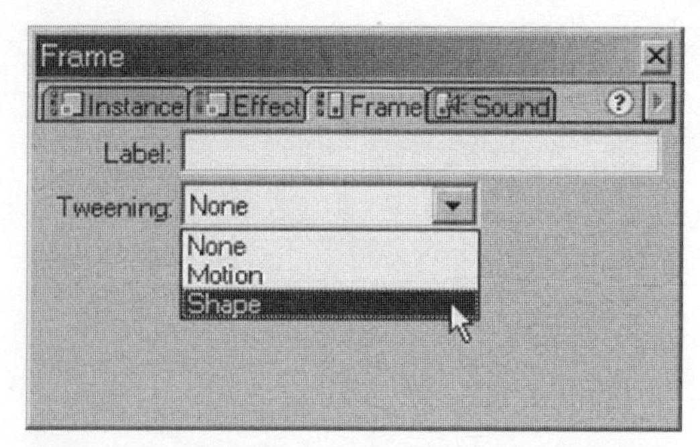

Fig.1.10 Select Shape from the Tweening menu

object, left-click on the current frame (frame 1) on the Timeline. The object you created should then change slightly in appearance to show that it is selected (Figure 1.8). If it does not, you probably clicked above the frame in the calibration area of the Timeline. Try again, this time making sure you left-click on the little rectangle that represents frame 1.

Now select Panels from the Window menu and Frame from the submenu (Figure 1.9). This will produce the small dialogue box of Figure 1.10. From the Tweening pop-down menu select the Shape option, which will produce a couple of additions to the dialogue box. The Easing setting controls the rate of change between frames, and you can type in a value or left-click on the downward pointing arrowhead to produce a scrollbar (Figure 1.11). A positive value results in a rapid change initially and a slower rate of change as the animation progresses. A negative value has the opposite effect with things starting slowly and accelerating towards the end. A value of zero gives a constant rate of change.

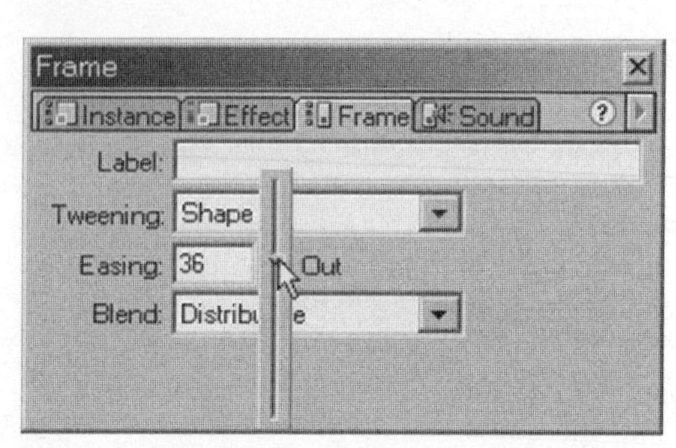

Fig.1.11 The Easing value can be adjusted using a slider control

There are two Blend options available, and the default is Distributive. This gives less jagged but less regular intermediate shapes. The Angular option tries to preserve straight lines and angles in the intermediate

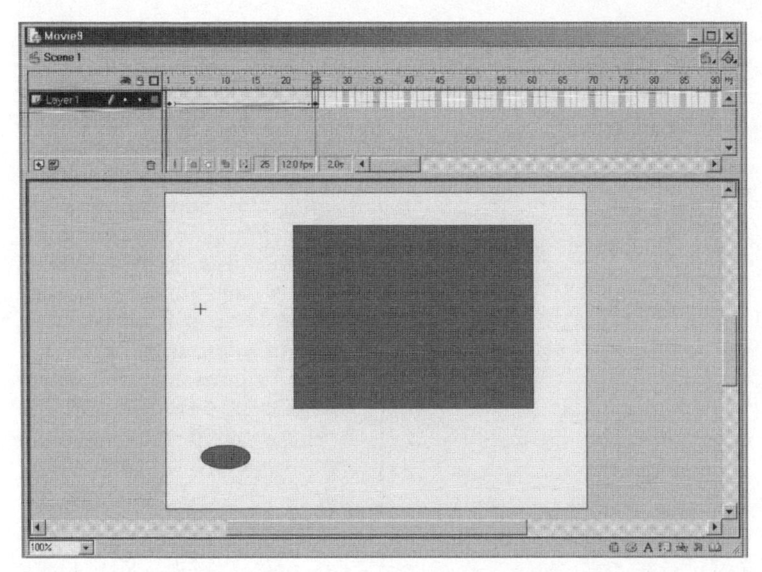

Fig.1.12 The ellipse with be shape tweened into the rectangle

shapes. Of course, this setting is only appropriate to shapes that have straight lines and angles, and Distributive blending will be used for inappropriate shapes. For testing purposes the Easing and Blend options are not too important, so use whatever settings you like or just leave the defaults. When you have finished, close the dialogue box by left clicking on the "X" in the top left-hand corner of the window.

Next select what will be the final frame in the animation, say frame 25, and select Keyframe from the Insert menu. Frames 1 to 25 will be coloured pale green and there will be an arrow through them to indicate that they are used for tweening. Position, colour, and shape can all be tweened, but for the present just settle for a new shape that can be anywhere in the drawing area that takes your fancy. I placed a large horizontal rectangle in the top right-hand corner of the screen (Figure 1.12). The new animation is then ready for testing and pressing the Enter key will run it. The second shape should grow from the original shape. Figures 1.13 to 1.16 show frames 2, 4, 10, and 20, and the way in which the transformation progresses can be clearly seen from these.

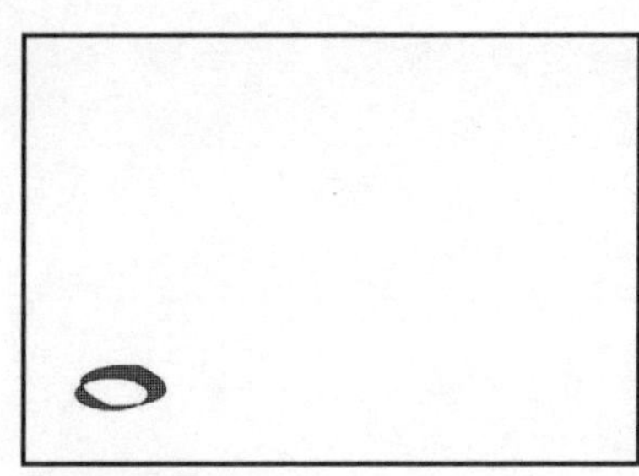

Fig.1.13 Frame 2

Fig.1.14 Frame 4

Fig.1.15 Frame 10

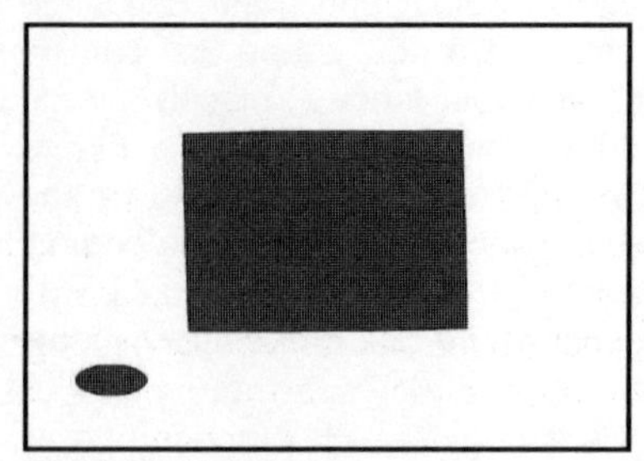

Fig.1.16 Frame 20

Frame by frame

Of course, you do not have to use tweening to produce animations using Flash, and it can be done the hard way if preferred. In other words, you can produce the animation manually on a frame-by-frame basis. In most cases it is not a matter of drawing each frame from scratch, but is more a case of altering the previous frame to generate the current one. Moving on to the next frame and choosing the Keyframe option from the Insert menu copies everything from the current frame to the new one so that the required modifications can be made. Use the Blank Keyframe option of the Insert menu to start "from scratch" with the new frame. Either way, this tends to be a relatively slow and painstaking approach. Its obvious advantage is that it provides complete freedom, and anything is possible using frame-by-frame animation.

I would certainly suggest you spend some time experimenting with this method once you have mastered the Flash editing tools. As an initial experiment to try out the frame-by-frame approach, start with a blank movie and place a shape or some shapes in frame 1 and then select Keyframe from the Insert menu or press function key F6. Select frame 2, move the objects slightly, use the menu to insert a key frame or press F6,

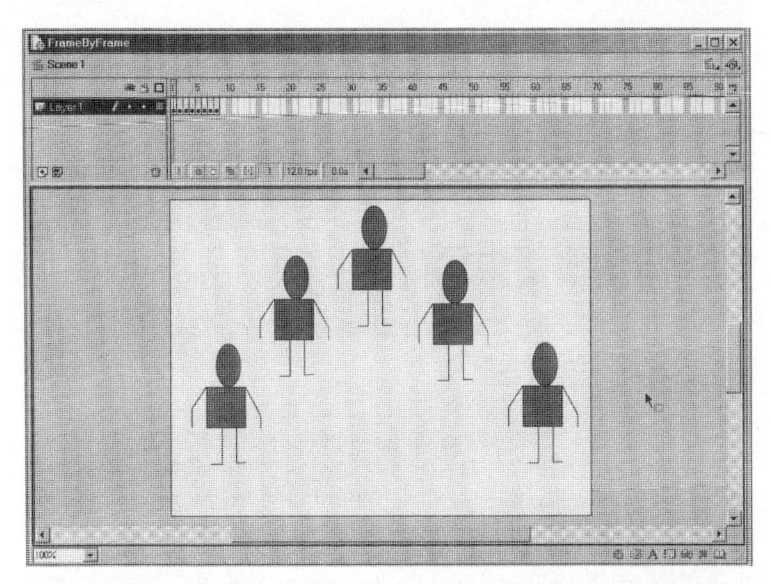

Fig.1.17 Frame by frame animation was used to make the figure jump

move on to frame 3, move the objects slightly again, and so on. Once you have put together a reasonable number of frames try pressing the Enter key to run the movie.

This gives a form of animation that is similar to motion tweening, but it is more versatile in that the objects do not have to go straight from point "A" to point "B". Figure 1.17 shows a composite version of five frames from my little frame-by-frame animation, and the figure has been made to jump up in the air and back to the ground while also moving forwards. The figure could also be rotated as it moved so that it did a somersault, it could be made to throw a ball, or anything else that you like.

Player

We have only "scratched the surface" here, but by trying out these three types of animation you should start to get the idea of the way in which Flash is used to produce animations. In order to play Flash movies it is necessary for users to have the correct player program, but a very high percentage of Internet users are equipped to run Flash movies. Recent versions of the most popular browsers are supplied complete with the necessary player software, which can also be downloaded free of charge from the Macromedia web site. Player programs are also supplied with Flash.

It is worth mentioning that Flash can also export animations in other formats, including the GIF type that is very popular for web use. However, bear in mind that a GIF version of an animation is likely to be several times larger than the standard Flash version, and download times will be increased accordingly. For a list of exportable file types, select the Export option from the File menu and then activate the Save as Type menu.

Line art

If you have experience with programs such as PhotoShop and Photo Paint Pro, it is important to realise that there is a fundamental difference between these programs and a program like Flash. Photo-editing programs are primarily designed to operate with images in bitmap form. In other words, the image is formed from thousands or even millions of dots of different colours. The dots are called pixels, and this method is the one used to produce the picture on the screen of a monitor.

Programs such as Corel Draw! and Adobe Illustrator, like Flash, are line art programs where the image is comprised of so-called graphics primitives or just primitives. These are lines, circles, etc., plus fill colours, patterns, etc. Objects are usually stored in the computer's memory using a co-ordinate system, and a straight line would be stored as a line from one co-ordinate to another, plus additional information such as its width, colour, and style (solid, dashed, etc.).

Line art, which is also know as "vector graphics", does not lend itself well to all types of image. In particular, it is not well suited to colour photographic images, which in most cases do not readily boil down into primitive objects, colour fills, and so on. Line art is well suited to charts, diagrams, cartoons, or anything of these general types. An advantage of line art in many applications is that the file sizes tend to be relatively small. With a really complex image the file size might actually go into the realm of megabytes, but in most cases files are measured in kilobytes rather than hundreds of kilobytes or megabytes. The file size is also independent of the final image size and resolution.

Images are usually stored using a high resolution co-ordinate system, which is scaled down to produce something like a small image on the screen of a monitor. For high-resolution output to a printer the co-ordinate

Fig.1.18 Vector graphics ensures that neat results are obtained even at high zoom levels

Fig.1.19 Enlarged bitmaps can look rather chunky and indistinct

system would still have to be scaled to suit the printer, but it would probably provide accurate placement of all the objects.

Line art makes the best of the available resolution, which is important when blowing up a small image to make it large, or when reproducing an image on a high resolution output device. Figure 1.18 shows some small text added to the drawing area in Flash, with the Zoom tool used to enlarge this part of the drawing so that it virtually fills the relevant section of the screen. The outline of the text makes full use of the available resolution, giving letters that are free from any obvious stepping or any other roughness on the edges.

A similar procedure with a bitmap in Adobe PhotoShop has not faired so well (Figure 1.19). The individual pixels have been scaled up to produce giant size pixels, and a few compromises have been made in order to get the text the right size. There are actually ways of enlarging bitmaps and smoothing out the rough edges, but scaling images up and down in size is easier with line art and the results are usually much better.

Size matters

With colour bitmaps the amount of data tends to be quite high even for just one frame. Using small images and compression techniques the size per frame can be kept reasonably small, but with something like a 100-frame animation the total amount of data is likely to mount up, and download times become quite long. A great deal of research is being carried out to reduce the size of movies based on bitmaps, and download speeds are likely to steadily increase with the passage of time. For the time being though, line art movies are a more practical proposition for most users, and are generally easier to produce as well.

I would not wish to give the impression that Flash is totally incompatible with bitmap graphics such as Jpeg and Png types. It is not possible to create bitmap images using Flash, but they can be imported and used in your page designs. Some editing of imported bitmaps is possible, such as altering colours and adding special effects, but the animation facilities are largely inoperative with this type of image. Probably the main use for bitmaps with Flash is as backgrounds. Anyway, Flash is not primarily for use with bitmaps, and if you intend to use this type of image you will need another program to produce them and undertake most or all of the editing.

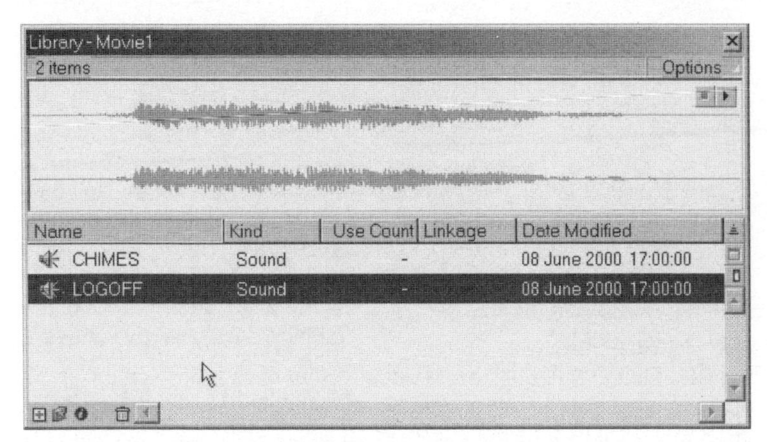

Fig.1.20 A waveform display in the Library panel

Finally

Although Flash is primarily a graphics program, it is has to be pointed out that it can also handle sounds. Waveform displays can be produced (Figure 1.20) and there are facilities to loop short sounds so that they play over and over again, together with some other simple controls and effects. Adding sound increases file sizes and download times, and it is clearly not a practical proposition unless you have some means of generating or obtaining the necessary sound files.

Producing your own sound files is not necessarily that difficult these days, with practically all computers having quite sophisticated sound recording capabilities. It depends on the type of sound required and the minimum quality that is acceptable. Sound can certainly add some oomph to your animations, and it is something that it is well worth giving a try. It is a subject that is covered in detail later in this book.

Flash can provide interactive content, and this is probably one of its main attractions for many users. This interactivity is provided using a programming language called Action Script, which has similarities to the better known JavaScript language. Fortunately, you do not have to learn Action Script in order to add interactivity to your web pages. In standard visual programming fashion, you tell Flash what must happen, and it writes the corresponding program code for you. Interactive content can be in the form of an animation that is triggered by the user in some way, or information can be entered by the user and then used in the

Fig.1.21 A menu using Flash buttons

displayed web pages. This is again something that is covered in detail in a later chapter.

A major use of Flash is producing fancy text and buttons. These do not have to be animated in some way, but usually are. For example, the text and background colours of text could be made to change when the pointer is positioned over the text. Apart from special effects, an advantage of Flash text is that it is free from many of the constraints of normal web page text. Very large sizes and fancy fonts are no problem. Well designed Flash buttons can give a much more professional look to web pages, and this is certainly an aspect of the program that is well worth exploring. In the example of Figure 1.21 a button seems to light up when the pointer is placed over it, and goes even brighter if the mouse is left clicked on the button.

Points to remember

Flash is mainly used to produce animations that are incorporated into web pages and sites produced using other programs, such as Macromedia's Dreamweaver. However, Flash can be used to generate complete web pages, and it can also be used to generate material for use on CD-ROMs.

Images generated using Flash are produced in standard line art fashion. Primitive graphics objects such as lines, circles and squares are added to the drawing area to build up the required image. Fill colours and graduated fill colours can be added to give more convincing results.

Flash can produce animations using motion tweening, where you specify the start and finish points for objects. Flash then works out the positions of the objects in each of the intermediate frames, saving you the bother of doing any manual animation.

Animations can also be produced automatically using shape tweening. You provide a starting shape and a finishing shape. Flash works out the intermediate frames as the original shape is transformed into the second one.

It is not necessary to use any form of automation when generating animations. The traditional frame-by-frame approach, where each frame is generated manually, is also possible. This method is much slower and requires more skill, but it is ultimately much more versatile.

A player program is needed in order to run Flash animations. Most modern browsers are supplied with this software, which is also included with Flash and can be downloaded from the Macromedia web site.

It is possible to export images and animations from Flash, and the popular GIF format is one of the available export options. However, animations are generally much more compact in their native Flash format.

Flash can be used to add sounds to animations, etc., and it provides some useful facilities for manipulating sounds. However, you can only add sound if you can make or obtain suitable sound files, and anything beyond a few simple sound effects might prove to be more difficult than you expected.

Fancy text and buttons can be produced using Flash. Flash text can live up to its name and buttons can light up. These are very popular uses of Flash that can give much more professional looking web pages.

2

Menus

From the top

Before starting a detailed investigation of the finer points of Flash it is worthwhile taking some time to learn about the user interface. By experimenting with the various aspects of the user interface and sidetracking occasionally to try some simple animations you will be well on the way to mastering Flash. This chapter covers some basic concepts and the main toolbar, but is primarily concerned with the menu system. Subsequent chapters cover the Tools palette and the panels, which are the other main ingredients of the user interface.

The Flash interface may take some getting used to if you are only familiar with programs that have a very basic user interface sporting little more than the usual menu and toolbars at the top of the screen, and a status bar at the bottom. In common with most graphics oriented programs, Flash has a very lively user interface with a variety of floating panels that control all manner of things.

However, you are not obliged to have all the panels on the screen at once, and in practice would probably never do so. Panels are brought onto the screen when they are needed and closed again when you have finished using them. This shuffling of onscreen control panels is a standard part of using many pieces of modern software, and is something that you have to acclimatise to as quickly as possible when using a program such as Flash. Of course, you can ignore the panels as far as possible and stick to the traditional menus if preferred, but the menu approach is likely to be slower and you will not be able to access all the facilities that you require in this way.

Menus and panels

With the panels switched off and the main toolbar and status bar switched on, the screen will look something like Figure 2.1. Which panels, toolbars, etc., are enabled is controlled via the Window menu, which we

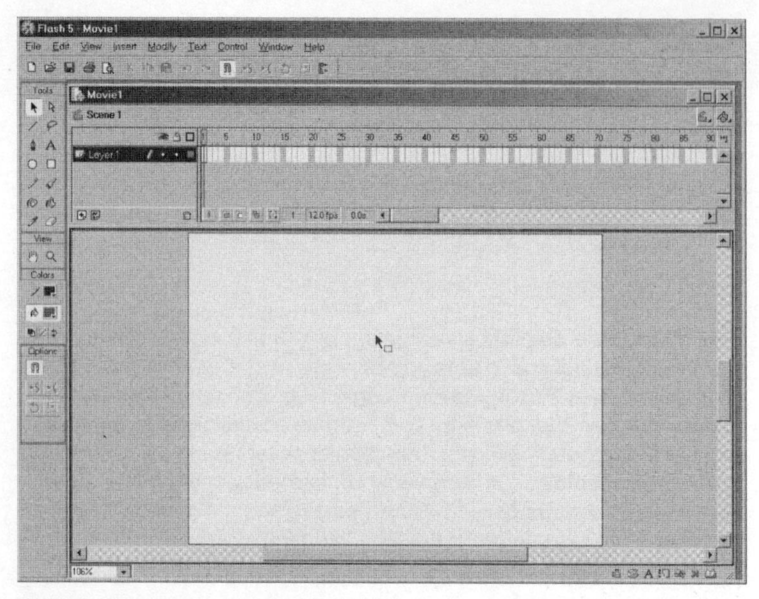

Fig.2.1 The screen obtained with the panels switched off

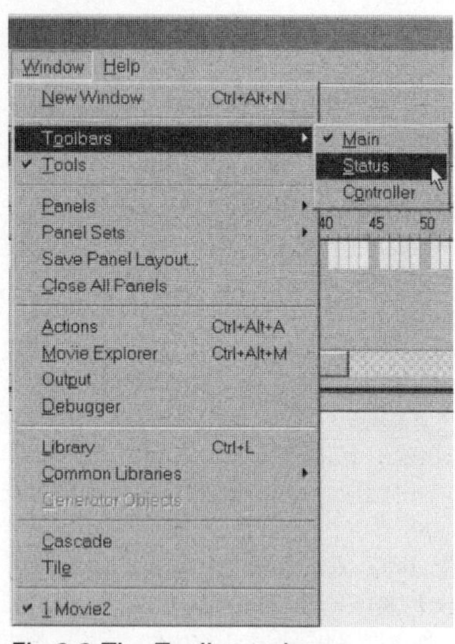

Fig.2.2 The Toolbar submenu

encountered in chapter 1. A submenu (Figure 2.2) controls the toolbars, and in addition to the Main toolbar there is also a Status option that adds a status bar at the bottom of the screen, and a Controller option. The latter provides tape recorder style controls in a floating window (Figure 2.3). Try selecting this option and using it with one of the simple animations produced when trying the exercises in chapter 1. The usual Play, Stop and Rewind options are available, and it is also possible to step backwards or forwards one frame at a time, or to jump to either end of the animation.

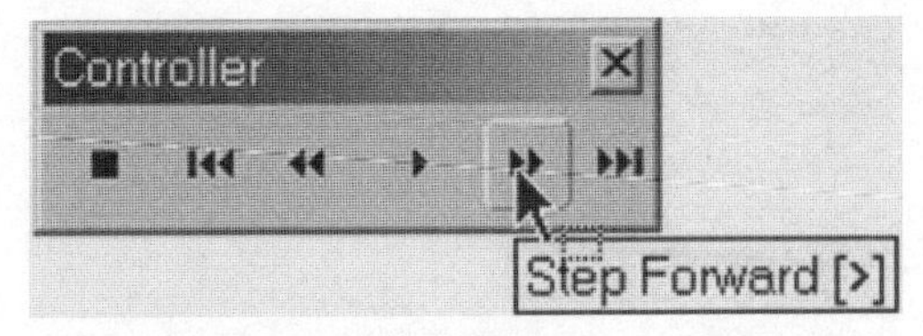

Fig.2.3 The Controller window

The Menu system provides access to many features of Flash, but this is not a program where everything can be controlled via the menu system, and toolbars, etc., are merely offered as an alternative. While there is some overlap between the menu system and the other methods of control available, there would appear to be a huge number of features that are not available via the menus. I have not made detailed checks on this point, but the drawing facilities and many of the editing facilities of the Tools palette are two obvious omissions from the menu system. This lack of features is presumably because there are simply too many to include in a usable menu structure. Hence toolbars and panels are the sole method of implementing many features.

Undo/Redo

Many of the features provided by the menus are the usual things that are found in most programs. For example, there are the usual commands such as Save, Open, Import and so on under the File menu, and the usual Cut, Copy, and Paste in the Edit menu. Two important features found under the Edit menu are Undo and Redo. There is no History facility in Flash that enables you to review all the recent commands and go back X number of commands if required. On the other hand, the Undo and Redo facilities offer more than undoing and redoing the last command.

Flash has a multilevel undo and redo facility, so it is possible to step back through a number of commands by repeatedly using the Undo command, and you can move forwards again using the Redo command as many times as necessary if you change your mind. Note that it is not only drawing commands that can be undone and reinstated. Editing commands such as moving and rotating objects can also be undone and redone. Even minor things such as object selection can be undone and redone.

Although Flash does not have a full History facility, the multilevel undo and redo feature is effectively the same, albeit in a relatively crude version. The number of commands that can be undone is not infinite. The user can control the number of commands that can be undone, and as usual

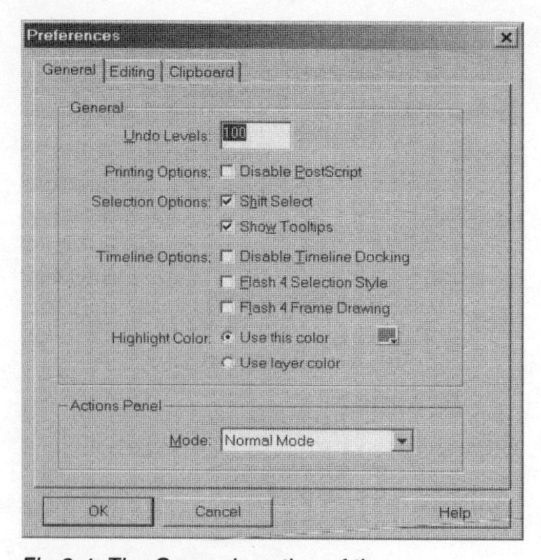

Fig.2.4 The General section of the Preferences dialogue box

with this type of thing it is necessary to find a good compromise. It is clearly helpful to be able to go back through a large number of commands, but this tends to use large amounts of memory. If your computer has suitably large amounts of memory this will not be of great importance, but it could impair performance in other respects with a computer that has a relatively small amount of memory.

The range of the Undo facility can be altered by first selecting Preferences from the Edit menu. This produces the dialogue box of Figure 2.4. The Undo Levels text field is edited to the required figure, and the default is 100. Being able to undo 100 commands is adequate for most users, but you might like to use a higher figure if your computer has plenty of memory. If your computer is not well blessed in the memory department it might be beneficial to reduce the figure to 50, which is still more than adequate for most purposes. Once the figure has been amended, left-click the OK button to implement the change and return to the main program.

View

The View menu controls what is actually shown on the screen, but note that many elements are controlled by way of the Window menu and not the View menu. The Timeline can be toggled on and off, and it can sometimes be beneficial to switch it off so that more of the screen can be used for the drawing area. Also, you may sometimes need to produce a straightforward illustration rather than an animation, and the Timeline then serves no useful purpose. The Work (drawing) area can also be switched on and off, but this is perhaps a rather less useful feature.

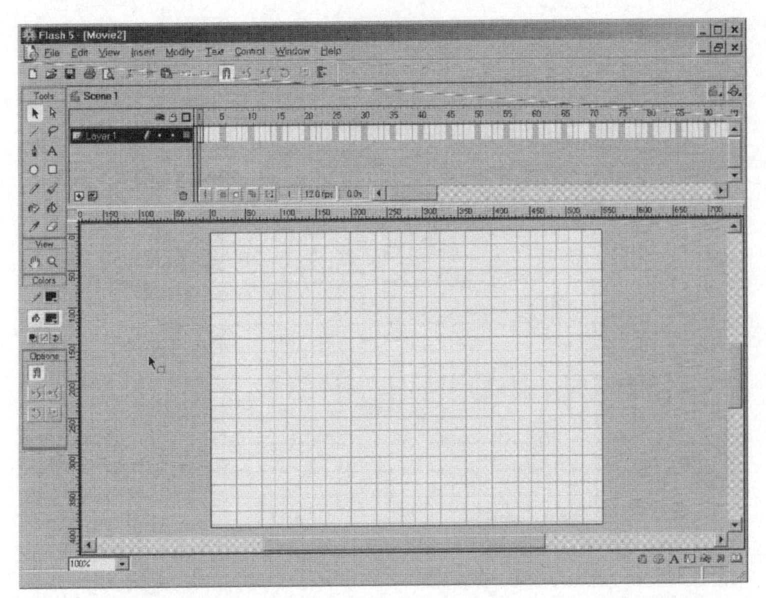

Fig.2.5 A grid of lines appears on the drawing area when the Show grid option is selected

It is also possible to toggle rulers and a grid. Often Flash is used to produce things where precise alignment and sizes are not required. You simply adjust things “by eye” to give what you feel is the best result. However, there are occasions when precision and uniformity are required, such as when producing charts and diagrams. The rulers enable accurate measurements to be made and the grid also makes it easier to get things the right size. Markers indicating the current pointer position appear in the horizontal and vertical rulers at the appropriate times, such as when a drawing tool is in use, making it easy to use the rulers to produce precise results.

A grid is also useful when elements in a diagram must be accurately aligned. Figure 2.5 shows the drawing area with the rulers and the default grid enabled. You will notice that there are two types of grid available in the Grid submenu (Figure 2.6). The Show Grid option is used to toggle the visible grid on and off. With the grid switched on it is still possible to draw straight lines between any two points in the drawing area, so it is necessary to take great care in order to get lines precisely where you need them.

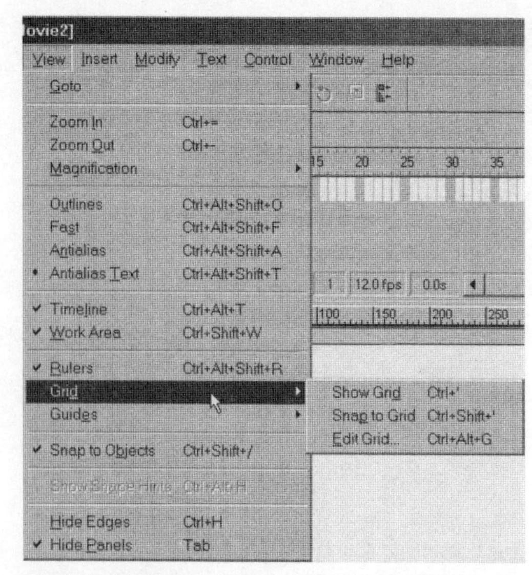

Fig.2.6 There are three options in the Grid submenu

When the Snap To Grid option is used it is only possible to draw lines to and from points where lines of the grid intersect. It is not just straight lines that are affected by the snap grid. Figure 2.7 shows some freehand lines drawn with the snap grid enabled, and it clearly shows how the program has tried to tidy things up. Wherever possible the lines are made up of straight segments running between grid

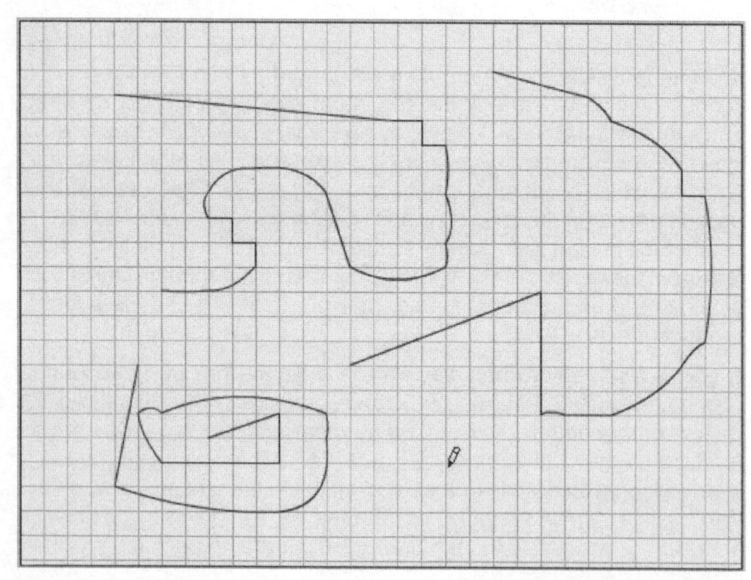

Fig.2.7 The snap grid will work when drawing freehand lines

points. Regular curves have been used where this treatment is inappropriate. Using the snap grid also affects shapes such as circles and rectangles, where constraints are placed on the sizes and positions.

There is separate control over the snap and visual grids, so it is possible to have one or other of them switched on, or both. The third option in the Grid submenu produces the dialogue box of Figure 2.8, which enables the grid parameters to be adjusted. The checkboxes enable the visible and snap grids to be enabled or disabled. The gap between lines in the grid can be set separately for vertical and horizontal spacing, and the figure is the spacing in screen pixels at normal screen magnification. There are four options in the Snap Accuracy menu, and they are described briefly here:

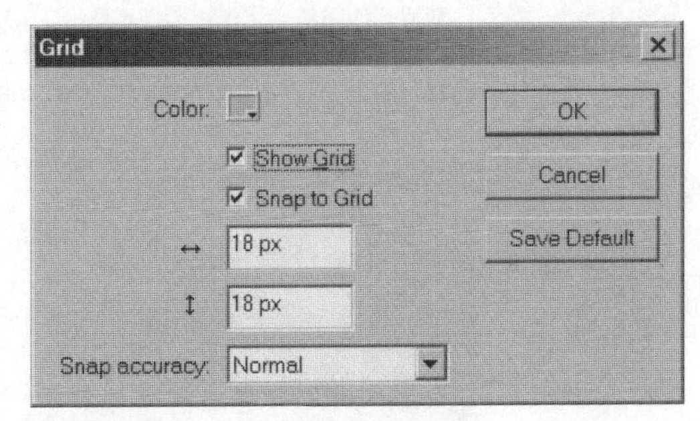

Fig.2.8 The Grid dialogue box

Must be Close

With this option the snap grid only works with points that are quite close to an intersection of two grid lines. Using points slightly away from the grid points does not give the snap effect. It is a good mode to use if accurate alignment will sometimes be needed but you also require the ability to draw and position objects between the grid points.

Always Snap

With this mode lines will always be drawn between grid points, and objects will snap to them. It does not matter how coarse the grid happens to be, or how far away the pointer is placed from a grid point, the nearest grid point will always be used. Clearly this mode is only suitable for charts and diagrams where everything is aligned to the grid.

Can be Distant

With a fine grid this is identical to the Always Snap option. With a coarse grid it is possible to use points that are off the grid, but only if they are well away from a grid point.

Normal

This mode is roughly half way between the Must be Close and the Can be Distant snap modes. The snap action only occurs for points that are reasonably close to an intersection point. The Normal mode is the default setting, and is also the one that is best for most purposes.

Left clicking on the colour button brings up the colour swatch and "eyedropper" tool of Figure 2.9. Use the "eyedropper" to select one of the colours in the chart, or from anywhere within one of the Flash windows. A normal pointer is obtained outside the Flash windows, but with my computer system left clicking on an area of screen still selects the corresponding colour. This may not work with all computers though. Once the required parameters have been selected, operate the Save Default button if you wish to use them as the defaults, and then operate the OK button to exit the dialogue box.

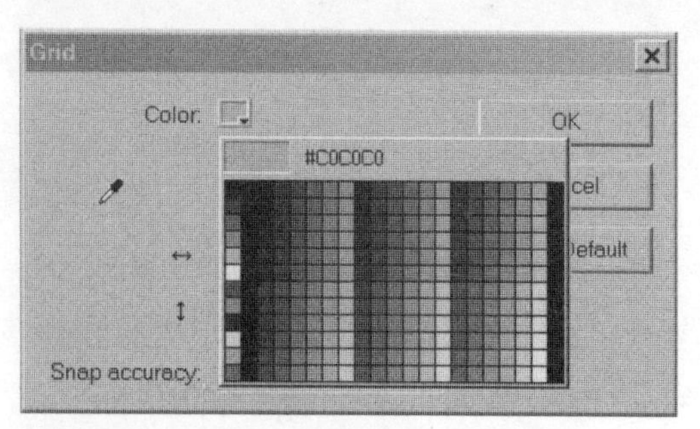

Fig.2.9 The colour swatch

Guides

There is a Guides option in the View menu, and a submenu offering a further four options (Figure 2.10). Guides are simply lines that are placed on the screen to aid the positioning of points, but they are not placed at regular intervals like a grid. You place them at strategic positions on the screen, one at a time. In order to produce a horizontal guideline, position the pointer over the horizontal ruler and drag the line to the required position. A vertical guideline is produced in the same way, but by dragging from the vertical ruler.

Once a guideline has been placed on the screen it can be dragged to a new position using the Arrow tool or the Subselect type (the two tools at the top of the Tools panel). The pointer has to be very close to the line in order to drag it, but the pointer will change slightly when it is close enough. The rectangle below the pointer changes to a short line and a tiny arrowhead. Figure 2.11 shows some guidelines added to the drawing area.

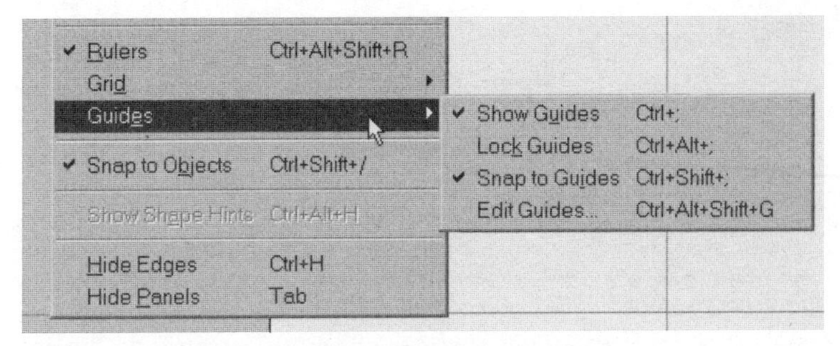

Fig.2.10 There are four options in the Guides submenu

The Guides submenu enables a snap action to be switched on and off. If you use this feature it is important to realise that it does not merely provide a snap action to points where two guidelines cross. If the pointer is placed near a guideline it will gravitate towards the line. Another option enables guidelines to be shown or hidden from view. Note that unwanted guidelines can be removed altogether by simply dragging them back to their ruler of origin. By using the Lock Guides option the

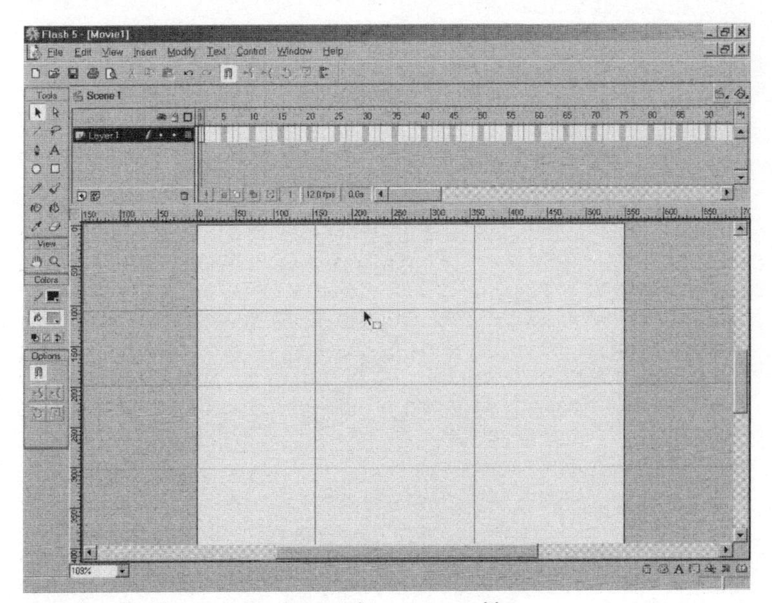

Fig.2.11 Guides can be dragged to new positions

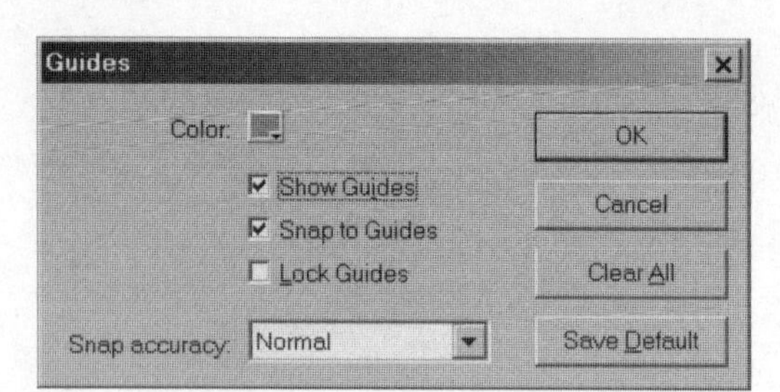

Fig.2.12 The Guides dialogue box is similar to the one for grids

guidelines can be fixed in position so that they can not be moved using the Arrow and Subselect tools. This avoids the possibility of the lines being accidentally moved during editing operations. The Edit Guides option produces the dialogue box of Figure 2.12, which is similar to the grid editing dialogue box.

Object snap

There is a further form of snap available in the View menu via the Snap to Objects option. With this option the pointer gravitates to lines and shapes within the drawing, making it easy to ensure that one object

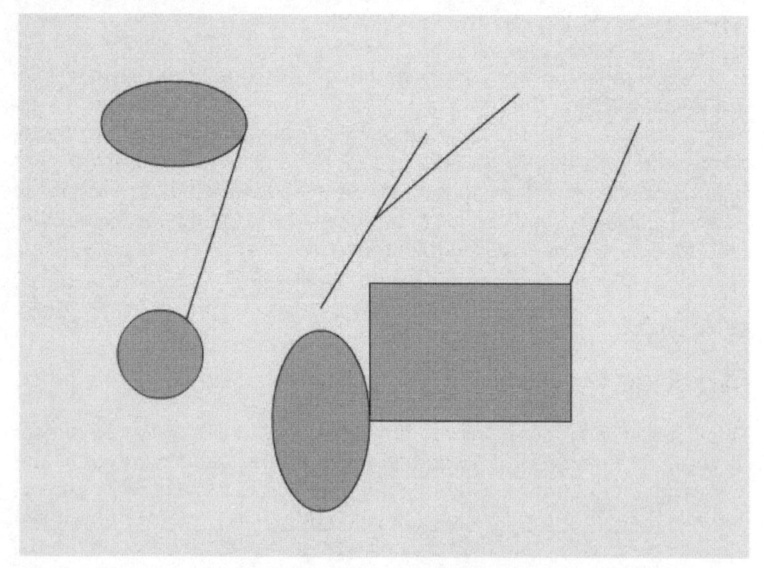

Fig.2.13 Lines and objects joined using the object snap facility

joins another correctly with no gap. Figure 2.13 shows various objects that have been joined using the object snap feature.

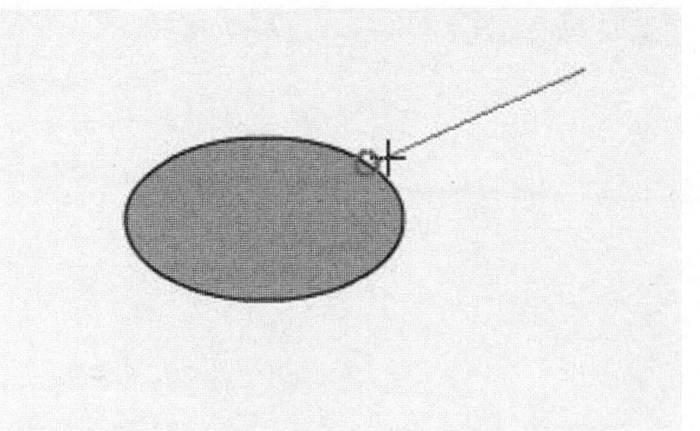

Fig.2.14 The pointer changes when an object snap occurs

Note that you can always see when any form of snap is in operation because a circle appears in addition to the normal pointer. Figure 2.14 shows this circle where the object snap has caused a line to snap to the ellipse. When drawing lines the circle sometimes appears for no apparent reason. This happens when the line is nearly vertical or horizontal, and it is actually snapping to an exactly vertical or horizontal position. This feature is disabled when the object snap facility is switched off.

Insert and Modify

The Insert menu is used to add things like additional frames in a sequence, keyframes, and new layers. The subject of layers is an important one, which is covered in detail later in this book. The Modify menu is used to modify general settings rather than editing artwork. For example, it can be used to change the frame rate of a movie. The Group facility enables several objects to be selected and then grouped together so that they act as a single object for some purposes. In particular, if you move one object the rest of the group will move with it. The Ungroup option can be used to break up the group into its constituent parts again.

Arrange

If you have used illustration programs you will be familiar with the concept of arranging the order of onscreen objects. The standard options are available in the Arrange submenu (Figure 2.15), but this facility does not work in quite the standard fashion with Flash. If two objects are drawn on the screen with one overlapping the other, things appear quite normal with the object drawn second appearing to be on top of the one placed on the screen first. The object drawn second partially obscures the object drawn first, as in Figure 2.16 where the ellipse was drawn first and then the square was added. Where things depart from normal is when the two objects are separated. With most programs that produce line art this would leave a complete ellipse and the square would also be fully intact.

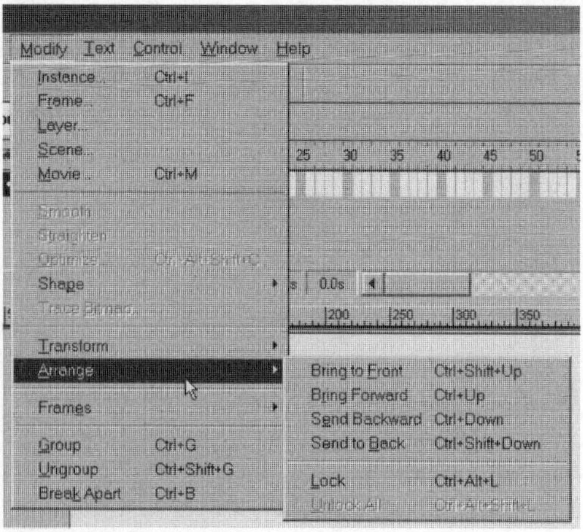

Fig.2.15 A number of options are available in the Arrange submenu

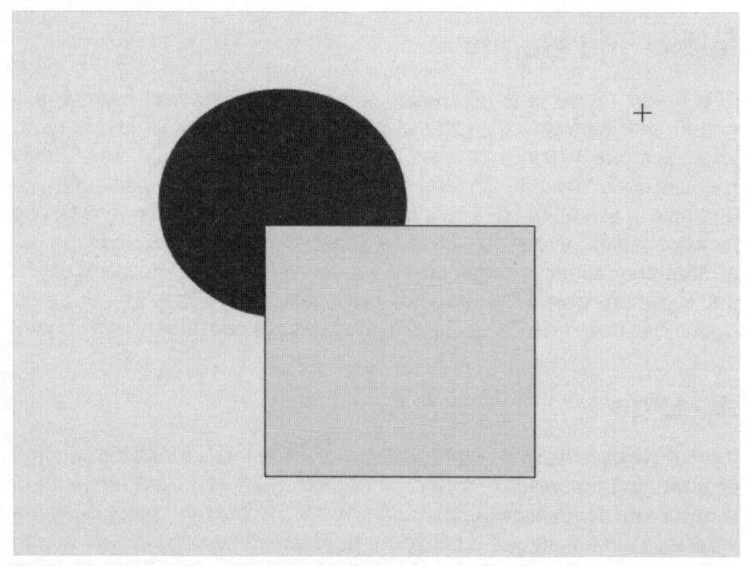

Fig.2.16 Although the square appears to be on top of the ellipse, it has actually obliterated part of the ellipse

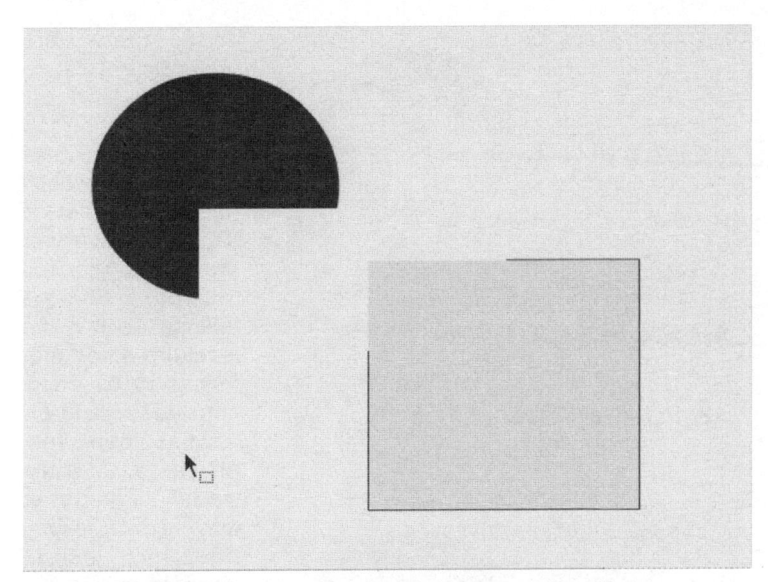

Fig.2.17 Moving the square shows the damage to the ellipse

Figure 2.17 shows the result of separating the two objects in Flash. By placing the square over the ellipse, the part of the ellipse that was obscured by the square has been removed, or "nibbled" as some people term it. Also, the outline of the square has been removed at the point where it overlapped the ellipse. This nibbling of the outline does not always occur, since it only happens when the outline is the same colour as the object in the background.

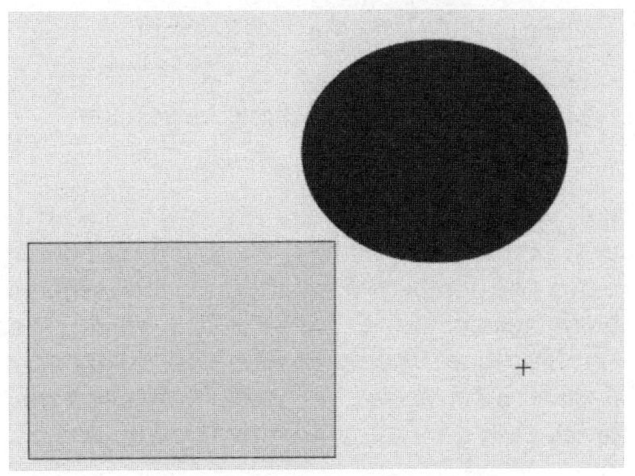

Fig.2.18 The rectangle and square are separate objects at this stage

The nibbling effect also occurs if the two objects are drawn separately and then moved so that they overlap. In Figure

Fig.2.19 The rectangle has been moved over the ellipse

2.18 there are separate objects on the screen, which are an ellipse and a rectangle. In Figure 2.19 they have been moved together so that they overlap. The rectangle was moved over the ellipse, so it is the rectangle that appears to be on top, and the ellipse that is partially obscured. In Figure 2.20 the rectangle has been moved away, leaving the ellipse incomplete.

Fig.2.20 Moving the rectangle reveals the nibbling effect

It is easy enough to try this out for yourself. Drawing shapes with the Oval and Rectangle tools was covered in chapter 1. In order to select an object and move it, double-click on it and then drag it to the new position on the screen. By double clicking on a filled object you select both the outline and the area of colour it contains. Note that the nibbling does not occur if you move one object over another, and then remove the top object without it being deselected. Consequently, while an object remains selected you can "fine tune" its position without erasing bits of any background object each time it is moved. To deselect an object simply select another object or left-click on a blank area of screen.

Grouping

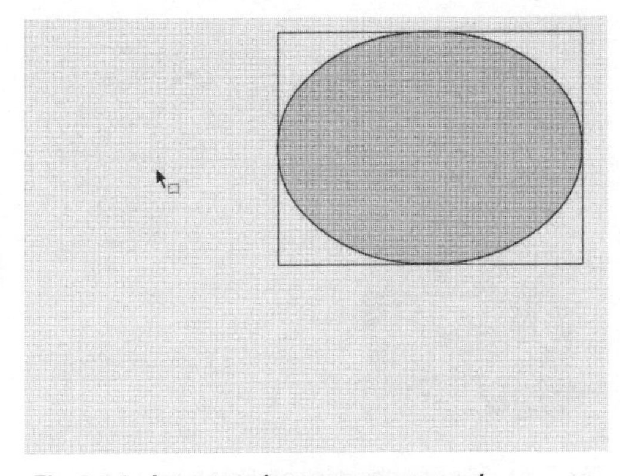

Fig.2.21 A rectangle appears around a group when it is selected

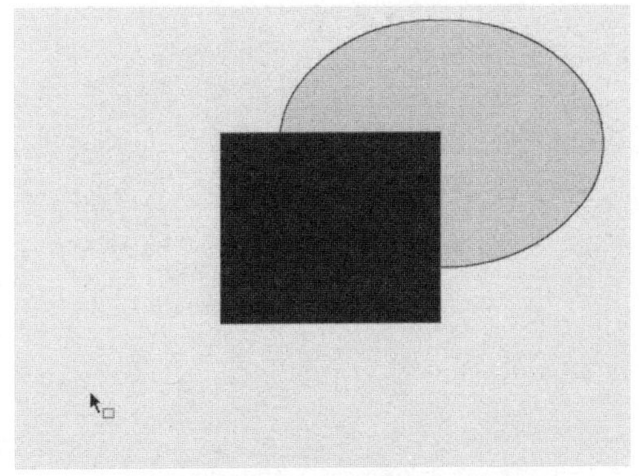

Fig.2.22 Both objects are groups, and no nibbling of the ellipse will occur

In order to make use of the facilities in the Arrange submenu it is necessary to work with groups of objects. Try drawing an ellipse on the screen and then double-click on the object to select it. Next select the Group option from the Modify menu. A blue rectangle will then appear around the ellipse to show that it is a group, as in Figure 2.21. In this case there are just two objects in the group, which are the ellipse and the filled area within the ellipse. If you try dragging the ellipse around the drawing area using the Arrow tool you will find that the ellipse itself, the fill colour, and the blue rectangle all move together. Left-click on a blank part of the drawing area to deselect the ellipse, and then left-click anywhere on or within the ellipse. This will select the group, and the blue rectangle will appear again to show that it is a group that you are dealing with.

Next draw a rectangle somewhere on the screen where it will not overlap the ellipse. Double-click on the rectangle and select Group from the Modify menu. Drag the rectangle onto the ellipse using the Arrow tool so that something like Figure 2.22 is obtained. Then drag the rectangle clear of the ellipse again. This time there should be no bits missing from the ellipse and something like Figure 2.23 should be obtained. Now try

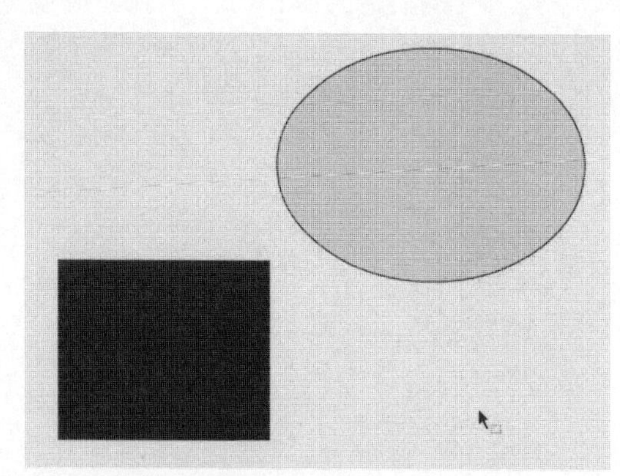

Fig.2.23 Moving the rectangle leaves the ellipse intact

dragging the rectangle back over the ellipse and selecting the Send to Back option from the Arrange submenu of the Modify menu. This should produce something like Figure 2.24, with the ellipse partially covering the rectangle rather than the opposite state of affairs.

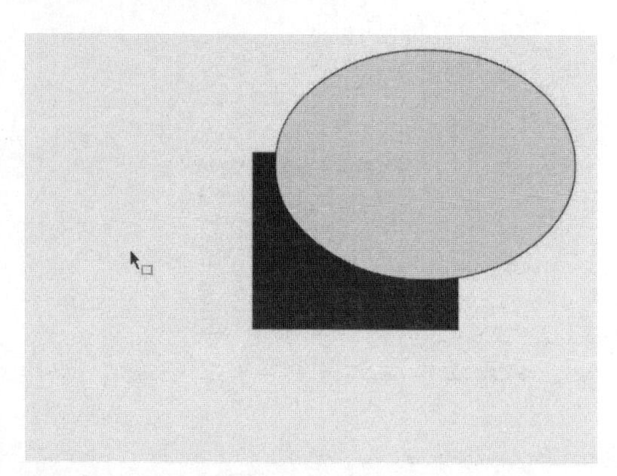

Fig.2.24 The rectangle has been set to appear behind the ellipse

In this example we grouped both objects, but it is only necessary to group one or the other in order to avoid the nibbling effect. However, with one object grouped and the other not, it is always the grouped object that will appear at the front. This can not be reversed using the Arrange submenu. Try selecting one of the groups and then using the Ungroup option of the Modify menu. If the objects are made to overlap and then moved apart there will be no nibbling effect, but the grouped object will always be at the front when they overlap.

Try using the Send to Back option from the Arrange submenu on the grouped object. It will still always appear in front of the ungrouped object. Incidentally, with grouped objects it is the last group to be produced that appears at the front, the group created prior to that is the next one back, and so on. With both objects ungrouped things return to normal, and overlapping the objects will restore the nibbling effect.

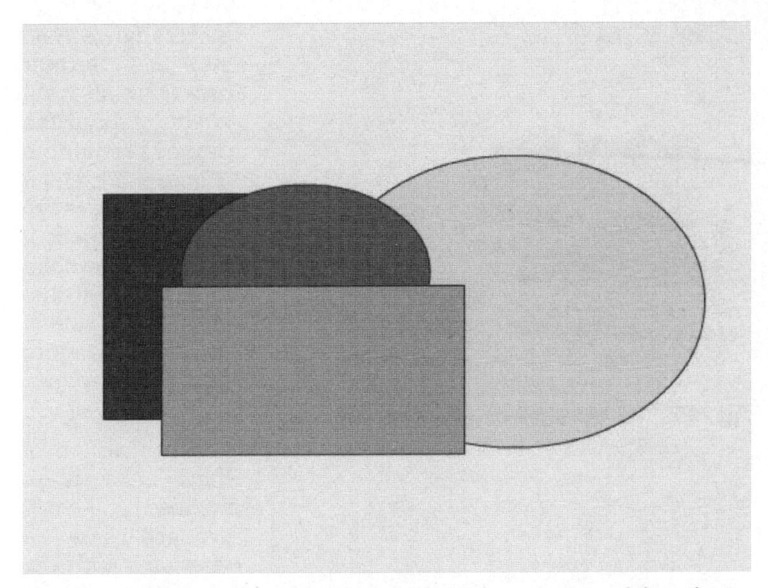

Fig.2.25 A number of groups can be stacked one on top of the other

Multiple groups

So far we have only considered using two groups, but large numbers of groups can be used if desired. The Arrange submenu can then be used to place the groups in any desired order. In Figure 2.25 the lower rectangle is the object at the front of the stack of four objects. In Figure 2.26 the Send Backward option of the Arrange submenu has been used, and the rectangle has moved back behind the smaller ellipse, but it remains in front of the other two objects. Repeating the

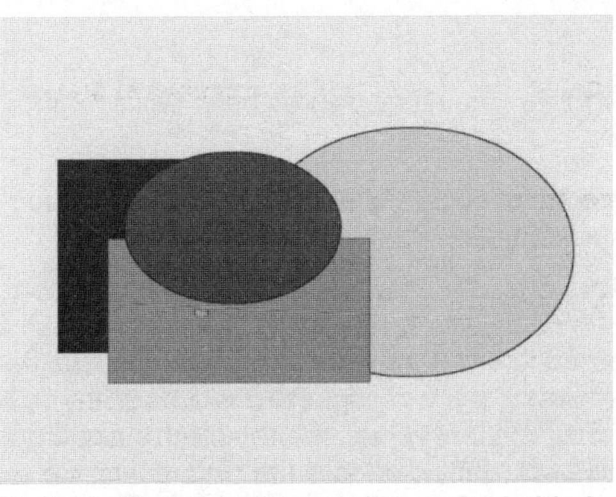

Fig.2.26 The rectangle has been sent behind the ellipse

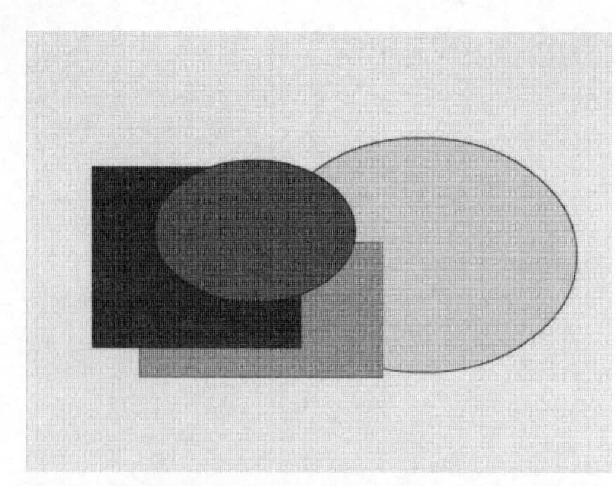

Fig.2.27 The rectangle has been moved one step further back

process moves it one step further backwards so that it is also behind the other rectangle (Figure 2.27), and a further move backwards takes it behind the second ellipse so that it is almost totally obscured (Figure 2.28).

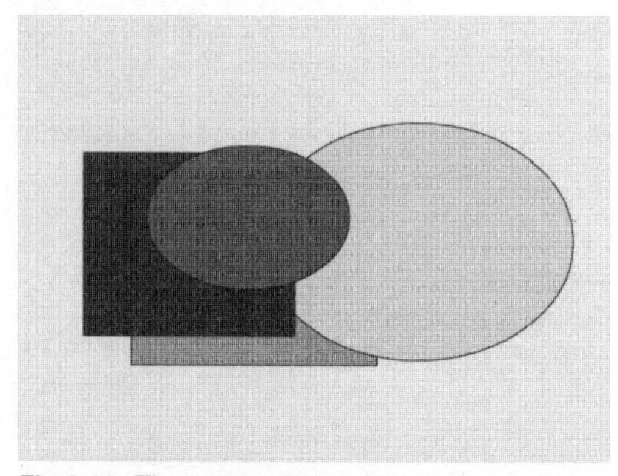

Fig.2.28 The rectangle has been moved right to the back

By using the Bring Forward option of the Arrange submenu this process can be reversed, with the rectangle being brought to the front again, one step at a time. The Bring To Front option would bring it to the front in a single step, and the Send To Back command would take it right to the back of the stack again. A few minutes experimenting with groups of objects is all that should be required in order to learn how to stack objects in the required order.

This is a very easy way of getting a pseudo three-dimensional effect, with complete objects being drawn and then stacked in the appropriate order. The computer then hides any parts of the objects that should not be visible. If you change the positions of any objects there is no redrawing work. You simply drag the objects to the new positions and the computer almost instantly redraws the picture with the obscured parts of objects removed. For this to work well it is of course important to get the perspective at least semi-plausible, with background objects being used at suitably reduced scales.

Transform - Scale

The Transform submenu of the Modify menu (Figure 2.29) provides some very useful features. Draw a rectangle on the screen and then double-click on it to select the rectangle and its fill. Then go to the Modify menu and select Scale from the Transform submenu. Eight small squares will then appear on the outline of the rectangle, as in Figure 2.30. These are generally called "handles", but I have encountered other terms such as "hooks". By dragging any of the four handles in the corners the rectangle it is possible to resize it, and its aspect ratio will remain unchanged.

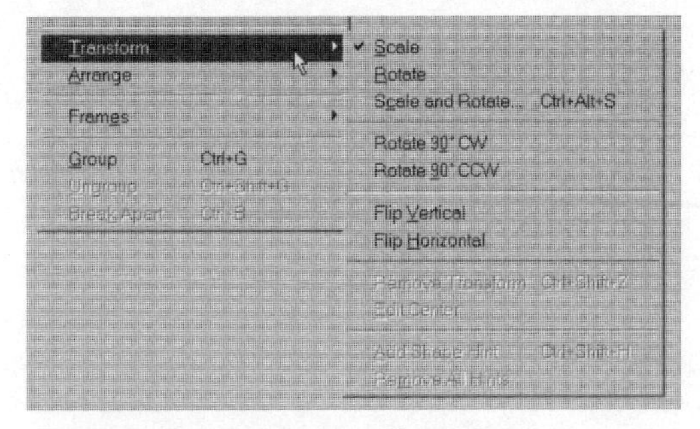

Fig.2.29 The Transform submenu

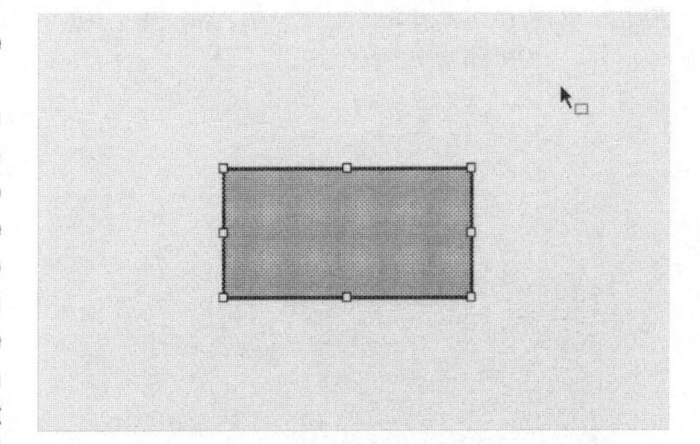

Fig.2.30 Eight handles permit changes in the scaling of objects

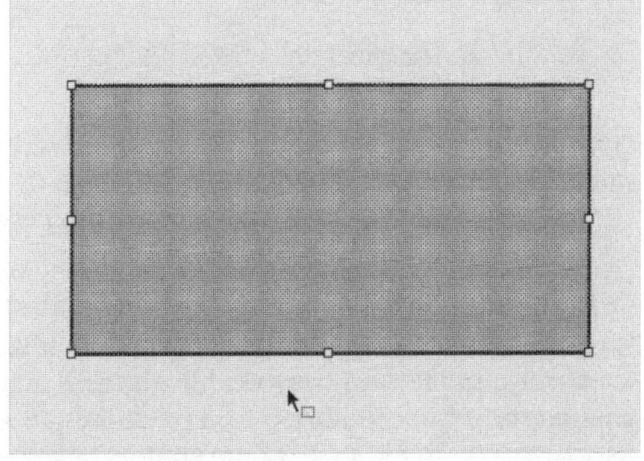

Fig.2.31 The enlarged version of the rectangle

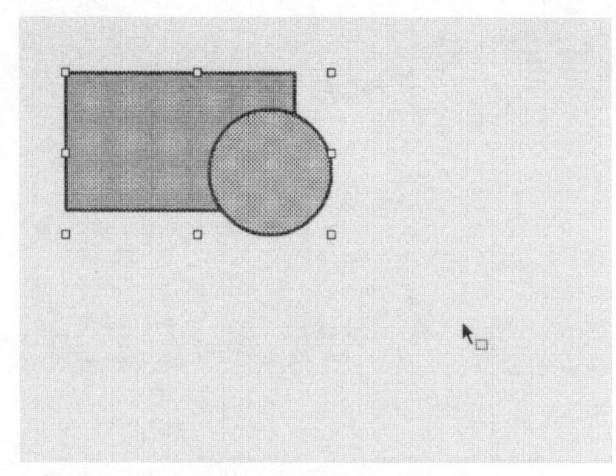

Fig.2.32 A group of objects can also be transformed

This method has been used in Figure 2.31 to enlarge the original rectangle without altering its aspect ratio. Note that only a limited number of sizes will be available if the snap grid is in operation, so for this exercise it is a good idea to have it turned off. Using the other four handles it is only possible to stretch or contract the rectangle in one dimension at a time, and any changes will therefore alter its aspect ratio.

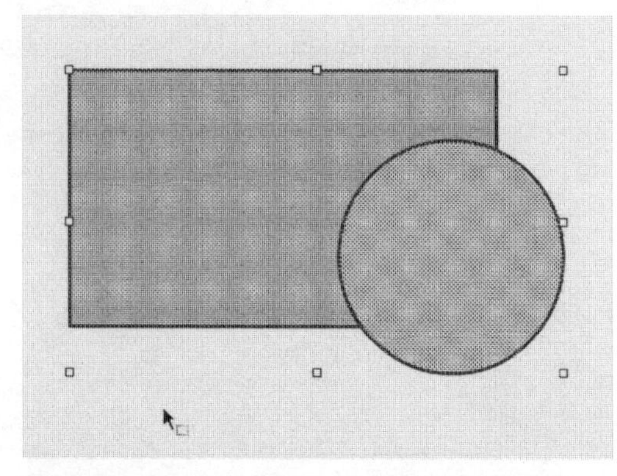

Fig.2.33 Here the group has been scaled up

Scaling is not limited to one object at a time. Try drawing a rectangle and a circle or ellipse in the top left-hand section of the drawing area. Next select the Arrow tool and drag a rectangle around both shapes to select them. Make sure that both shapes fall entirely within the rectangle. Then select the Scale option from the Transform submenu, which should produce something like Figure 2.32.

Once again there are eight handles, and they are on a rectangle that is just large enough to completely surround both shapes, but the rectangle is not displayed on the screen. Things operate in much the same way for several objects as they do for a single object. In Figure 2.33 the shapes have been dragged to a much larger size while retaining their aspect ratios. In Figure 2.34 the shapes have been shrunk horizontally, giving a very obvious change in the aspect ratios of both. Scaling can be applied to a group, and it again operates in much the same way with eight handles appearing. The only minor difference is that the rectangle indicating the group will appear on the screen, and the handles will appear on this instead of an "imaginary" rectangle (Figure 2.35).

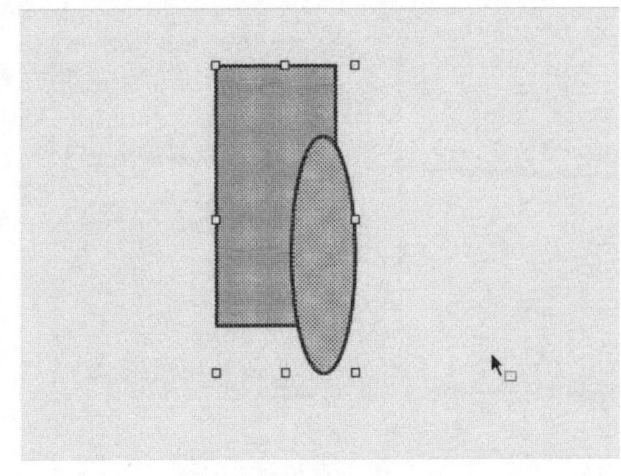

Fig.2.34 Here the group has been compressed horizontally

Transform - Rotate

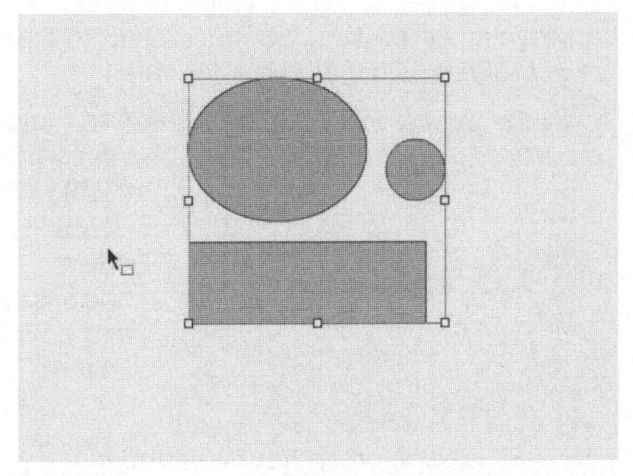

Fig.2.35 The handles appear on the rectangle when a group is scaled

The Rotate option in the Transform submenu enables an object or group of objects to be rotated and (or) skewed. To try out this facility place a large square or rectangle in the drawing area and then select it by double clicking on it. Next go to the Modify menu and select Rotate from the Transform submenu. The object now has eight handles, but these are round rather than square (Figure 2.36) in order to distinguish them from the handles used for scaling operations. When the pointer is placed near one of the four corner handles it changes to four arrows in a circle, as in Figure 2.37. This indicates that the pointer has latched on to the handle, and the object can then be dragged through the required degree of rotation.

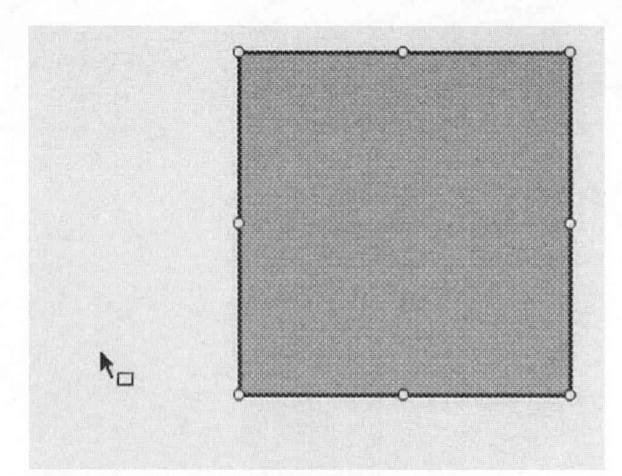

Fig.2.36 *Round handles appear when the Rotate option is selected*

The object stays in place on the screen, but an outline follows the pointer so that you can see where the rotated object will be deposited when the mouse button is released (Figure 2.38). The outline disappears when the mouse button is released and the object is automatically erased and redrawn in the new position (Figure 2.39). By default the object or group is rotated around its centre. Once the object or group has been rotated the eight handles are still present, but they return to their normal positions and are not rotated with the object.

When the pointer is placed near the four handles that are not at the corners, it changes to a line having an arrowhead at each end (Figure 2.40). The arrows show the directions in which that side of the object or group can be moved, and this is horizontally for the top and bottom sides, and vertically for the left and right sides. Figure 2.41 shows a square that has been skewed by having the top moved to the right, and Figure 2.42 shows a square that has had its left side moved downwards. You are not restricted to either rotating objects or skewing them, and the two can be freely mixed, as in Figure 4.43.

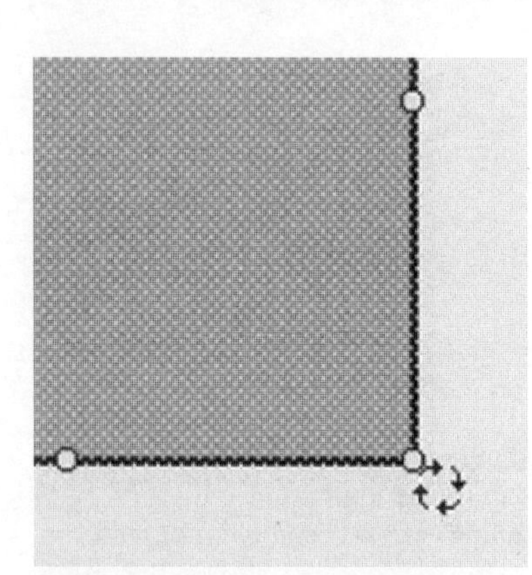

Fig.2.37 *The pointer changes when it locks onto a handle*

The rotation and skewing effects are not restricted to simple two-dimensional shapes. Suppose you have the clipart jet fighter of Figure 2.44, which is almost perfect for your needs except you require the plane

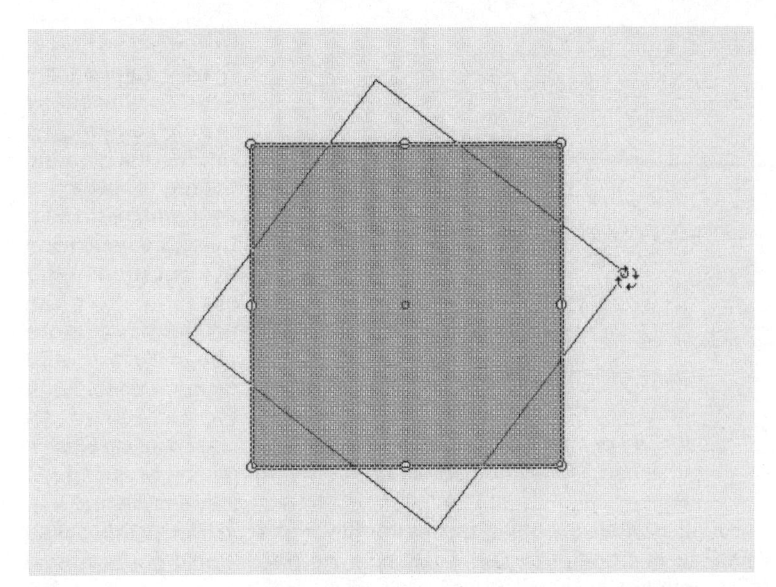

Fig.2.38 Dragging a handle shows the new position as an outline

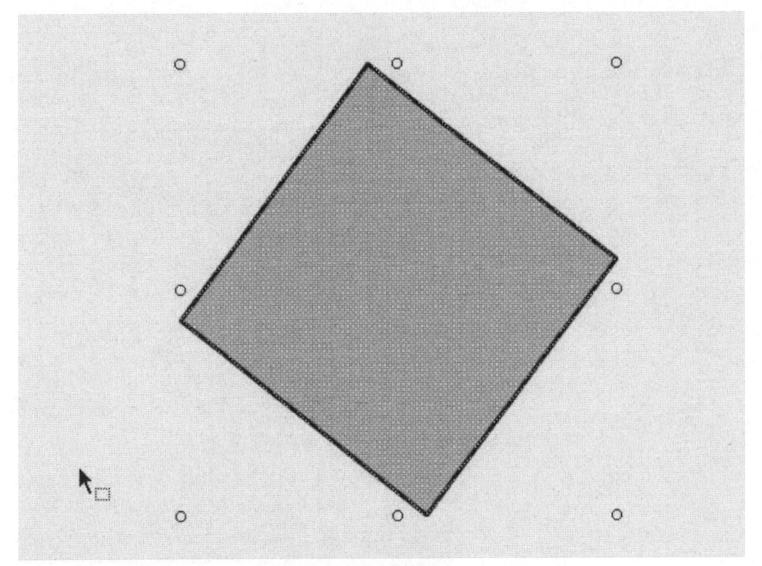

Fig.2.39 The rotated version of the square

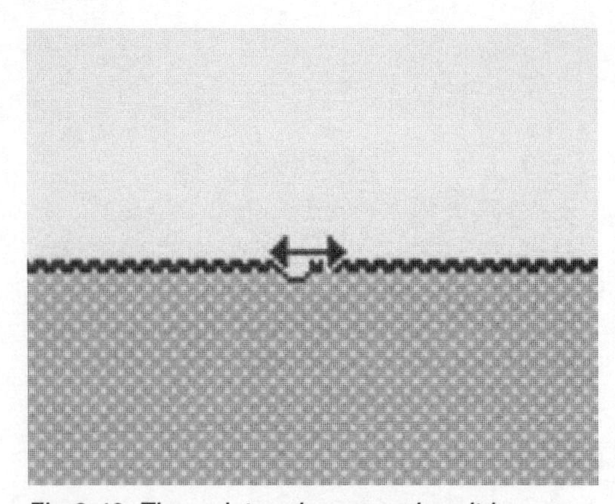

Fig.2.40 The pointer changes when it is near a handle that permits skewing

to be in a dive. Simply rotating the image will usually give reasonable results provided the degree of rotation is kept within reason. Using a combination of rotation and skewing often produces a more convincing and dynamic effect, as in Figure 2.45. Of course, using Flash's motion tweening it is very easy to make an animation where the object moves from its original position to the rotated and skewed position. In this example the plane would go from level flight into a dive.

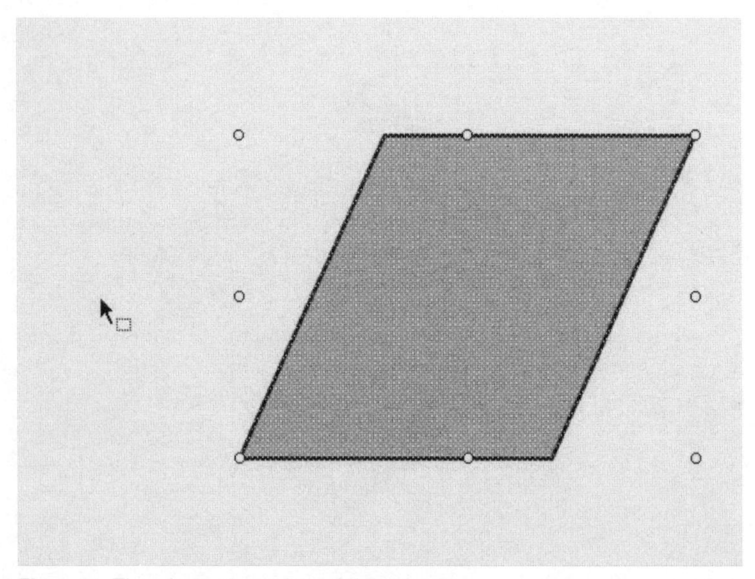

Fig.2.41 The skewed version of the square

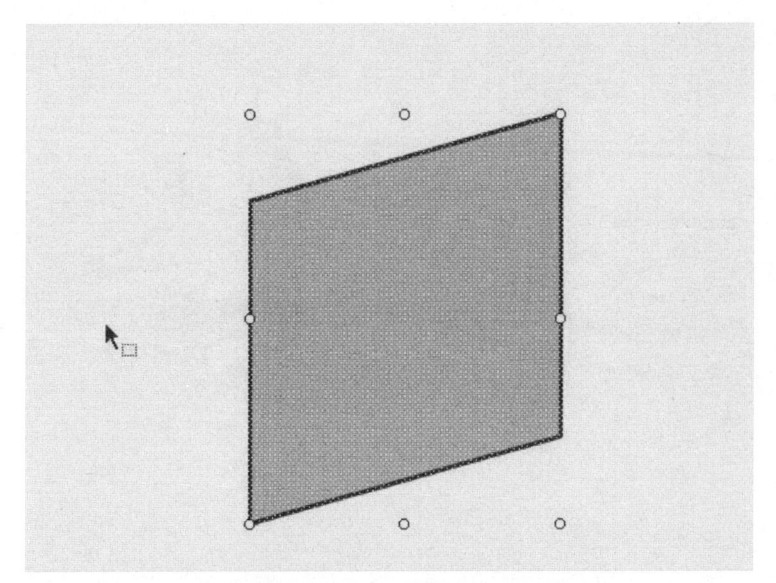

Fig.2.42 Vertical skewing has been applied to this square

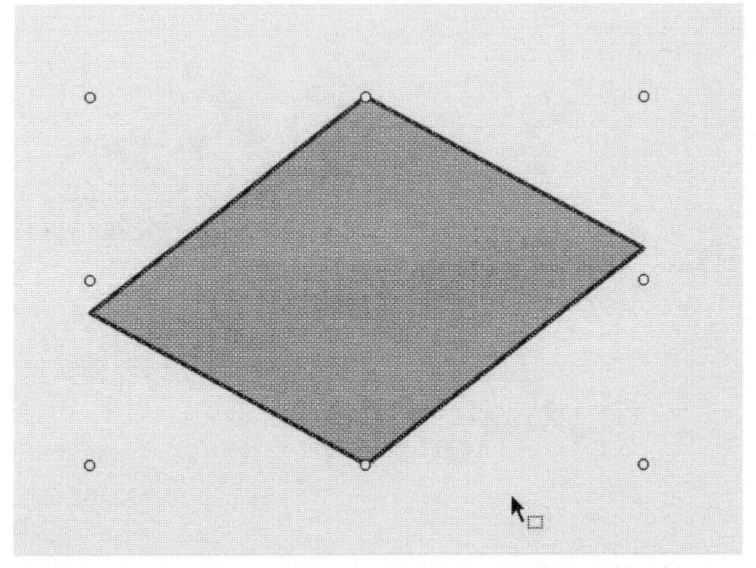

Fig.2.43 Skewing and rotation have both been applied to this object

Fig.2.44 The original version of the jet plane

Fig.2.45 Skewing and rotation have placed the plane in a dive

Fig.2.46 The first frame of the jet plane animation

Rotate and tweening

If you have some suitable clipart it is well worthwhile experimenting with some simple animations based on rotation and skewing. Refer back to chapter 1 for details of producing animations using motion tweening. With the plane example it will look something less than totally convincing if the image is simply rotated and skewed. If the image starts in the top right-hand corner of the screen and finishes in the bottom left-hand corner the effect is

Fig.2.47

Fig.2.48

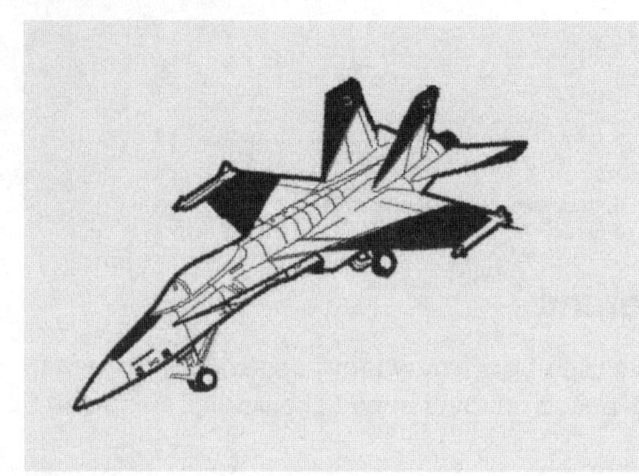

Fig.2.49

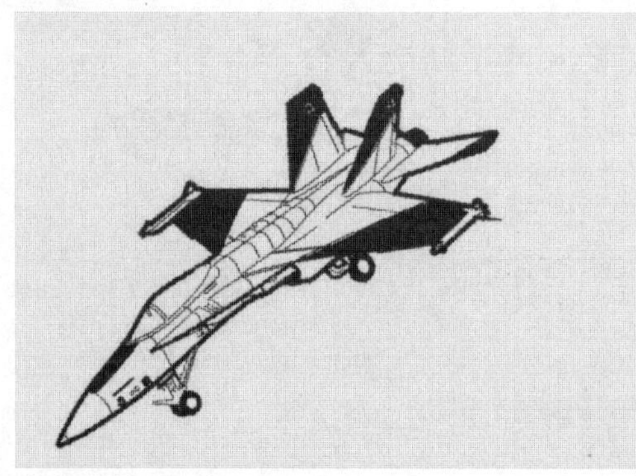

Fig.2.50 The final frame

about a million times more convincing. It is not even necessary to have a large amount of movement across and down the screen. Figures 2.46 to 2.50 show the start and finish frames of my simple test animation, plus three intermediate frames generated by Flash.

The movement across and down the screen is clearly minimal, but the effect obtained is very definitely one of the plane going into a dive. Without the movement the plane seems to rotate while hovering in mid-air. This makes the important point that minor changes such as this can make a huge difference to the way an animation is perceived by viewers. A little attention to details such as this can make the difference between your Flash movies working well and failing to impress at all. Worse still, people might put a completely wrong interpretation on the animation. If you produce a movie that does not give the desired effect, a little thought and some careful editing will often rescue the situation. With something like the jet plane example a simple sound effect would also greatly enhance results.

Scale and Tweening

Scaling can also be used to good effect with motion tweening, giving the impression that something is moving towards the viewer or moving away from them. Figures 2.51 to 2.55 show five frames from an animation produced using another piece of clipart, and this time it is a picture of Concorde. For this method to work it is usually essential to have an image that is (more or less) a rear view or, as in this case, a front view. Although still quite advanced technically, Concorde can not fly sideways. In this example the plane is not viewed from directly in front, and it is clearly aimed slightly to the viewer's right. The initial image is therefore quite small and in the bottom left-hand corner of the drawing area. The final image has been scaled up

Fig.2.51 The first frame of the animation that uses scaling and motion tweening

Fig.2.52

Fig.2.53

and moved to the opposite corner of the drawing area.

When run, the animation gives the impression that the plane is moving towards the viewer and across his or her field of view. Even though the real plane would be going very fast, its apparent progress would be quite slow as it is largely moving towards the viewer. I therefore used more frames for this animation. Things seemed to be about right with 75 frames at 12 frames per second. The plane goes much higher in the frame as it approaches, giving the impression that it is taking off. The opposite effect with the plane apparently coming in to land could be given by starting it in the top left-hand corner and finishing the animation with it in the bottom right-hand corner. Having the plane quite high initially and slightly higher at the end should give the impression of level flight.

Fig.2.54

Scale plus rotation

Often the best results are obtained using a mixture of scaling and rotation. In the Figures 2.56 to 2.60 the original jet plane movie has been modified slightly, with the initial image of the plane being reduced in size. Rather

Fig.2.55 The final frame of the movie with the fully expanded plane

than just diving, the plane also seems to come towards the viewer. This gives a more convincing effect than the original and it is also produces a more dynamic result. It is well worth while experimenting with scaling, rotation, and some clipart. Combined with motion tweening and a small amount of shape changing from the first frame to the final one it is possible to produce some very good results in rapid time. There is not exactly a world shortage of clipart, which is often included on the front cover discs of computer magazines and with graphics software. There is also plenty of it

Fig.2.56 The first frame of the movie that uses scaling, rotation, and motion tweening

Fig.2.57

available on the Internet. Unless you require something pretty bizarre there is a good chance of finding suitable clipart. Even if you are "artistically challenged", it is still possible to produce some excellent animations using Flash.

Of course, if you use clipart in web sites, CD-ROM presentations, etc., it is essential to check the copyright conditions. The restrictions on the use of clipart are usually minimal, if there are any at all. Clipart having endless "strings attached" would be a bit pointless. However, it is still essential to read the "fine print" to ensure that you stay strictly within the rules. For example, in some cases it is a requirement that the source of the clipart is acknowledged, and it is often a requirement that it will not be used in a way that will bring the owners of the copyright into disrepute. The rules are often different depending on whether the clipart is published in paper or electronic form. For example, there may be restrictions on the maximum resolution that can be used if the artwork is published in electronic form, such as on the Internet or on a CD-ROM.

Fig.2.58

Fig.2.59

Fig.2.60 The final frame with the fully processed image

Precision

Returning to the Transform submenu, the Scale and Rotate option brings up the simple dialogue box of Figure 2.61. This enables objects or groups to be scaled and (or) rotated by specified amounts. Flash is not really intended for things like technical drawings, but with charts, diagrams, and even general illustration work it can be useful to do things precisely rather than "by eye". The scaling factor is a percentage, which is set below 100 percent to provide a reduction in size, or over 100 percent to provide an increase. Decimal points are allowed, so very accurate scaling can be achieved in theory. Bear in mind that the "real world" accuracy is likely to be limited by the accuracy of the output device, especially if that device is the screen of a monitor.

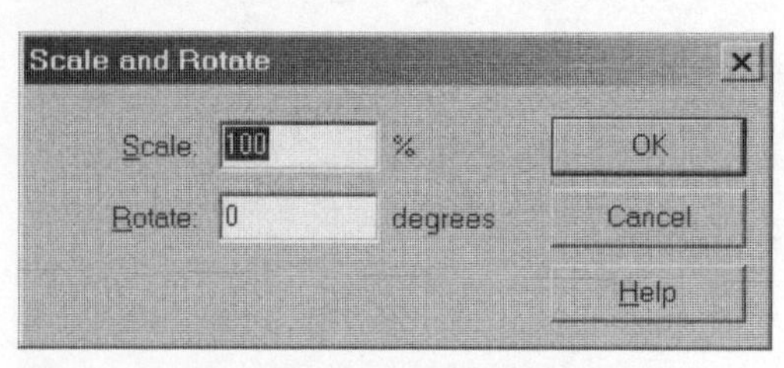

Fig.2.61 The Scale and Rotate window

The rotation is given as an angle in degrees, and decimal points are again permitted. Once more, bear in mind that the true accuracy obtained is likely to be dictated by the output device rather than Flash's mathematical prowess. The rectangle in Figure 2.62 has been rotated by 18.5 degrees, and clockwise rotation has been produced. A negative value is used where rotation in a counter-clockwise direction is required. The Rotate 90° CW and Rotate 90° CCW, as one would expect, simple rotate the selected object or group by 90 degrees in a clockwise or counter-clockwise direction.

Fig.2.62 The rectangle has been rotated by 18.5 degrees

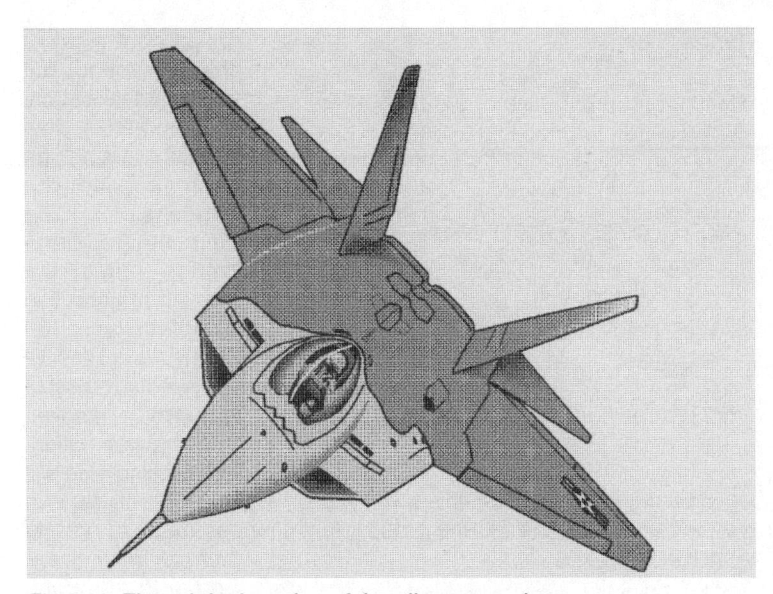

Fig.2.63 The original version of the clipart aeroplane

Flip

The Flip options in the Transform submenu converts the selected object or group into a "mirror" image of the original. Figure 2.63 shows the starting image while Figures 2.64 and 2.65 respectively show vertically and horizontally flipped versions. In Figure 2.66 both horizontal and vertical flipping have been applied.

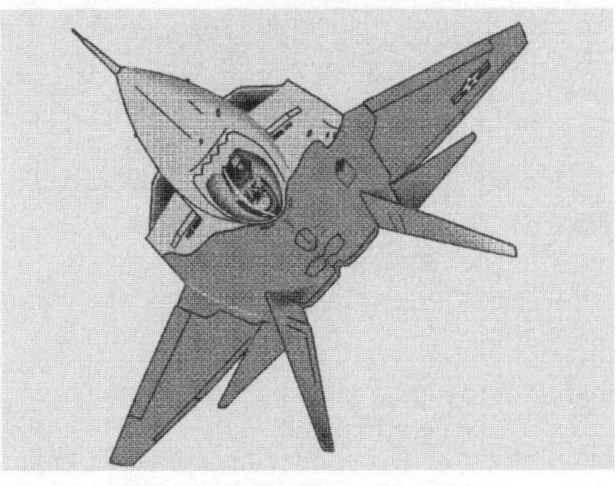

Fig.2.64 The vertically flipped image

It is possible to remove all transformations by stepping back a suitable number of commands using the

Fig.2.65 The horizontally flipped image

Undo command of the Edit menu, but this could take some time and other work could also be undone in the process. The Remove Transform option in the Transform submenu enables all transformations of the selected object or group to be removed in a single operation, but nothing else will be altered. Note that using this command on a group will only remove transformations applied to the group. Any changes made to objects before they were added to the group will not be undone. Furthermore, it is not possible to undo these transformations by ungrouping the objects and then selecting them individually. It is possible to manually reverse any changes using this method, provided you can remember exactly what you did in the first place.

Fig.2.66 This version has been flipped horizontally and vertically

Text

Text is a subject that will be covered in detail later in this book, so the Text menu will not be considered in detail here. The available options (Figure 2.67) should look familiar if you are used to word processors, graphics programs, or just about any programs that can handle text. There are the usual facilities to control text size, alignment, font, etc.

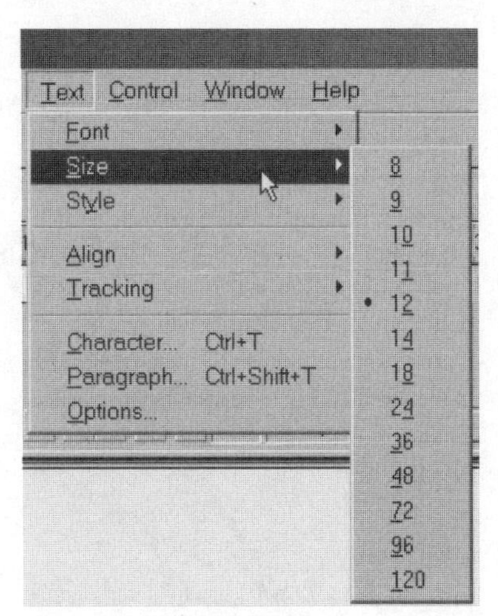

Fig.2.67 The Text menu

Control

The Control menu (Figure 2.68) enables movies to be played, rewound to the beginning, or single stepped backward or forward. The Test Movie option first saves the movie as a standard swf Flash file using the current filename plus a swf extension. Any existing file of the same name and type will be overwritten, so be careful not to obliterate a file you still need when using this option. Once the file has been saved the Flash Player is

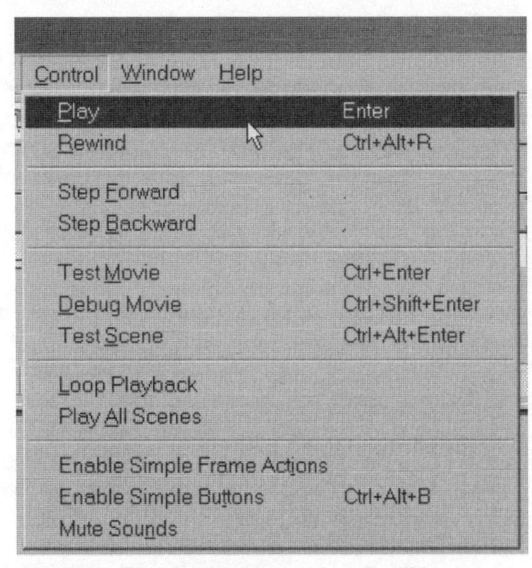

Fig.2.68 The Control menu has facilities to control the playing of movies within Flash

Fig.2.69 The Test Movie option in action

launched and then the movie file is played (Figure 2.69). I suppose that it is a good idea to check any finished movie using the Flash Player program prior to using the movie in earnest. However, this feature is of most use when the movie has interactive content that can only be tested properly using a player program or a suitably equipped browser. To exit the player left-click on the cross in the top right-hand corner of the player's window.

There are options to aid debugging of movies, but we will not consider these here. Try loading one of the simple animations produced during earlier exercises, select the Loop Playback option from the Control menu, and the press the Enter key to start the animation. After it has completed a single run the movie is automatically rewound to frame 1 and run again. This process continues indefinitely, but selecting Stop from the Control menu will bring the movie to a halt. Another option in the Control menu enables any sounds to be switched off.

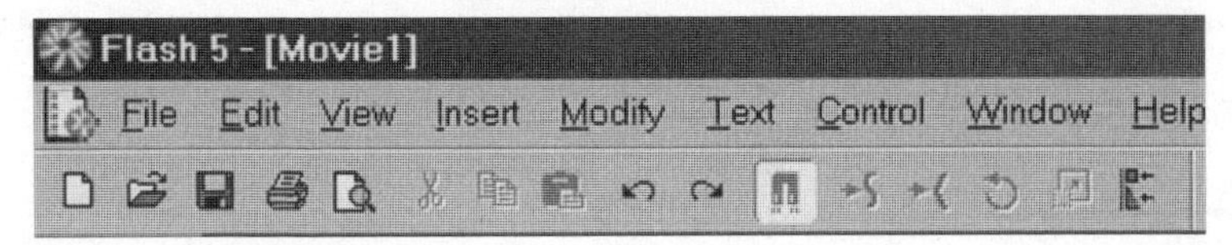

Fig.2.70 The Main toolbar

Main Toolbar

The Main Toolbar (Figure 2.70) provides rapid access to the most commonly used commands, and largely duplicates facilities available via the menu system. Working from left to right, the first button opens a new and totally blank movie so that a new one can be built from scratch. The next three are the standard Open, Save, and Print commands. Most users of Flash are primarily interested in producing a finished result that will appear on-screen rather than in print, but the ability to print out artwork is more than a little useful.

Fig.2.71 The Print Preview facility enables page layouts to be checked prior to printing

Fig.2.72 The Print Preview facility can provide zoomed views

The same is true of the Print Preview facility provided by the next button in the toolbar. This provides a visual representation of the printed page (Figure 2.71) so that you can check that everything is as required prior to actually printing a copy. Since colour printers are often extremely slow and have high running costs, it is definitely a good idea to habitually use the Print Preview facility before printing things out. The row of buttons towards the top of the Print Preview screen enables the view of the page to be zoomed in and out. Figure 2.72 shows a zoomed view of the page.

The usual scrollbars permit scrolling around a zoomed view. Operate the Print button to go ahead and print the page or the Close button to return to the normal Flash interface. If the page layout is not to your liking there are various settings that can be changed by way of the Page Layout option in the File menu. This produces the dialogue box of Figure 2.73. This is very straightforward, with settings for the margin widths, centring, scaling, and so on. The dummy page in the top left-hand corner of the window shows how the settings will affect the appearance of the printed page.

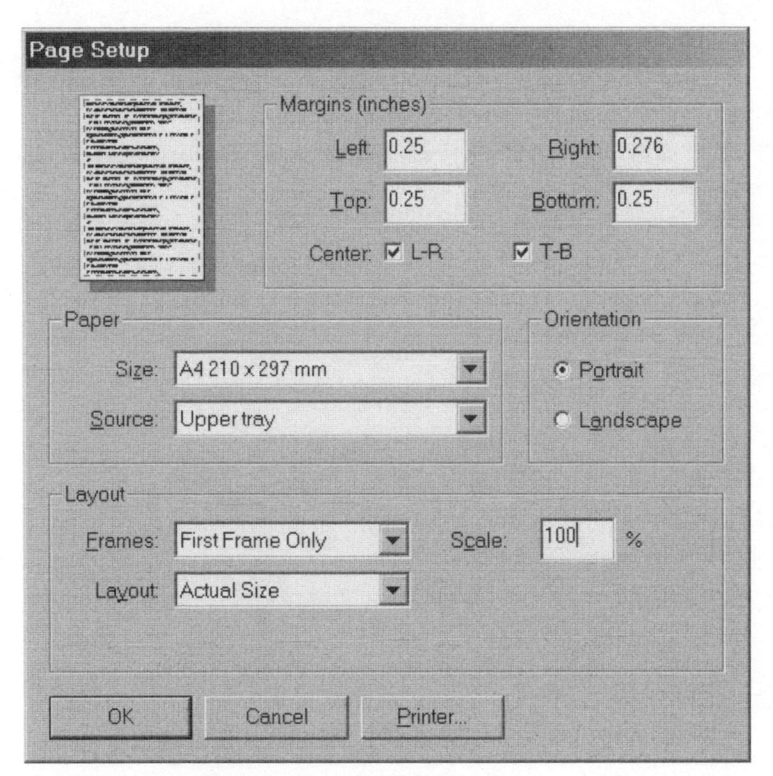

Fig.2.73 The Page Setup dialogue box

The buttons described so far duplicate functions available using the File menu. The next five buttons in the Main Toolbar duplicate functions available under the Edit menu. Working from left to right they provide the standard Cut, Copy, Paste, Undo, and Redo functions. The next button toggles the Snap to Objects function on and off, and this duplicates the facility available under the View menu.

Smooth and Straighten

Next along the Main Toolbar are the Smooth and Straighten buttons. The effect of the Straighten button is the more obvious, so we will start with this one. As its name implies, this command turns curved lines into straight lines. Figure 2.74 shows a line that has been scribbled onto the

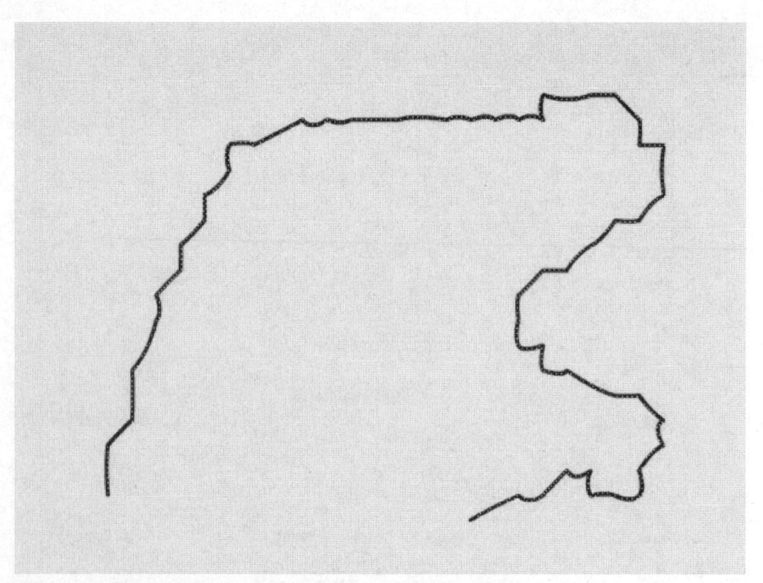

Fig.2.74 The original version of the scribbled line

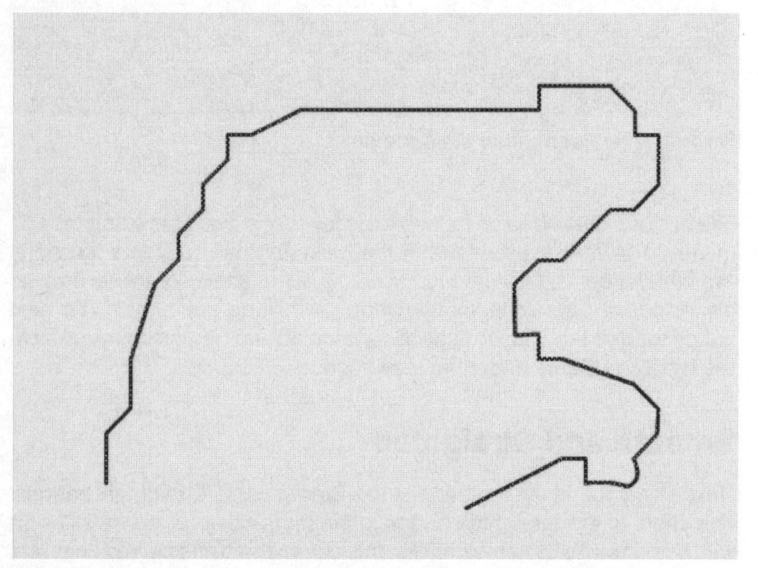

Fig.2.75 The effect of the Straighten facility is clearly visible

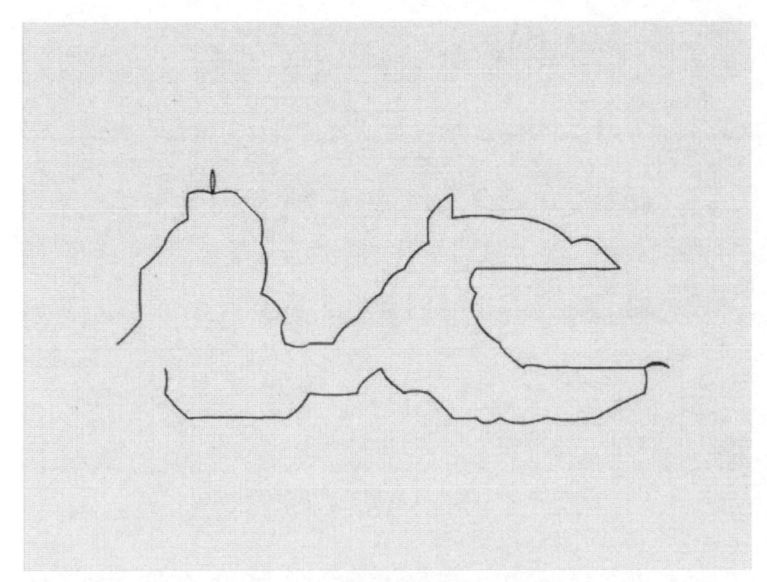

Fig.2.76 The line prior to smoothing being applied

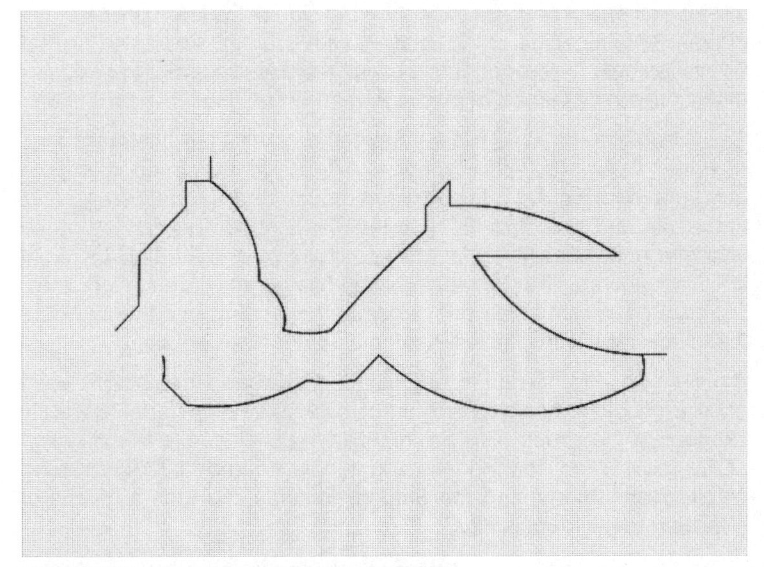

Fig.2.77 The line after repeated smoothing

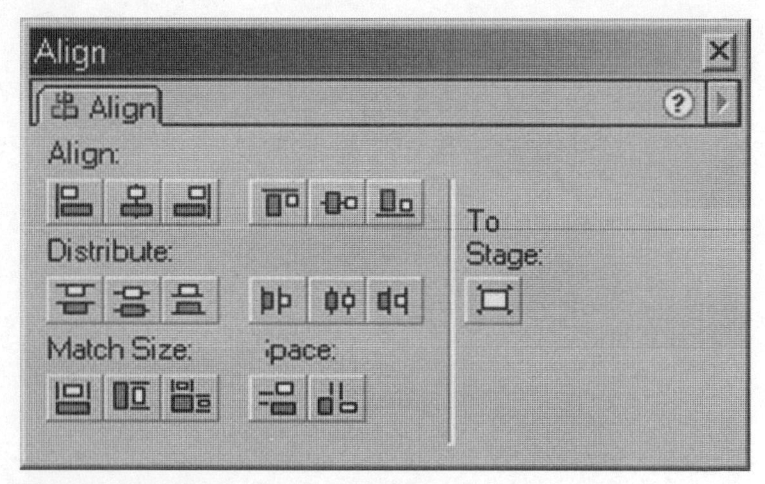

Fig.2.78 The Align panel offers a range of alignment options

screen and then selected using the Arrow tool. Operating the Straighten button produced the result shown in Figure 2.75. It would be a slight exaggeration to say that all the curves had been removed, since there is still a small one present on the right-hand side of the line. However, the curves have been largely replaced with straight lines. Using the Straighten button a second time is usually sufficient to remove any curves that survived the first set of processing.

The Smoothing effect is more subtle, and its effect is often less than obvious. It removes small bumps and lumps in lines in an attempt to give long regular curves. In doing so it reduces the number of segments in the line and simplifies it. Note that the Smooth function is not the opposite of the Straighten facility, and that it does not convert straight lines into curves. The Smooth function has no effect on straight lines. Figure 2.76 shows a line prior to smoothing being used, and Figure 2.77 shows the same line after smoothing has been applied.

Because the effect tends to be quite limited when smoothing is used once, it has been used over thirty times in this example in order to grossly exaggerate the effect. This has resulted in considerable simplification of the line. When drawing freehand curves it can be difficult to avoid small imperfections, and the Smooth function provides a means of removing these irregularities.

Alignment

Fig.2.79 The two rectangles prior to alignment

Finally, the last button in the toolbar is the Alignment button. When operated this button launches the panel of Figure 2.78, which gives various alignment options. Here we are talking about the alignment of the selected objects and not text alignment. Various options are available and it is not too difficult to work out what most of them do. As a couple of examples, Figure 2.79 shows two objects on the screen prior to alignment, and Figure 2.80 shows them after the Align Left Edge option has been used. The lower rectangle has been moved to the left so that its left edge is aligned with the same edge of the upper rectangle. In Figures 2.81 and 2.82 the Align Vertical Centre option has been used to align the three blocks vertically.

Fig.2.80 The rectangles after the Align Left Edge option has been used

In most cases it is better to draw objects with the aid of the visual and snap grids so that they are correct in the first place, rather than rely on the Alignment function to correct errors of placement or size. However, this feature can be useful in situations where for some reason it is difficult to get the alignment accurate using other methods. It can also get things back into kilter if careless editing has allowed objects to “wander”.

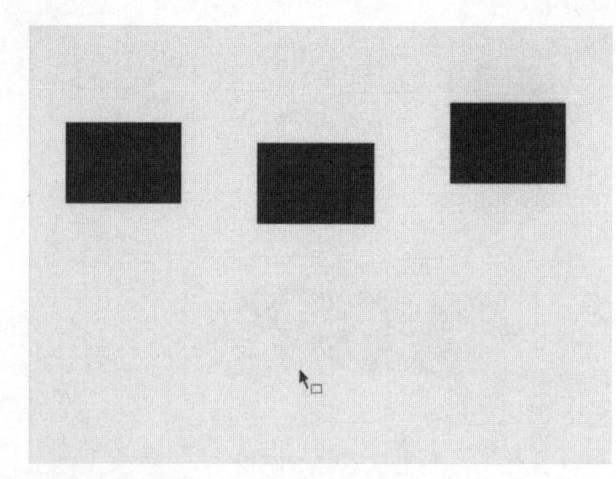

Fig.2.81 Three rectangles prior to alignment

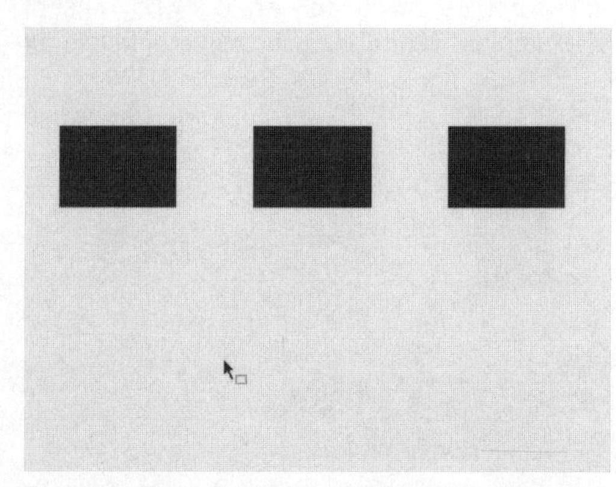

Fig.2.82 The effect of vertical centre alignment

The Main Toolbar is an optional extra that can be switched off via the Window menu in order to save screen space. However, it provides almost instant access to a number of commonly used features, including the Undo and Redo facilities, and it is probably best to leave it permanently in place. It will almost certainly save a great deal of time and fully merit the small amount of screen area that it occupies.

More menus

Right clicking will sometimes produce a pop-up menu, but exactly what appears (if anything) depends on what is right clicked. Right clicking on an object in the work area selects that object and produces the menu of Figure 2.83. This gives rapid access to editing facilities such as Cut, Copy, Rotate, and Scale. If a group or collection of objects is selected, right clicking on one of the objects in the collection or group will produce the same menu. However, editing facilities such as Cut and Rotate will then apply to all the objects in the collection or group. Right clicking on a blank part of the work area produces the pop-up menu of Figure 2.84. This menu gives quick access to the Paste facility, plus the settings for rulers, grids, and guides.

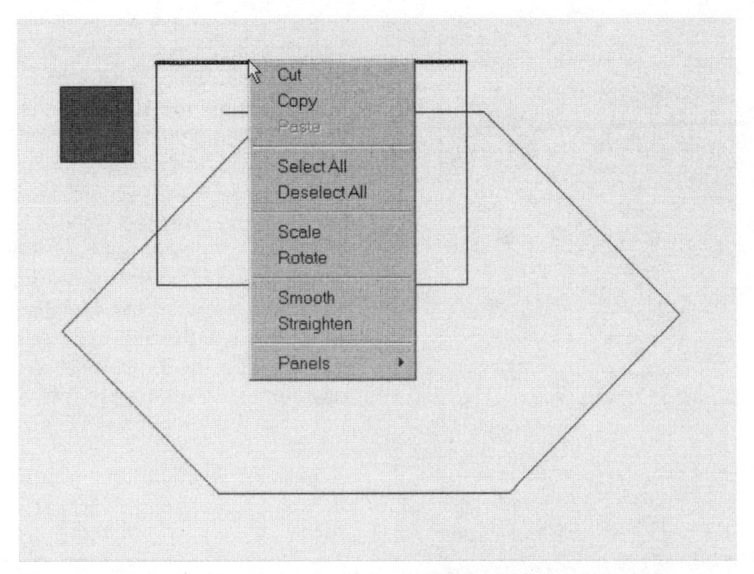

Fig.2.83 Right clicking on a drawing element produces this menu

Paste

You will probably have noticed that there are two versions of the Paste command. The standard Paste command places the objects in the centre of the stage. Once deposited on the drawing the objects can be dragged to the required positions. The Paste in Place command deposits the objects at whatever position on the screen they were copied from. If the original is still in place, the copy will be placed directly on top of it. However, the copy will be selected automatically when it is placed on the stage, and it can be dragged to a new position, leaving the original intact.

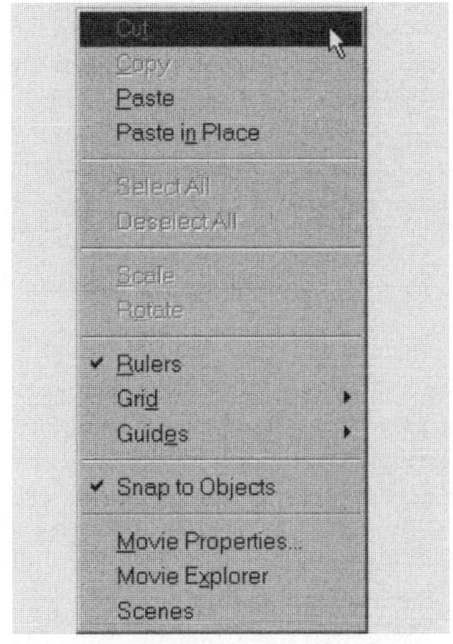

Fig.2.84 Right clicking on a blank area produces this menu

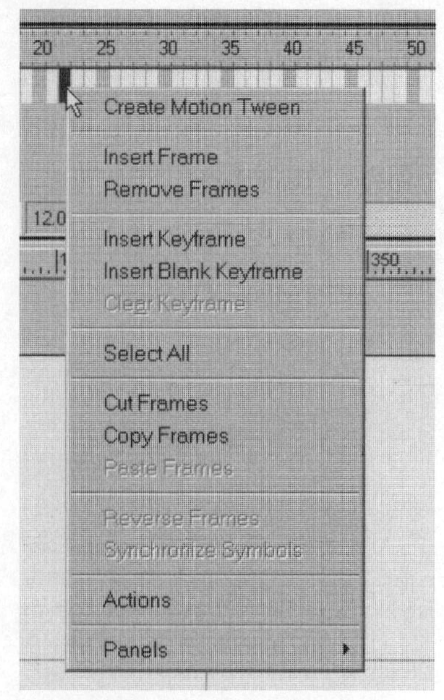

Fig.2.85 The popup frame menu

Right clicking on a frame in the Timeline produces the menu of Figure 2.85, which offers some useful frame related options. Right clicking on most other parts of the Flash interface has no effect, apart from panels, and these are covered in later chapters. We have not covered all aspects of the menu system here, but most of the facilities available via the menus have been described. More are covered in subsequent chapters.

Points to remember

The menu system provides access to a huge range of functions, but it is not possible to operate Flash using the menu system as the sole method of control. For example, many functions, including the drawing tools and some editing facilities, can not be accessed via the menu system. In common with most graphics programs, Flash is controlled using a combination of menus, toolbars, and panels.

You only have to display parts of the user interface that you actually need at the time.

The File menu has the usual options such as Save, Open, New, and Print. There are also various import and export options that enable images to be loaded in various standard formats, and to be saved in a range of formats. For example, the popular GIF format can be imported and exported.

The Edit menu has the usual Cut, Copy, and Paste features. There are also Undo and Redo options. Although Flash has no History facility, the multilevel Undo and Redo commands give similar capabilities, and by default the last 100 actions can be undone.

Using the View menu it is possible to switch some windows on and off, but this facility is largely controlled via the Window menu. The View menu controls the zoom level for the work area, and is also used to control grids and guides. Guidelines, visual grids, snap grids, rulers, and object snaps are all useful when drawing with precision rather than "by eye".

With the Insert menu it is possible to add or remove frames and add keyframes. Other things can be added, including layers.

The Modify menu provides access to a huge range of editing facilities. These include the ability to group and ungroup objects, rotate and scale individual objects or groups, and to arrange the order of groups in order to give simple three-dimensional effects.

It is not possible to add text using the Text menu, but a full range of typographical settings is available. These include text size, font, style, and alignment. Use the Text tool to add text.

The Control menu provides Play, Rewind, and single stepping controls for movies. It also permits the sound (if any) to be switched on and off, movies to be looped, and the movie to be tested using the Flash Player program.

Using the Window menu it is possible to select which windows will be displayed. It is sometimes necessary to do a fair amount of juggling with the windows, keeping a reasonable amount of the screen clear for the work area by only displaying those windows that are needed at the time.

The Main Toolbar provides rapid access to commonly used facilities, and it largely duplicates features that are available via the menu system. New, Open, Save, Print, Undo, and Redo are some of the commands provided by this toolbar.

Right clicking on an object brings up a menu that provides some editing facilities. Right clicking on a blank area of the work area produces a menu that gives rapid access to, amongst other things, the settings for rulers, guides, grids, and object snapping.

3

Drawing tools

Line Tool

The Tools palette (Figure 3.1) is optional and can be switched off to conserve screen space. However, it is central to drawing and editing images, and you will probably wish to have it permanently displayed on the screen. The Tools palette is divided into several sections, and we will start with upper section, which contains the tools that you will use most often.

The Line tool is used to draw straight lines, and it is used by first placing the pointer over the start point and then holding down the left mouse button. The pointer is then moved to the finish point of the line, and a line will join the start point to the current position of the pointer. As the pointer is moved, the line will be continuously redrawn so that there is always a straight line from the start point to the pointer (Figure 3.2). This is known as "rubber-banding" incidentally. When the pointer is at precisely the required finish point, release the left mouse button and the line will be drawn on the screen. Multi-section lines and shapes must be drawn using individual lines joined together (Figure 3.3), but the object snap ensures that there is no difficulty in getting the lines joined together properly. As will be explained in detail later, enclosed shapes can be given a fill colour.

Often it is necessary to draw lines precisely horizontally or vertically. Switching on the snap grid helps to avoid accidentally drawing lines that are fractionally off the vertical and horizontal, or the Shift key can be pressed while drawing lines. Rather than following the pointer precisely, the rubber-band line will get as close as possible while producing lines that are horizontal, vertical, or at 45 degrees. This is similar to the orthogonal mode of many technical drawing programs.

Although arcs can not be drawn using Line Tool, it is possible to draw a straight line and then edit it to produce an arc. Try drawing a line in the drawing area and then select the Arrow tool. When the pointer is placed near the line it changes slightly, with an arc appearing in place of the

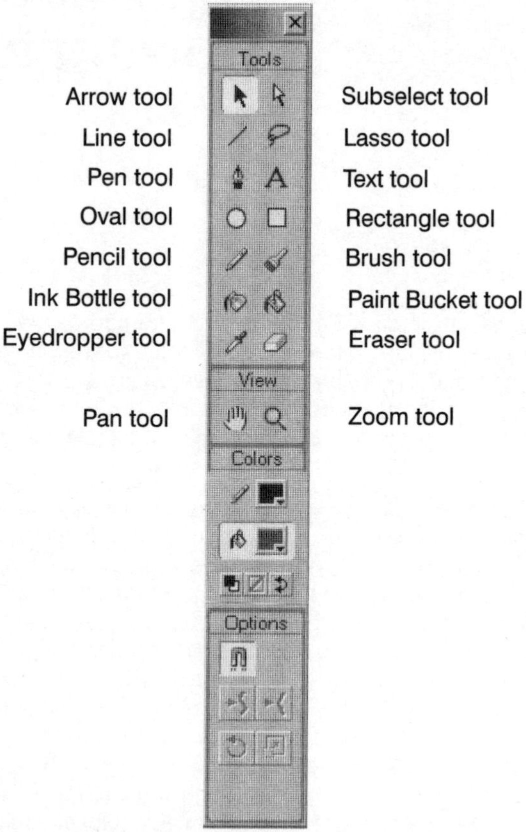

Arrow tool
Subselect tool
Line tool
Lasso tool
Pen tool
Text tool
Oval tool
Rectangle tool
Pencil tool
Brush tool
Ink Bottle tool
Paint Bucket tool
Eyedropper tool
Eraser tool
Pan tool
Zoom tool

Tools
View
Colors
Options

Fig.3.1 The tools available from the Tools palette

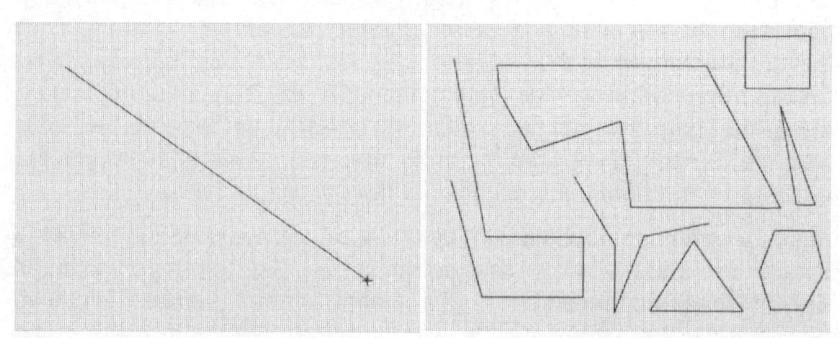

Fig. 3.2 A rubber-banded line

Fig.3.3 Results using the Line tool

usual rectangle at the bottom of the pointer (Figure 3.4). The line can then be dragged into an arc (Figure 3.5), and the type of arc obtained depends on the point on the line that is dragged, and where it is dragged. The further it is dragged, the greater the curvature of the arc. Figure 3.6 shows some arcs produced using this method. If you put some lines on the screen and then try dragging various points on the lines around the screen you will soon grasp the way in which this facility operates.

Fig.3.4 An arc apears under the pointer when it is in range of a line

The nibbling effect that occurs with shapes was described in the previous chapter, and it is important to bear in mind that a similar effect happens when lines cross other objects. Due care needs to be taken in order to avoid accidentally slicing objects in two using lines. In the example of Figure 3.7 a line has been drawn through a filled ellipse. This looks fine, but trying to select the ellipse and the fill colour to move them can not be achieved by simply double clicking on the object using the Arrow tool. The ellipse has been split into two separate entities, as demonstrated in Figure 3.8 where the two sections have been move apart slightly. In fact further damage has occurred because the outline of the ellipse is the same colour as the line. This has resulted in the middle part of the line being erased as well.

Of course, the problem can be overcome by turning the ellipse and its fill

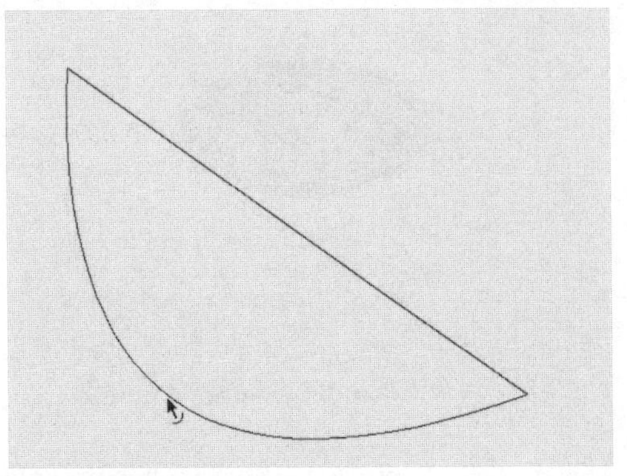

Fig.3.5 Pulling a line into an arc

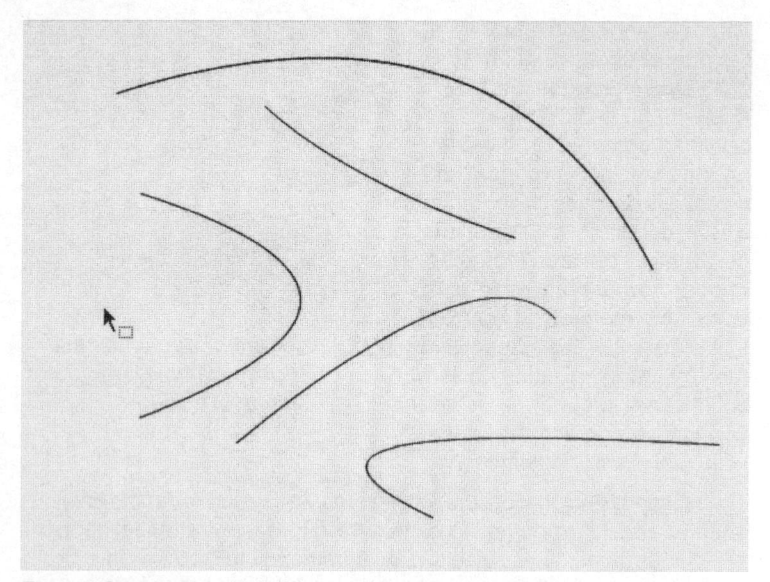

Fig.3.6 Some arcs produced by dragging straight lines using the Arrow tool

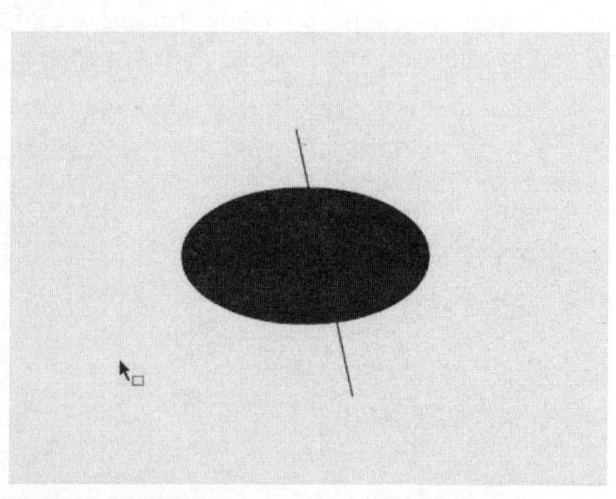

Fig.3.7 The line has cut the ellipse in two

into a group prior to adding the line. However, this results in the line being stacked behind the ellipse, even though it was added afterwards (Figure 3.9). A group always appears over non-grouped items, and using the Send to Back option from the Arrange submenu will not change this. There is a way around the problem, and this is simply to group the line. Even though it is a single object, it can still be turned into a group. With the options in the Arrange submenu it can then be

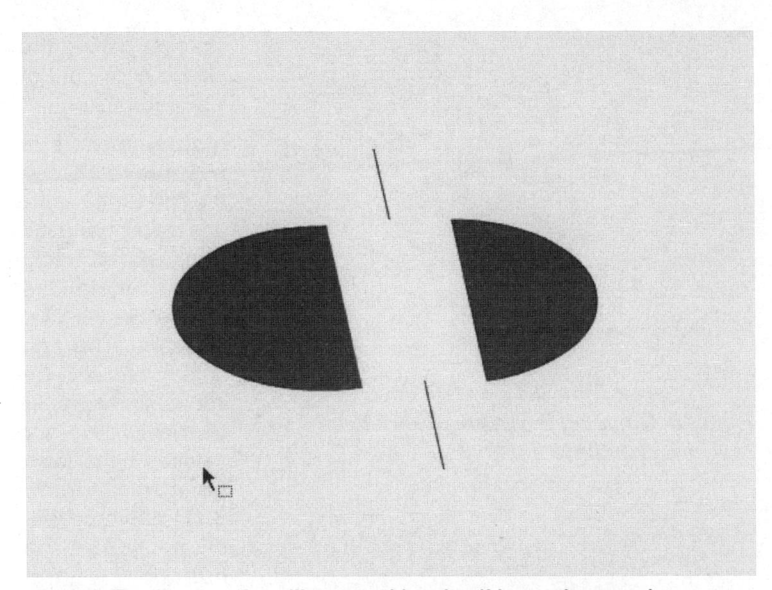

Fig.3.8 The line cut the ellipse, and has itself been damaged

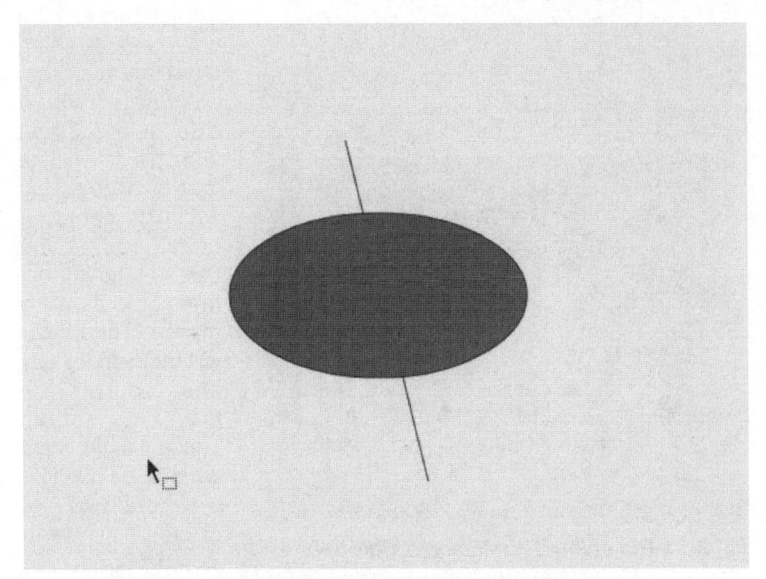

Fig.3.9 Grouping the ellipse results in it covering the line

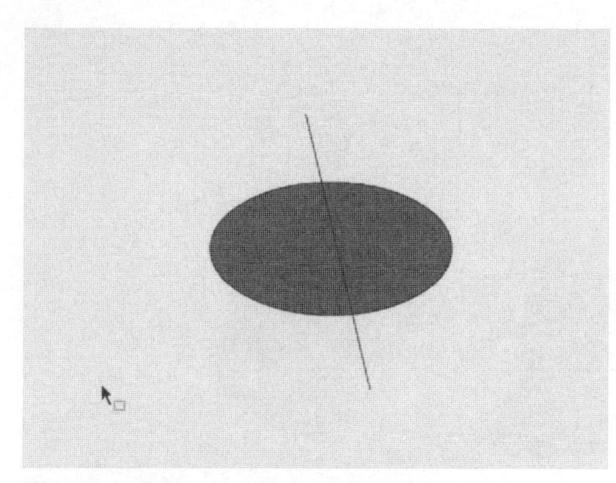

Fig.3.10 Grouping the line enables it to be brought to the front

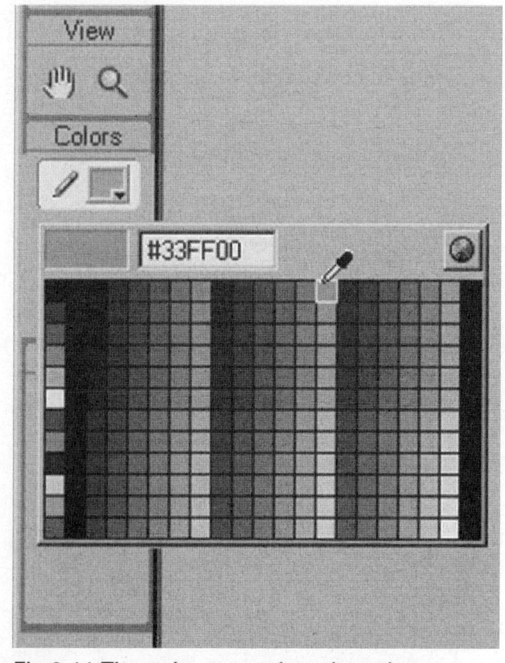

Fig.3.11 The colour swatch and eyedropper

stacked behind the ellipse or in front of it (Figure 3.10).

Incidentally, it is possible to change the line width, style, and colour using the Stroke panel. Using the panels is covered in the next chapter. The line colour can also be set using the upper of the two colour palettes in the Tools palette (Figure 3.11). Simply left-click on the button and then use the "eyedropper" to select one of the colours in the chart, or a colour from anywhere within one of the Flash windows. The button will be filled with the selected colour so that you can see the current line colour at a glance. This colour will be used for any lines drawn on the screen subsequently, and it will also be used for the outlines of circles and rectangles.

Oval tool

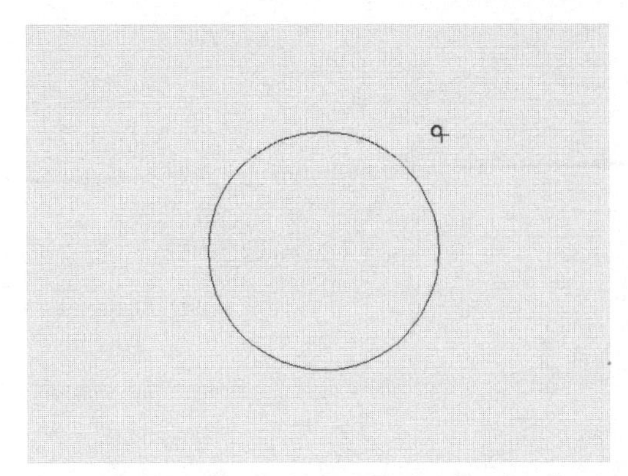

Fig.3.12 Drawing a circle with the Oval tool

We did some dabbling with this tool in chapter 1, so you should have no difficulty in using it to produce circles and ellipses. Simply operate the left mouse button with the pointer at a suitable position in the work area, and then drag a circle or ellipse of the required size. A circle is obtained if the pointer is at 45 degrees to the start point, and a small circle then appears just above the pointer to indicate that the pointer has snapped into circle mode (Figure 3.12). The same thing happens using the pointer at angles of 135, 225, and 315 degrees from the starting point.

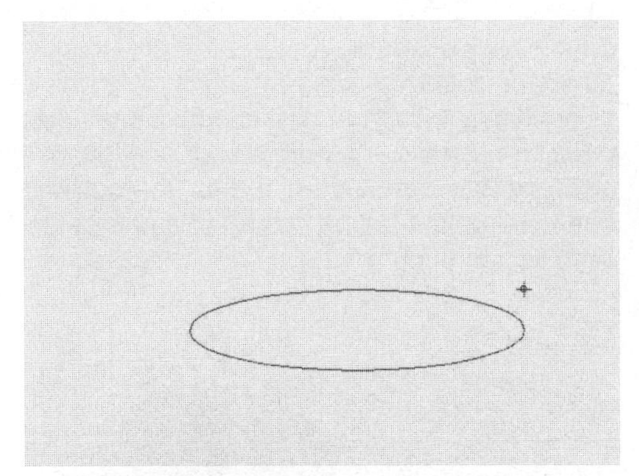

Fig.3.13 Ellipses can also be produced using the Oval tool

Positioning the pointer at an angle of other than 45 degrees, etc. causes it to be squashed into an ellipse (Figure 3.13). Although this tool is called the Oval tool, it actually produces circles and ellipses, and not what are generally accepted as ovals. Note that this tool can be forced to produce circles by holding down the Shift key while dragging the pointer to the second point (Figure 3.14). The angle from the second point from the starting point is then irrelevant. The distance is all that matters, and this governs the size of the circle.

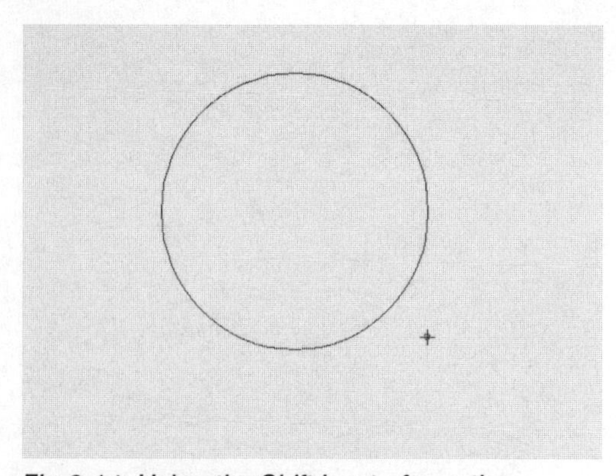

Fig.3.14 Using the Shift key to force the production of a circle

Do not forget that circles and ellipses consist of two separate parts, which are the outline and the fill. If you draw a circle or ellipse and then click on the fill to select it, it can then be dragged clear of the outline (Figure 3.15). The two parts can be used together as a single entity, or treated as separate objects, as preferred. To select the outline and the fill, simply double-click on the fill. This system of single clicking to select part of an object or double clicking to select all of it is used a great deal when using Flash. It can be used to select one section of a line or the whole thing for example. As pointed out previously, changing the line colour also changes the colour used for the outlines of circles and ellipses. The lower colour button in the Tools palette is used to select the colour used for fills (Figure 3.16).

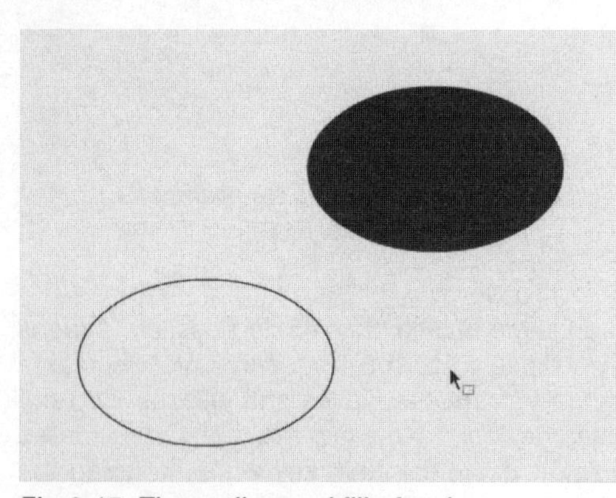

Fig.3.15 The outline and fill of a shape are separate entities

We saw previously how the Arrow tool changes when it is placed near a straight line, and that the line can then be dragged into an arc. Something similar occurs when the Arrow tool is placed near a circle or an ellipse, enabling the object to be dragged into a new shape. A rubber-band line shows the new shape that will be obtained (Figure

3.17). Note that the object must not be selected when performing this type of operation, or it will be moved around the stage rather than being distorted. By repeatedly dragging edges of the object it is possible to produce a wide variety of shapes. If the object is filled, the fill will adjust to all changes in the shape of the outline so that the object is always filled properly (Figure 3.18).

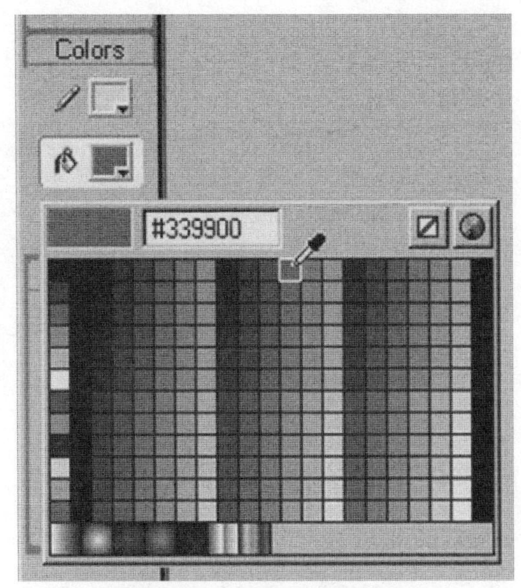

Fig.3.16 Fill colours are selected in the same way as line colours

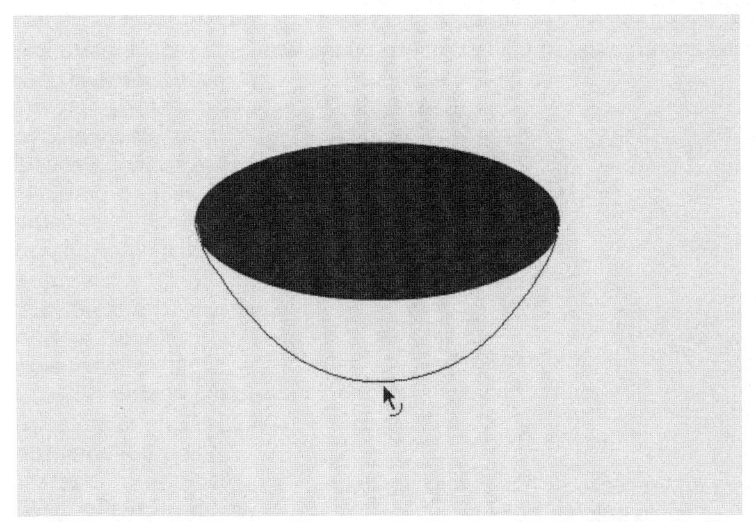

Fig.3.17 The outline of a shape can be dragged using the arrow tool

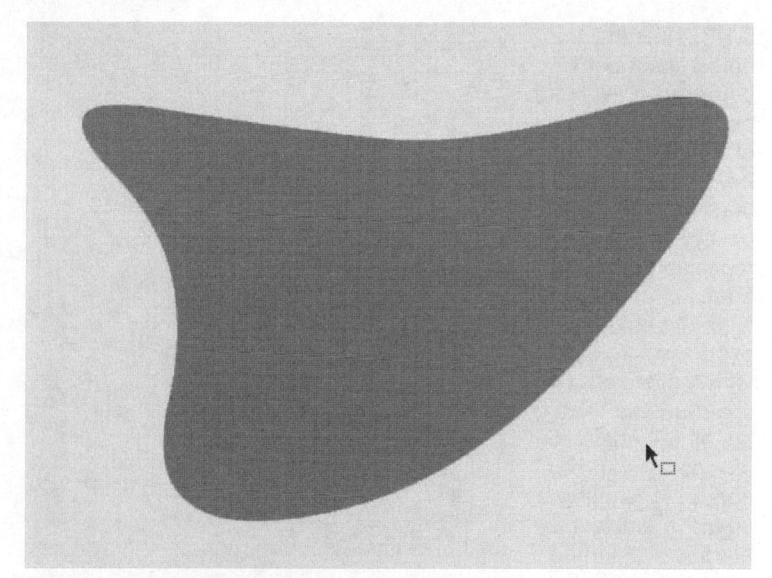

Fig.3.18 Elaborate shapes can be made from simple beginnings

Rectangle tool

The Rectangle tool is very straightforward in use. Drag a rectangle onto the screen, release the left mouse button when the required size and aspect ratio has been achieved, and the rectangle appears on the screen. A square is easy to produce, because the rectangle will snap to produce a square when the aspect ratio is close to 1 to 1. A circle appears near the pointer to indicate that a snap action is in operation (Figure 3.19). Alternatively, hold

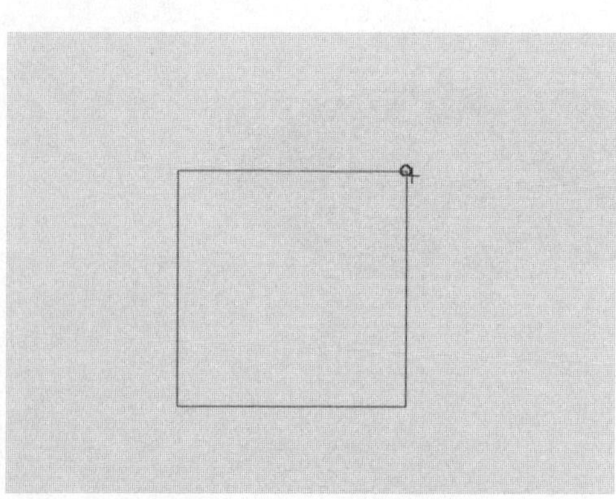

Fig.3.19 Producing a square using the rectangle tool

down the Shift key while dragging the rectangle and it will only be possible to produce a square (Figure 3.20).

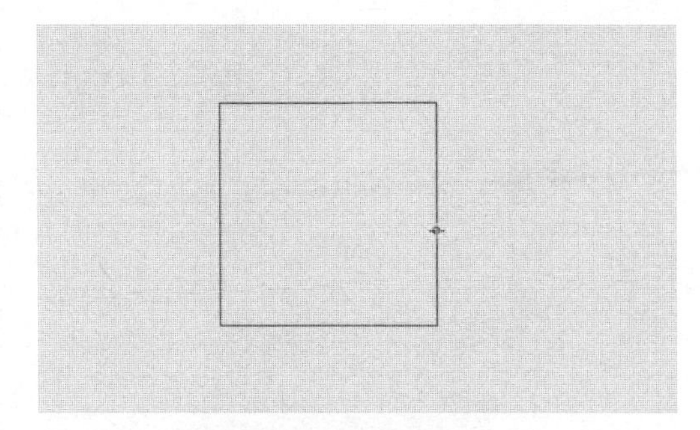

Fig.3.20 Producing a square with the aid of the Shift key

The sides of the square can be dragged into arcs using the arrow tool, and this operates in the same manner as dragging a straight line into an arc (Figure 3.21). Using repeated operations of this type it is possible to produce some elaborate shapes that have little in common with the original rectangle (Figure 3.22). At the bottom of the Tools palette there is a section labelled Options, and for the Line and Oval tools this area is blank.

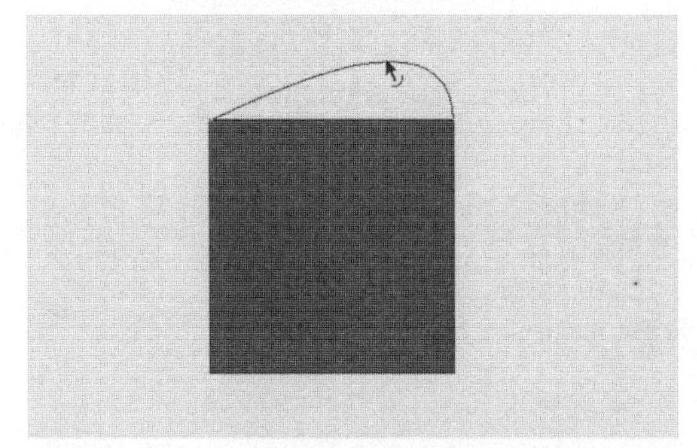

Fig.3.21 The outline can be adjusted using the Arrow tool

However, there is one option available when the Rectangle tool is selected, and this is the Round Rectangle Radius option (Figure 3.23). This enables the corners of rectangles to be rounded. When this

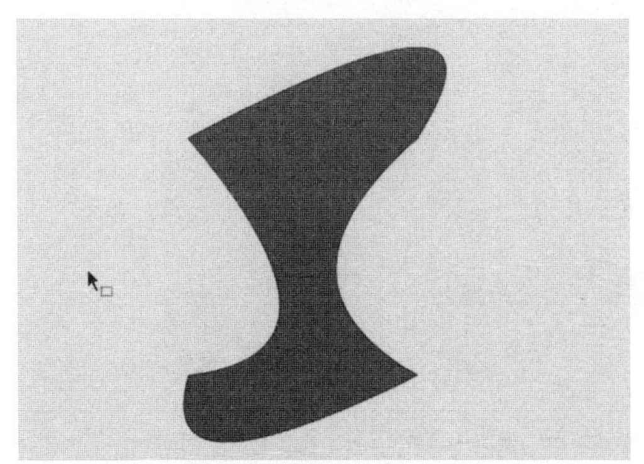

Fig.3.22 Elaborate shapes can be produced

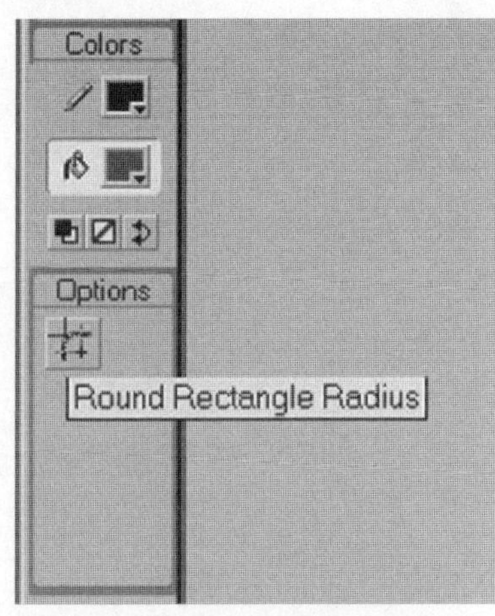

Fig.3.23 Rectangles can have rounded corners

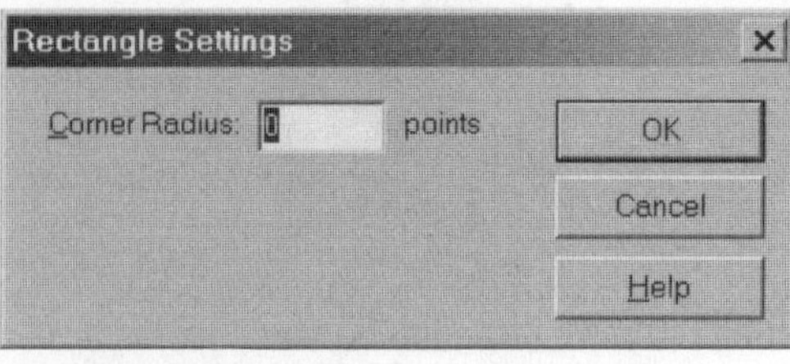

Fig.3.24 The Rectangle Settings window

Fig.3.25 A rectangle with rounded corners

button is operated the dialogue box of Figure 3.24 appears, and a radius for the corner can then be entered. The figure used is a point size incidentally, but it will probably be necessary to use a little trial and error to find the value that provides the desired effect. Figure 3.25 shows a rectangle that has a corner radius of 20 points.

Pencil tool

At first the pencil tool seems to be much like equivalent tools in many bitmap drawing programs. Freehand lines can be drawn on the screen by holding down the left mouse button and moving the mouse. As the pointer is moved around the work area it leaves a line showing the course it has taken. The mouse button is released when the line has been completed. It is at this point that it becomes apparent that the Pencil tool is not a normal freehand drawing tool. There are some obvious changes in the line on the screen when the mouse button is

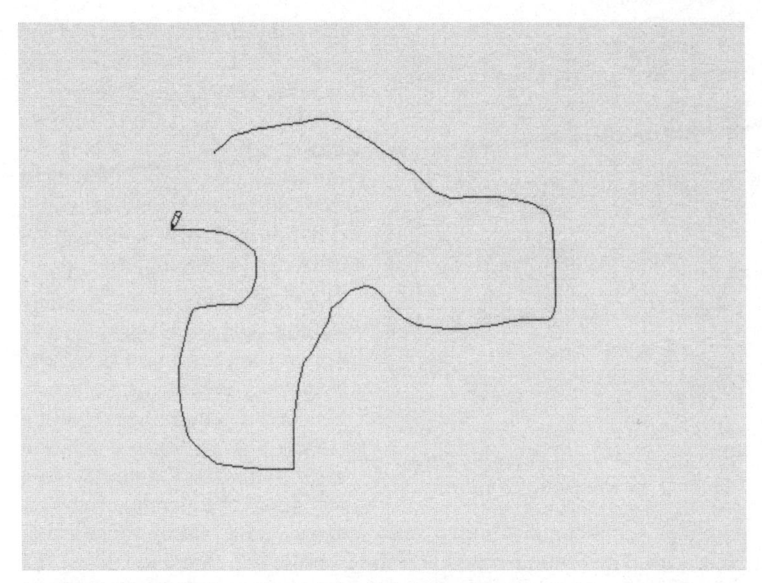

Fig.3.26 The "raw" version of the line being drawn

released. The "before" and "after" versions of Figures 3.26 and 3.27 show this effect very clearly.

So why does this happen? When using Flash it helps to bear in mind that it is not a bitmap graphics program. With a paint program the freehand drawing tools are simply changing pixels as the pointer is moved over them. Flash deals with lines, arcs, and fills rather than pixels, and anything you draw on the screen has to be converted into the graphics primitives. Exactly how Flash interprets what you produce with a freehand

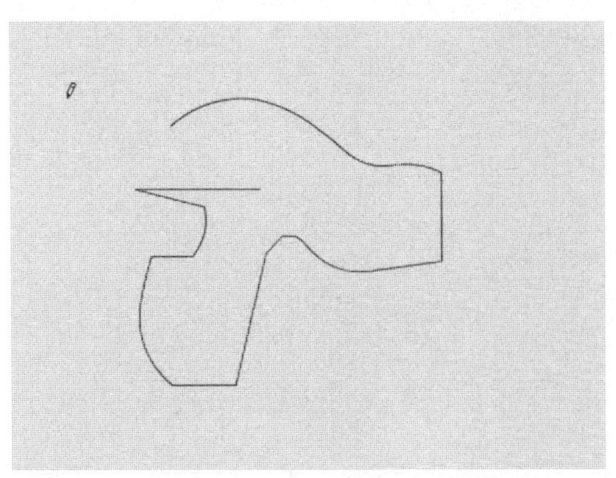

Fig.3.27 The processed version of the line

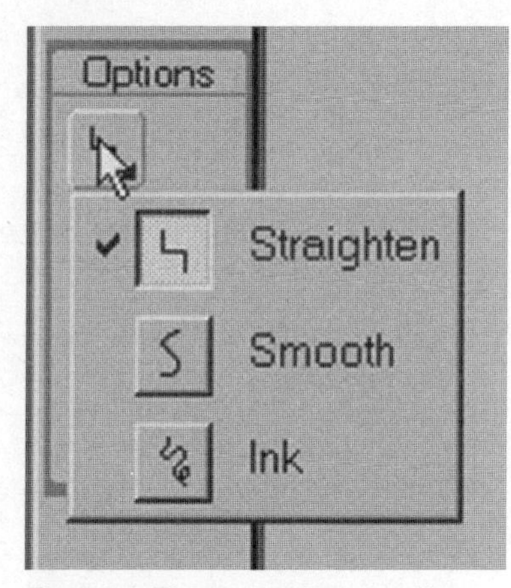

Fig.3.28 There are three modes for the Pencil tool

drawing tool depends on the mode in use. There is only one button in the Options section of the Tools palette when the Pencil tool is selected, and this is the Pencil Mode button. Operating this button produces a little pop-out panel that provides three drawing modes (Figure 3.28).

The Straighten mode is used by default, and this does its best to convert anything you draw into a series of straight lines. However, where straight lines are clearly inappropriate it will use arcs instead. Obviously this tidying up of your artwork can be helpful in some circumstances, but in others it could make nonsense of your work. The Smooth mode is better if something closer to the original line is needed. Figures 3.29 and 3.30 show "before" and "after" versions of the same line using the Smooth drawing mode.

The differences between the original and processed versions of the line are much smaller in this mode. The smoothing removes any small irregularities but otherwise leaves things much as they were. When drawing using a mouse it can be difficult to produce lines that are free from minor glitches. A graphics tablet plus a pen-like drawing implement is a much better choice for freehand drawing, but it can still be difficult to produce lines that are free from minor imperfections. The smoothing helps to remove small imperfections in lines without making any radical alterations to them.

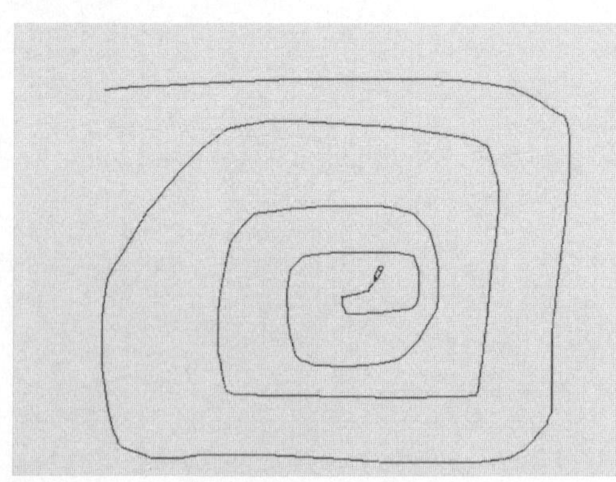

Fig.3.29 The "raw" version of the line prior to smoothing

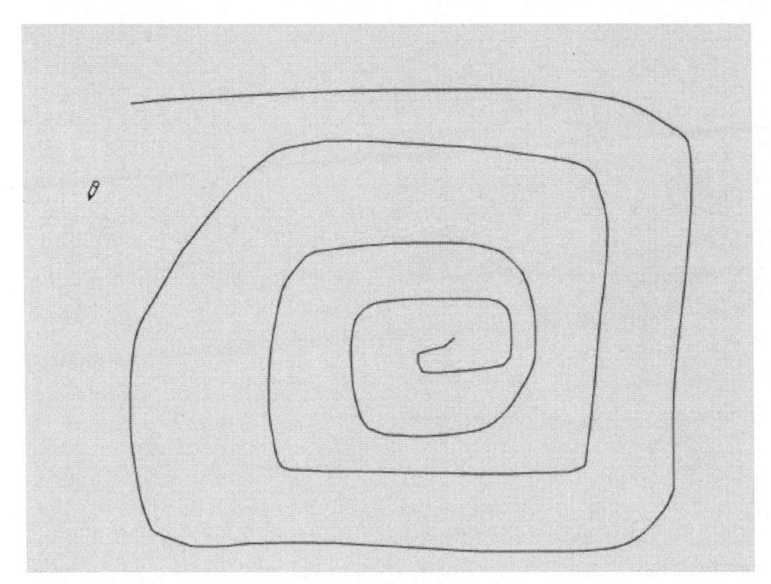

Fig.3.30 The smoothed version of the line

If you require the lines to be produced "warts and all", the Ink mode should be used. As can be seen from the original line of Figure 3.31 and the Ink mode version of Figure 3.32, this mode leaves your artwork with no significant changes introduced by the software. You are still not working in a bitmap mode when using either the Ink or the Smooth modes, even though the effect is superficially much like and equivalent tool in a bitmap editor. With all three modes the lines are produced by stringing together a series of straight lines and arcs.

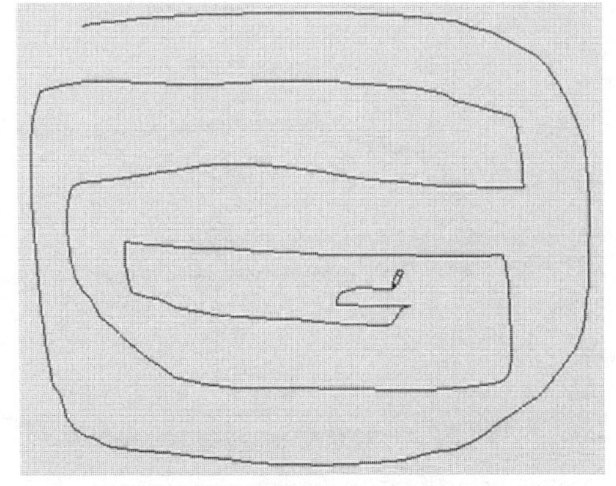

Fig.3.31 The Ink mode line prior to releasing the mouse button

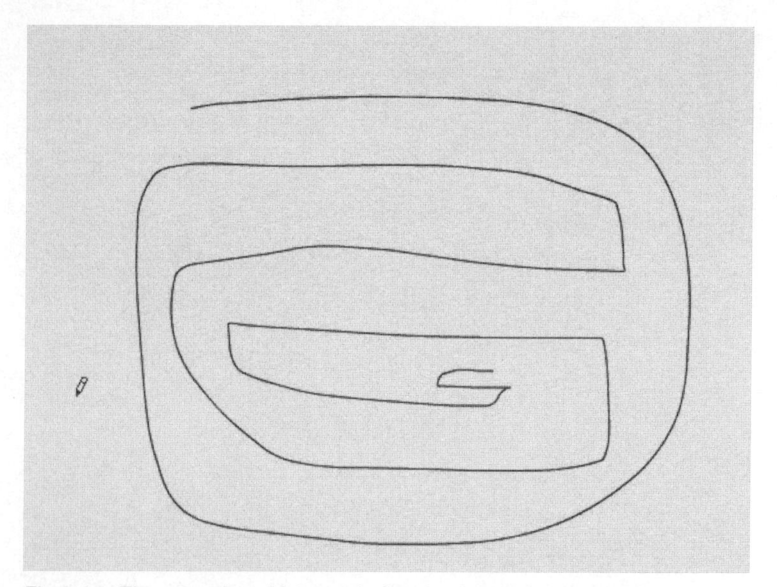

Fig.3.32 The completed Ink mode line is virtually unchanged

This point is demonstrated by Figure 3.33, which shows a highly zoomed view of part of the line shown in Figure 3.32. There are no signs of outsize pixels or rough edges, and the line is reproduced as accurately as the screen resolution permits. The Straighten mode greatly simplifies lines, the Smooth mode slightly simplifies them, and the Ink mode

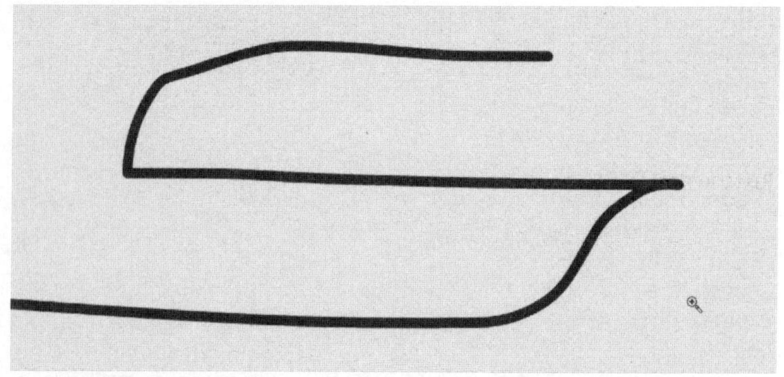

Fig.3.33 There are no outsize pixels in the zoomed view of the line

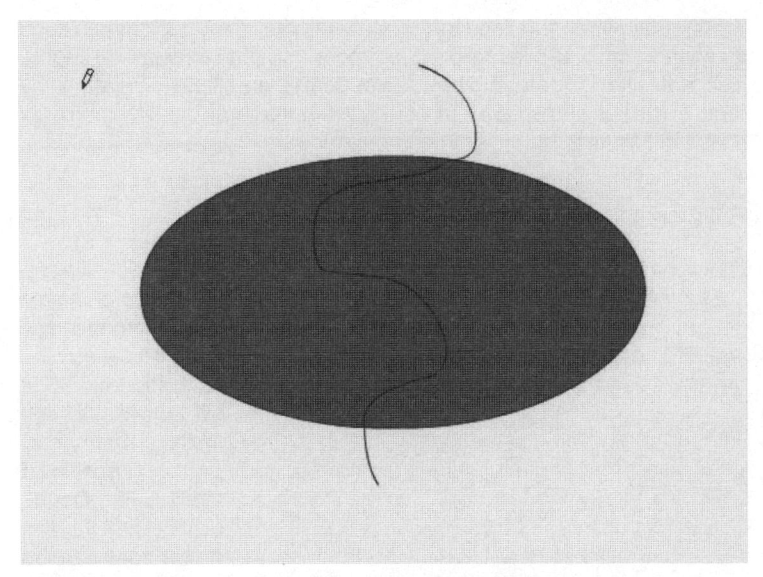

Fig.3.34 The freehand line has cut the ellipse in two

produces lines accurately no matter how many sections are required to do it. Bear in mind that complex lines having numerous sections will require more storage space and will take longer to download.

As pointed out previously, lines that run across other objects have a tendency to cut those objects in two. Freehand lines produced using the Pencil tool do this in just the same way as straight lines or arcs. This can be a problem if you accidentally run a line over another object, but it can also be very useful.

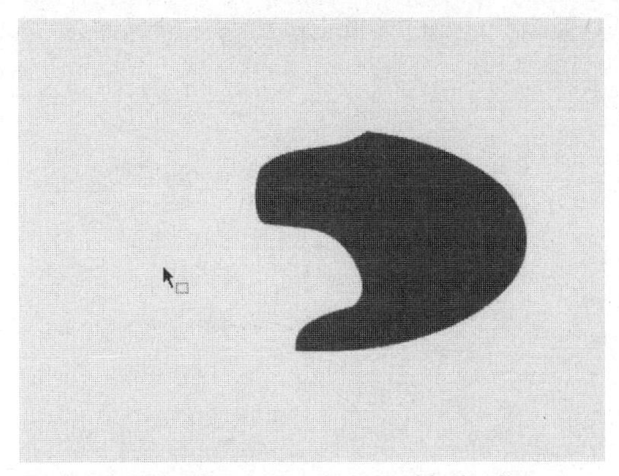

Fig.3.35 The shape that is left with the line and left-hand section of the ellipse removed

You can use freehand lines to carve pieces out of regular shapes such as squares and ellipses to produce more complex shapes. In Figure 3.34 a freehand line has been drawn across an ellipse. Deleting the parts of the line and shape that were not required produced the complex shape in Figure 3.35.

Shapes

There are tools specifically for drawing rectangles and circles or ellipses, but how do you draw other shapes using Flash. In the case of simple shapes having flat sides it should not be too difficult to produce the required shapes using the Line tool. If a triangle is drawn on the screen, as in Figure 3.36, it still consists of three lines that can be selected individually. On the other hand, the Arrow tool can be used to drag a corner of the triangle to a new position, as in Figure 3.37, and it then acts as a single entity.

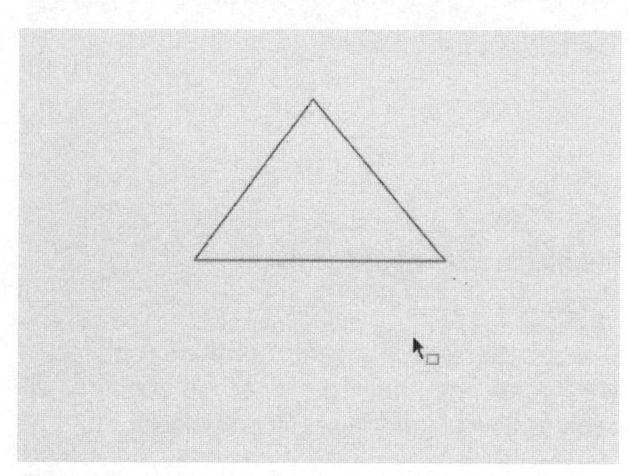

Fig.3.36 A triangle drawn using the Line tool

Remember that none of the lines in the shape should be selected when doing this type of editing, or some of the lines may be moved to a new position rather than being stretched to form a new shape. Also, make sure the pointer is near the corner that is to be dragged and not just near one of the lines, or you may

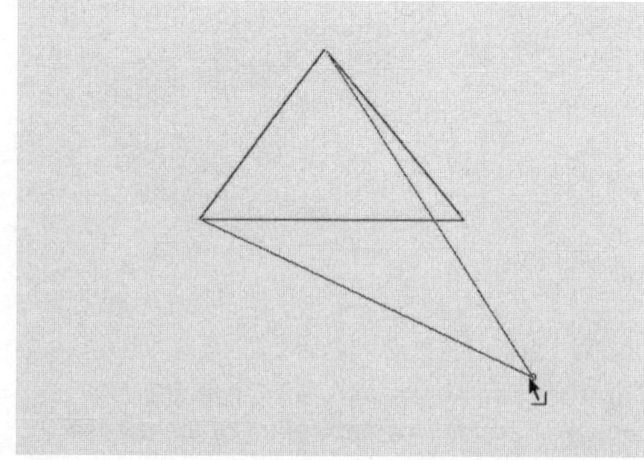

Fig.3.37 Editing the triangle with the Arrow tool

simply drag one of the lines into an arc. When the pointer is close enough to a corner of the shape the usual rectangle will be replaced by two lines at right angles (Figure 3.38).

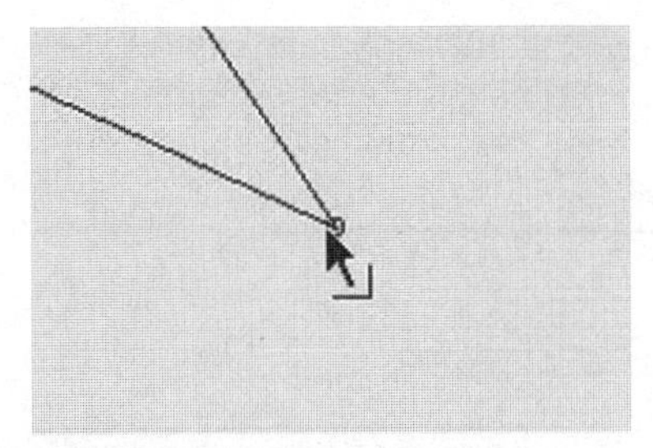

Fig.3.38 The changed pointer

Another method is to roughly draw the shape using the Pencil tool in the Straighten mode, and then hope that it will tidy up your rough drawing into the required shape. For rectangles, circles, and ellipses it is probably better to use the appropriate tools, but it can be useful to generate triangles in this way. Figure 3.39 shows a rather rough attempt at drawing a triangle, and Figure 3.40 shows the neat triangle produced from this using the straightening process. Of course, if the shape produced is not quite right a little dragging of the corners should soon correct the problem. Shapes having more than four sides can be drawn with the Line tool aided by the snap and visual grids or guides.

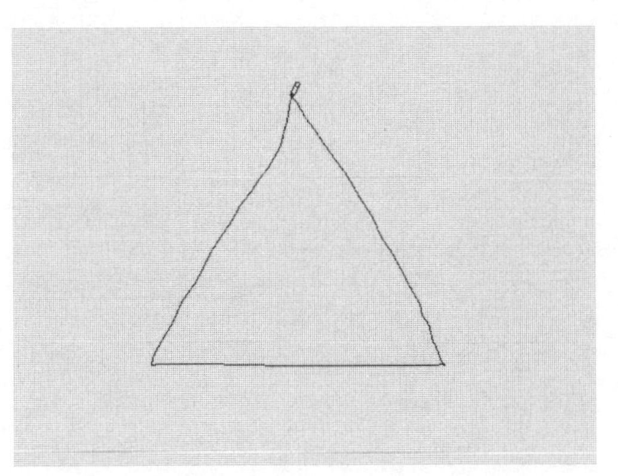

Fig.3.39 The rough version of the triangle

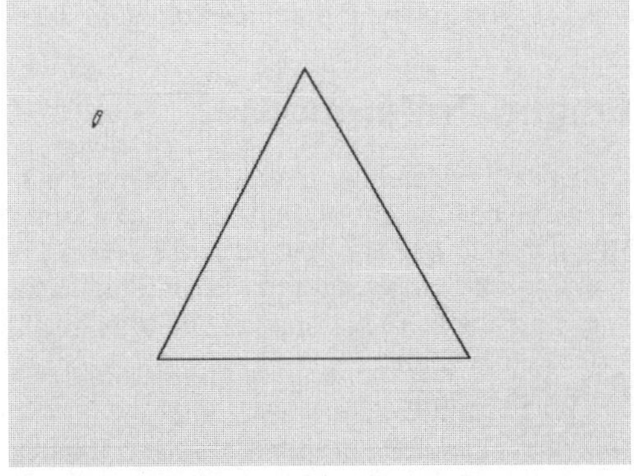

Fig.3.40 The tidied up version of the triangle

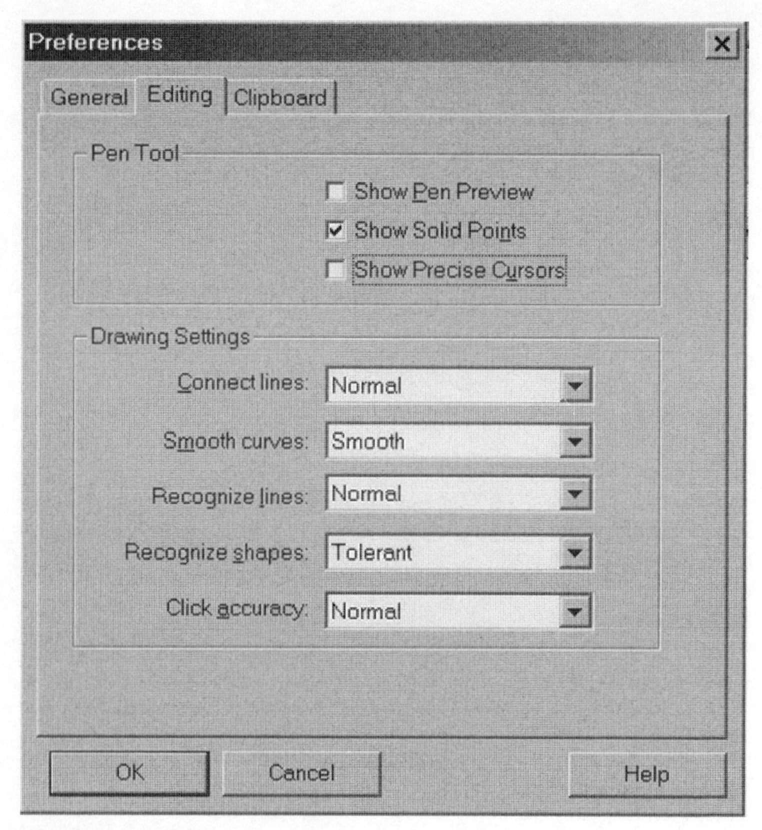

Fig.3.41 The Editing Preferences dialogue box

Editing Preferences

The Editing Preferences dialogue box (Figure 3.41) controls the amount of assistance Flash provides in tidying up your sketched lines and shapes. This dialogue box is obtained by selecting Preferences from the Edit menu and then operating the Editing tab in the window that appears. These are the available options and their functions:

Connect Lines

This determines how close the start and finish points of a line have to be in order to result in Flash closing the line to form a shape. The available settings are Must be close, Normal, and Can be distant.

Smooth Curves

The amount of smoothing used on curves is governed by this option. There is the option to switch off smoothing altogether, plus three levels of smoothing which are Rough, Normal, and Smooth. The latter gives the greatest amount of smoothing.

Recognise Lines

If a line is almost straight, Flash will remove all the curves and produce a perfectly straight line. This option controls the amount of imperfection Flash will tolerate and still produce a straight line. The rougher your sketching, the more tolerant Flash needs to be. This processing can be switched off, or enabled with three degrees of effectiveness (Strict, Normal, and Tolerant).

Recognise Shapes

Similar to the Recognise Lines option, this one determines how close you have to get to an ellipse, rectangle, or triangle before Flash will recognise it. The settings are the same as for the Recognise Lines option.

Click Accuracy

This parameter is concerned with how close the pointer must be to an object before left clicking will select that object. The options are Strict, Normal, and Tolerant, which in practice mean very close, close, and quite close.

When the required parameters have been set, left click on the OK button to make them take effect and close the dialogue box.

Fills

Enclosed shapes drawn with the Line and Pencil tools, unlike those drawn with the Rectangle and Oval tools, are not automatically filled with the current fill colour. However, any enclosed area can be filled using the Paint Bucket tool. To fill an area just operate the Paint Bucket button to select this tool, and then left click with the pointer within the outline of the shape. With small or spindly shapes it is important to make sure that the right part of the pointer is within the outline. The pointer looks like a paint can having paint pouring out, and it is the bottom end of the "paint" that must be within the outline of the shape. The reliable method of filling awkward shapes is to zoom in on them so that the pointer will comfortably fit inside the shape's outline.

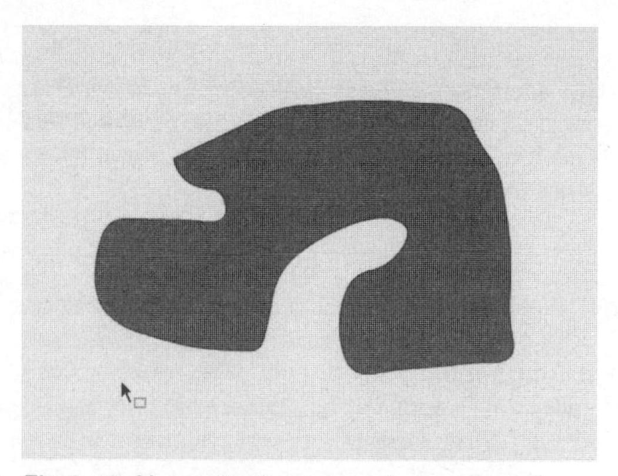

Fig.3.42 No matter how complex, a closed outline can always be filled

Note that it is not only simple shapes that can be filled in this way. It works just as well with complex shapes (Figure 3.42). Remember to make sure that the required fill colour is set in the Colors section of the Tools palette prior to filling a shape.

With many paint programs it is necessary to proceed carefully when using a Paint Bucket tool, since results can be dramatic if it is accidentally used on an outline that is not properly closed. The "paint" usually bleeds from the shape and goes all over the place. This does not happen with Flash's version of the Paint Bucket tool, and it will simply have no effect if it is used anywhere other than inside a closed outline. The Paint Bucket tool with not work using grouped objects either. They must be ungrouped before the fill is added, or the fill must be added before they are grouped.

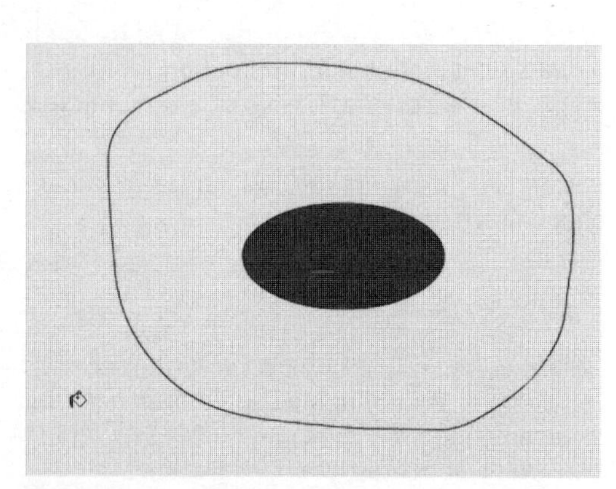

Fig.3.43 The screen before the fill is added

If there is an object within the outline that is to be filled (Figure 3.43), the fill colour will not cover the object. Instead, the fill colour will flow around the object, as in Figure 3.44. Of course, if the object is the same colour as the fill colour, it will then be covered by the fill and is effectively deleted by it. If an object already

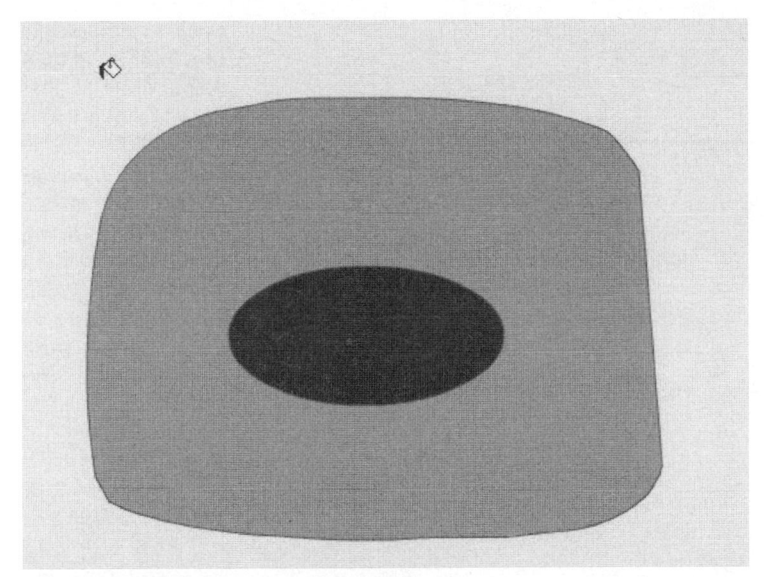

Fig.3.44 The fill does not cover the ellipse

has a fill colour, any colour added using the Paint Bucket tool will replace the original fill colour. Note that moving the inner object will not result in the fill automatically adjusting to suit. Instead, a "hole" will be left in the fill where the inner object used to be (Figure 3.45).

Ink Bottle tool

Fig.3.45 Moving the ellipse leaves a "hole"

The Ink Bottle tool is used to change the colour of lines. Try drawing some lines in the work area using the default colour, which will probably be black. Select the Ink Bottle tool and then use the Stroke Color

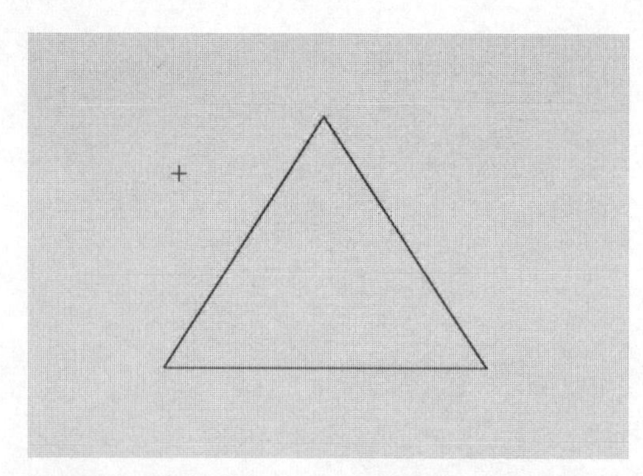

Fig.3.46 The original version of the triangle

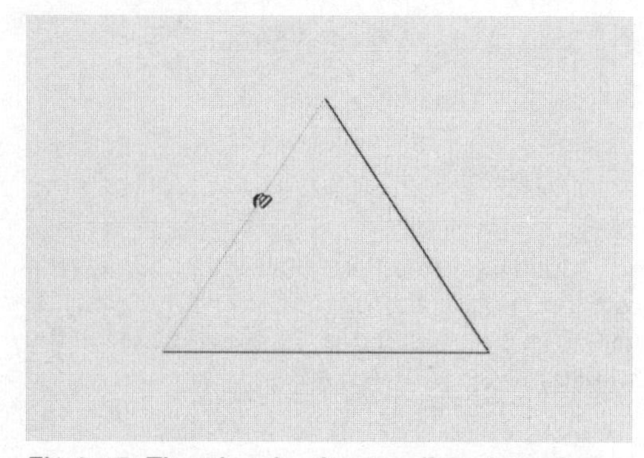

Fig.3.47 The triangle after two lines have been changed using the Ink Bottle tool

button in the Tools palette to bring up a colour chart so that a different stroke (line) colour can be selected. Choose something that is a good contrast to the original stroke colour. Then try left clicking on one of the lines using the Ink Bottle tool. The line should change from its original colour to the new colour (Figures 3.46 and 3.47). This tool will only work on lines, so there is no risk of accidentally changing the fill colour while editing the outline of a filled shape. Similarly, the Paint Bucket tool does not work on lines, so there is no danger of changing the outline colour when trying to alter the fill colour. The Ink Bottle tool will not work on objects while they are grouped.

Brush tool

The Brush tool is similar to the equivalent facility found in all paint programs, and it is a sort of "Jumbo" version of the Pencil tool. Its basic function is drawing thick lines, but it is actually a bit more sophisticated than this. If you are used to brush tools in paint programs it is important to remember that Flash does not deal in pixels, and that each line added using the Brush tool is a complete entity and not a just a set of separate

Fig.3.48 The default setting of the Brush tool produces broad lines

Fig.3.49 A closed outline drawn using the Brush tool

Fig.3.50 A fill can be added to the outline in the normal way

Fig.3.51 The Ink Bottle tool will not change the colour of a brushstroke

pixels. Objects drawn using the Brush tool can be selected and edited much like other objects.

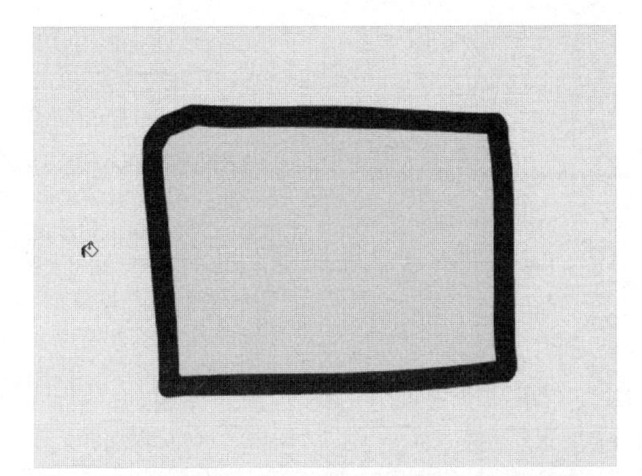

Fig.3.52 The brushstroke's colour changed using the Paint Bucket tool

To try out the brush tool just select it from the Tools palette and start doodling in the drawing area of the screen. The default setting produces quite thick lines (Figure 3.48), and the pointer is a filled circle that indicates the line thickness. In Figure 3.48 the pointer is in the top left-hand corner of the screen. When a closed shape is produced using the Brush tool it is not necessary to paint in a fill colour using the Brush tool. The Paint Bucket tool can be used in the normal way to add a fill to an object of this type (Figures 3.49 and 3.50).

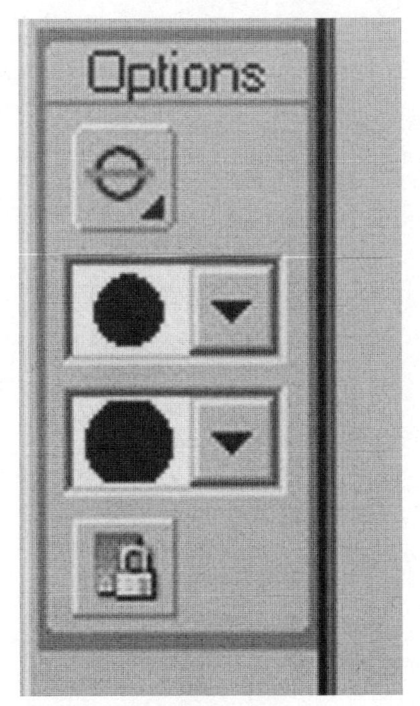

Fig.3.53 The brush options

Attempting to change the colour of a brushstroke using the Ink Bottle tool will not have the desired effect. In Figure 3.51 the Ink Bottle tool has been used in an attempt to turn the shape black. What has actually happened is that a fine black outline has appeared on the inner and outer borders of the thick line. In Figure 3.52 the same thing has been tried, but this time using the Paint Bucket tool, and this has produced the

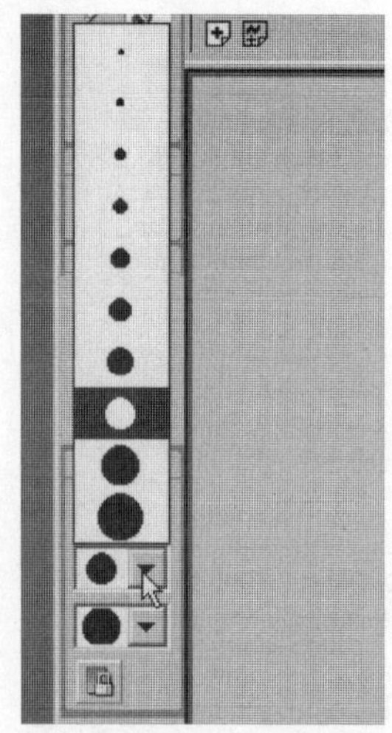

Fig.3.54 10 brush sizes are available

desired result. Note that it is the fill colour that determines the colour of brushstrokes and not the stroke colour.

Several buttons appear in the Options section of the Tools palette when the Brush tool is selected (Figure 3.53). There are two menus here, and the upper one is the Brush Size menu. Left clicking on the arrowhead produces the menu of Figure 3.54, which offers a range of 10 different brush sizes. Lines produced using the smallest, largest, and two intermediate sizes of brush are shown in Figure 3.55.

The lower menu gives access to nine brush shapes (Figure 3.56). The standard round brush is present, together with a square type. The others are designed to produce calligraphy effects, and it is more of a

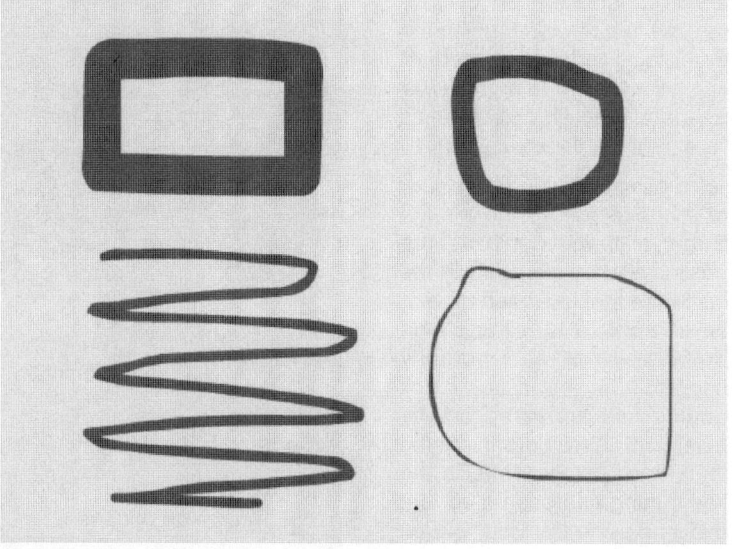

Fig.3.55 Brushstrokes of various widths

caligraphy pen tool than a brush tool when these are used. Figure 3.57 shows some lines drawn using the brush that has a horizontal rectangular shape. The horizontal lines are much thinner than the vertical ones, which are in turn thinner than the diagonal lines. The obvious use for the brushes of this type is for handwriting (Figure 3.58), but they have other uses such as big brush techniques, and it is well worth experimenting with them. The nine brush styles are each available in a range of 10 sizes, so in total there are some 90 brushes to choose from.

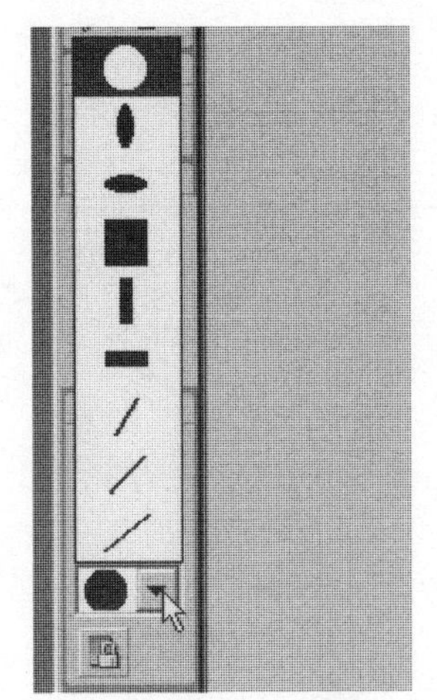

Fig.3.56 Nine brush styles are available

Fig.3.57 Lines drawn using a rectangular brush

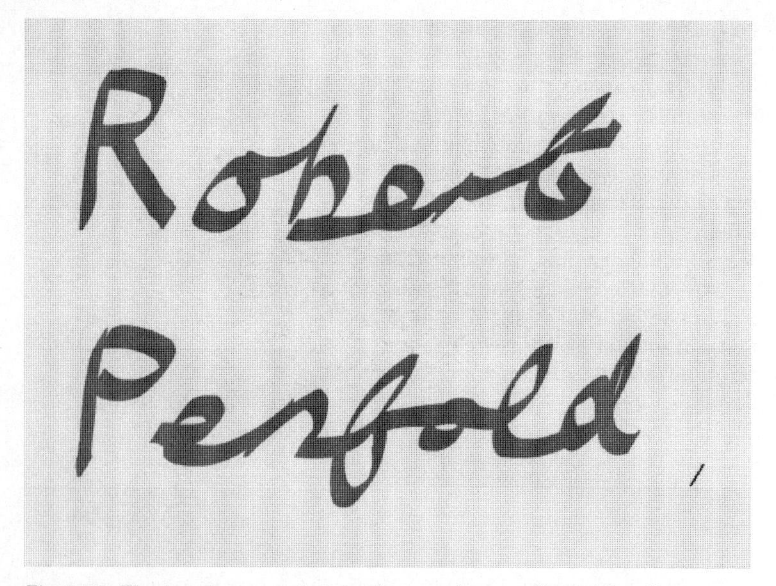

Fig.3.58 The brushes can be used to produce calligraphic effects

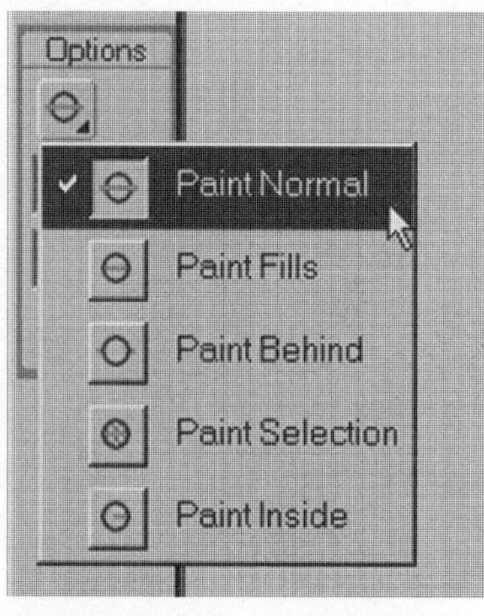

Fig.3.59 The brush mode menu

Brush Mode

The button at the top of the Options section of the Tools palette provides access to the five brush modes (Figure 3.59). These are mostly concerned with the way in which material added with the Brush tool will interact with any existing material. Here are details of the five modes:

Paint Normal

This is the default mode, and anything added using this mode interacts with existing objects in the normal way. If a brushstroke cuts through another object, as in Figure 3.60, it cuts the object in two (Figure 3.61). With a large

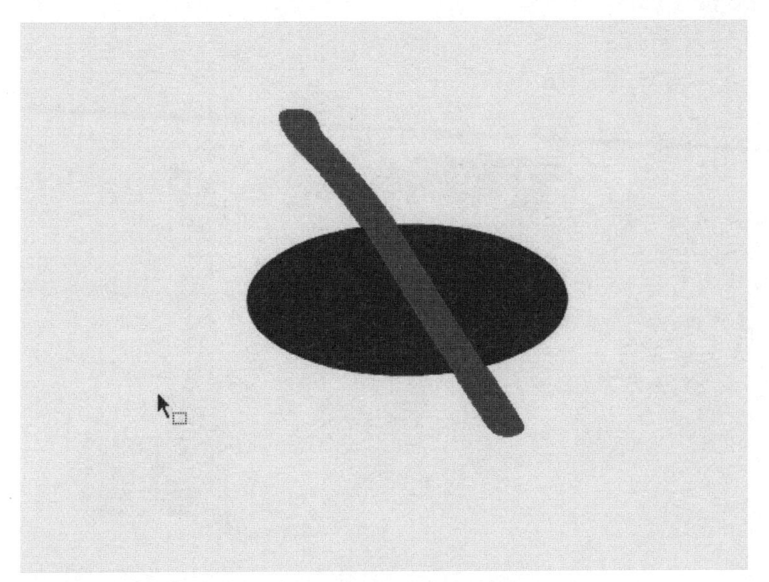

Fig.3.60 A brushstroke can cut other objects in two

brush size it actually does rather more than cut the object in two, since the part of the object covered by the brushstroke is obliterated.

Paint Fills

As its name suggests, in this mode the Brush tool only paints over fills. However, plain areas of the screen count as fills, so this mode is not quite as selective as it might at first appear. This mode has been used in Figure 3.62, but the line has not yet been completed so the appearance is the same as for

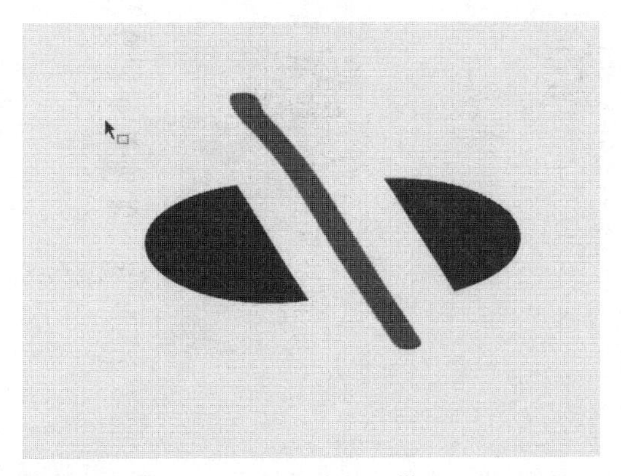

Fig.3.61 The two parts of the ellipse separate

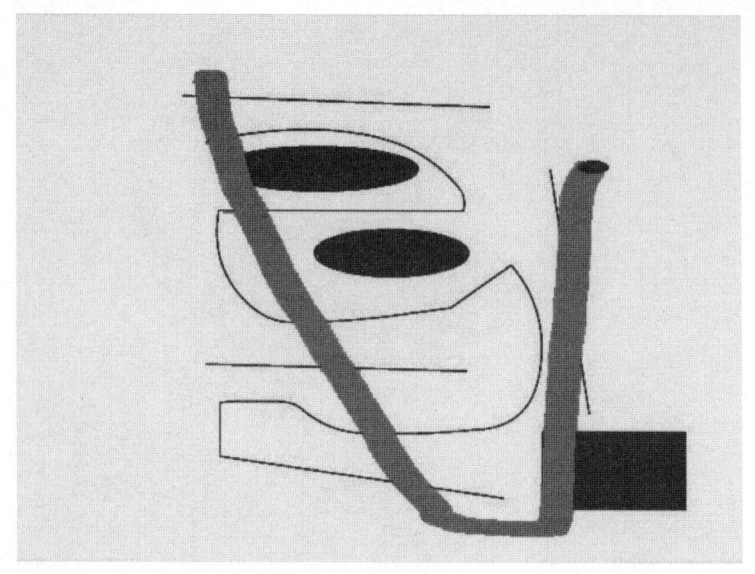

Fig.3.62 At this stage the brushstroke looks the same as normal

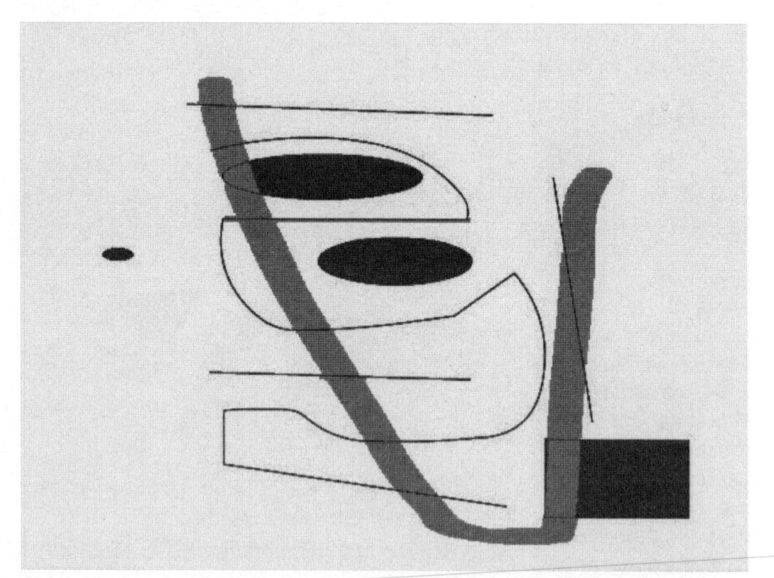

Fig.3.63 The completed brushstroke has correctly left lines untouched

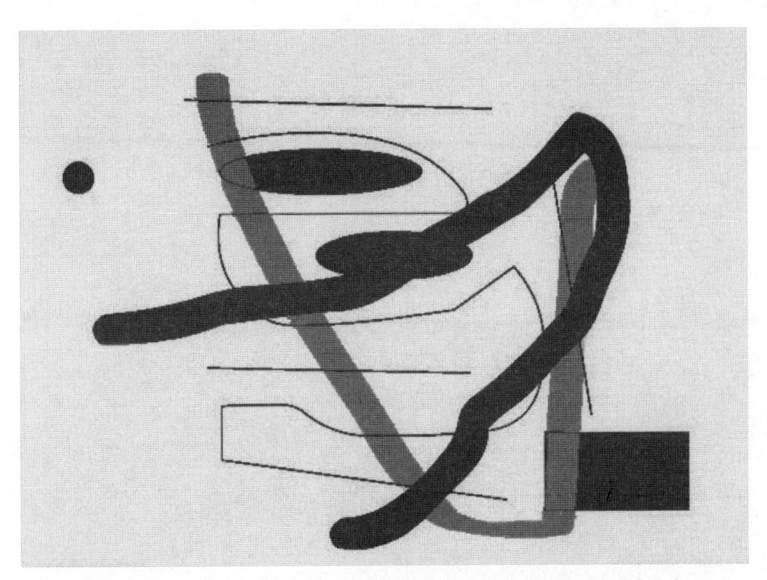

Fig.3.64 A second brushstroke has covered the original, which is not a line

Fig.3.65 In the Paint Behind mode only the background is covered

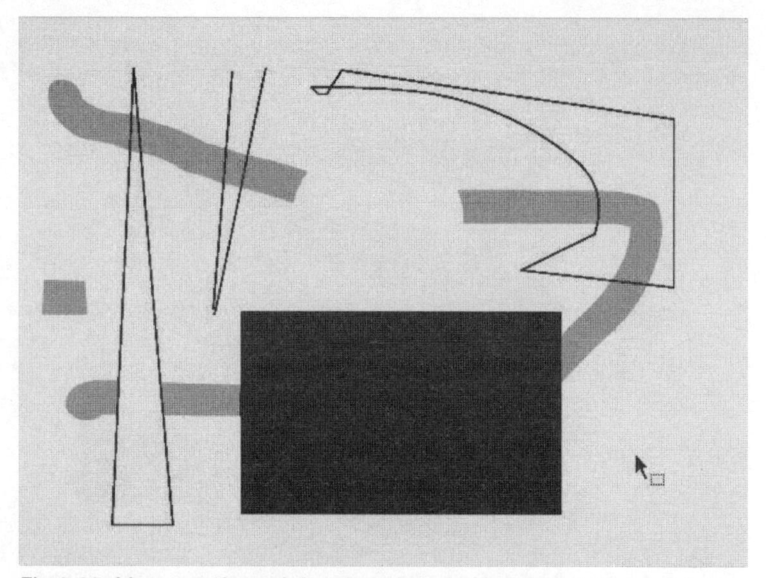

Fig.3.66 Lines cut through brushstrokes, turning them into a number of separate objects

the Paint Normal mode. In Figure 3.63 the brushstroke has been completed and Flash has done the necessary processing to provide the correct effect. Previously unused areas of screen have been painted over, as have parts of the fills on two objects. The lines on the other hand, including the outlines of one ellipse and the rectangle, are still "present and correct". In Figure 3.64 a brushstroke in a different colour has been added. This has once again failed to cover the lines, but it has covered the previous brushstroke. When you draw using the Brush tool you are painting with fills and not drawing lines.

Paint Behind

Paint Background might be a more apt name for this mode. It does not paint over any objects, whether they are fills or lines. This can be seen in the example of Figure 3.65 where the brushstroke has gone "behind" the lines and the filled objects. In reality you are not painting behind objects when this mode is used. In Figure 3.66 the circle has been erased, and there is no sign of the brushstroke where the circle used to be. The brushstroke is really painting over the background and nothing else, rather than painting behind objects.

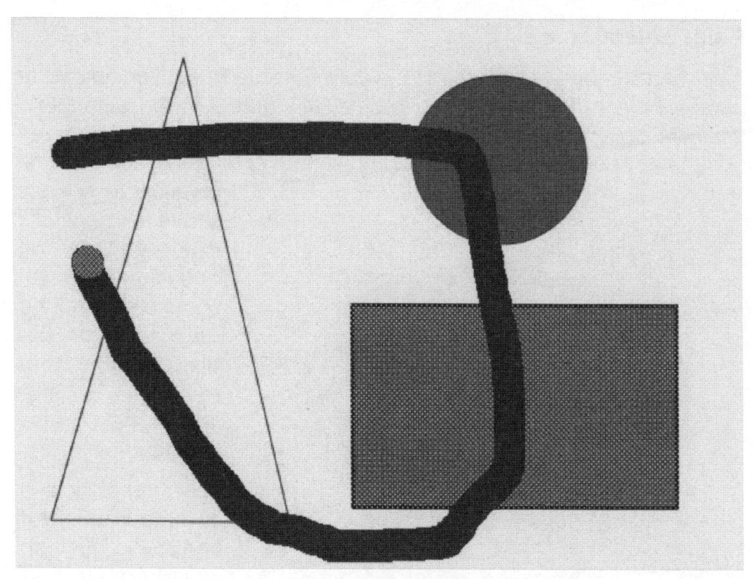

Fig.3.67 The brushstroke immediately prior to completion

Bear in mind that a single brushstroke can produce numerous objects when using a selective mode such as this. When a brushstroke crosses an object, the part of the stroke on one side of the object is a separate entity to the one on the other side. Even narrow lines produce this breaking up of brushstrokes. This effect is demonstrated in Figure 3.66 where the part of the brushstroke inside the triangle has been selected and moved without making any changes to the rest of the stroke.

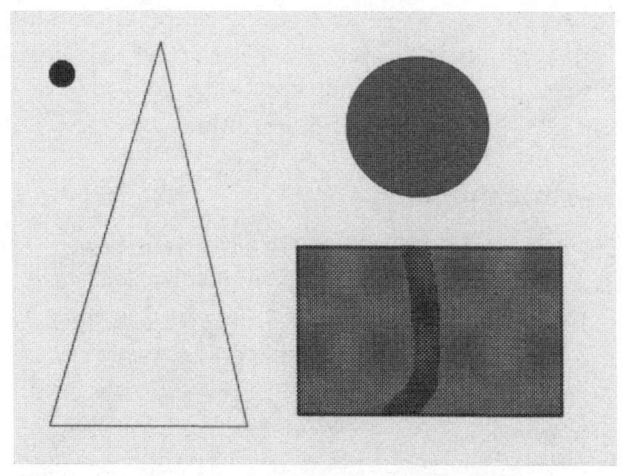

Fig.3.68 Only the rectangle, which was selected, has been covered

Paint Selection

As its name implies, in this mode it is only possible to paint on objects or parts of objects that have been selected. In Figure 3.67 the rectangle is the only object that has been selected. The brushstroke has been completed but the left mouse button has not yet been released so that possible to see the stroke in its entirety. In Figure 3.68 the operation has been completed, and the only part of the brushstroke that remains is the section that crosses the rectangle.

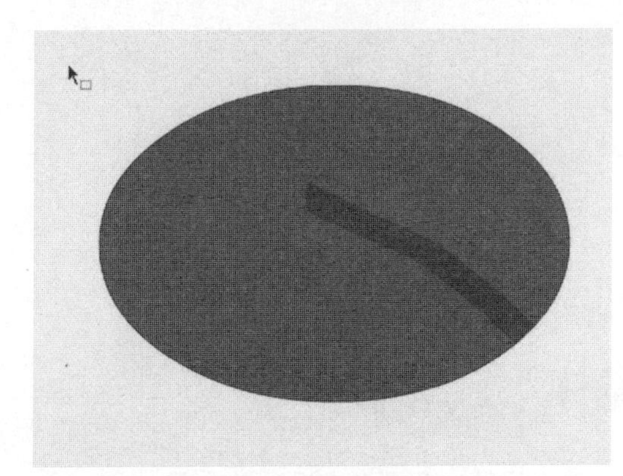

Fig.3.69 Objects can be partially selected

Selecting objects is covered in the next chapter, but an unusual feature of Flash is its ability to select parts of objects. In Figure 3.69 the right-hand section of the ellipse was selected, a brushstroke was added across it, and then the ellipse was deselected. Because the Paint Selection mode was used, the brushstroke only covers the part of the ellipse that was selected.

Paint Inside

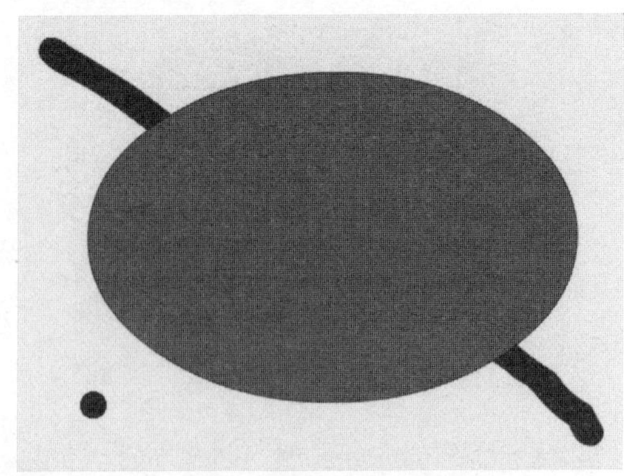

Fig.3.70 The Paint Outside mode in use

This is another slightly misleading name, in that it implies that it will only paint inside an object. In Figure 3.70 the exact opposite has occurred, and the only parts of the brushstroke that have been produced are the sections outside the ellipse. What tends to cause confusion with this mode is that you need to indicate to Flash exactly what it is supposed to paint inside. In this example the brushstroke was started outside the ellipse, and Flash has therefore assumed that the "paint" must be applied to the area outside the ellipse. Figure 3.71 shows a brushstroke that started inside the ellipse and extended well outside. This has produced the desired effect with the part of the stroke outside the ellipse being removed.

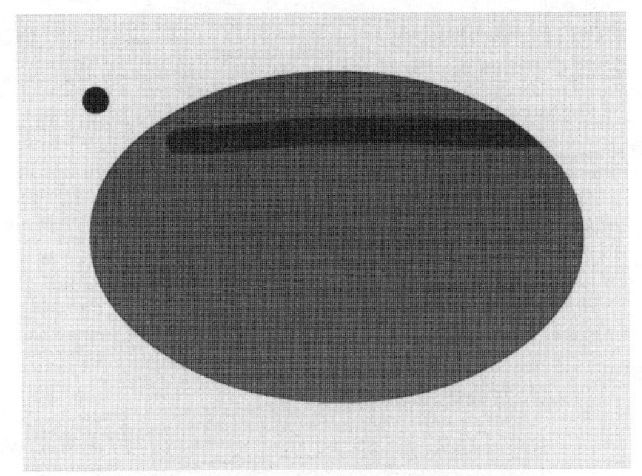

Fig.3.71 Here the right action has been obtained, with the brushstroke only inside the ellipse

In Figure 3.72 a rectangle has been placed inside the ellipse and a brushstroke has been taken across the rectangle. The part of the stroke that covered the rectangle has been removed. The Paint Inside name suggests that the stroke would be carried on through the rectangle, but this is not the way that it works. What actually happens is that Flash only paints on the object in which the stroke starts. It will not paint on objects that are inside or outside that object.

Of course, the point of all these modes is to make it easier to paint on the appropriate areas while avoiding the areas where you do not wish to paint. Using them can avoid the fiddly and

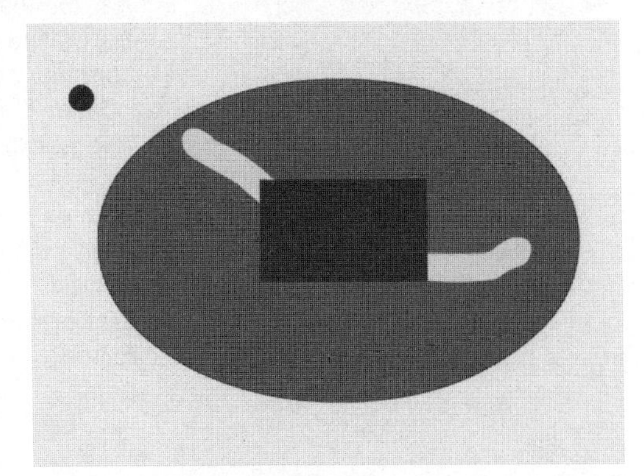

Fig.3.72 The rectangle has not been covered by the brushstroke

time consuming alternative of zooming in and painting very carefully up to the borders of objects, which tends to give poor accuracy anyway.

Lock Fill

The Lock Fill button at the bottom of the Options section of the Tools palette is only relevant when a brushstroke is filled with a bitmap or a gradient fill. These are subjects that are covered in a later chapter, and this subject will not be pursued further here.

Eyedropper tool

Fig.3.73 The pointer with the Eyedropper tool near a line

Fig.3.74 Here the Eyedropper tool is in a filled area

The Eyedropper tool is used to change the current stroke or fill colour by selecting the colour from an object in the work area. It also enables a colour from one line or fill to be transferred to another line or fill, or several lines or fills come to that. When the eyedropper tool has locked onto a colour a small addition to the pointer shows whether it is a stroke or fill colour that will be selected. In Figure 3.73 the tool has locked onto the line forming the outline of a rectangle, and the "pencil" below the eyedropper pointer shows that it is the line and not the fill that the tool has locked onto. In Figure 3.74 the pointer is inside the rectangle, and "paintbrush" has appeared beneath it to indicate that it has locked onto the fill colour. Editing colours is covered in detail in the next chapter.

Pen tool

After a few minutes experimenting with the Pen tool you could well come to the conclusion that its purpose is to generate random lines and curves. Even if you are used to drawing programs that have Bezier curves, you may still find the Flash version something less than obvious in use. A French gentleman of that name, who required a means of drawing complex curves using a computer, invented Bezier curves. He apparently needed them as an aid to designing vehicles for a French manufacturer that produced particularly curvy cars at that time. However, the versatility of Bezier curves is such that they can be used when drawing just about anything.

Fig.3.75 The first stage of drawing the curve

It is, of course, possible to draw curves using the Line tool, by first drawing a straight line and then dragging it into a curve using the Arrow tool. This only gives a relatively limited range of curves though, because the curvature is controlled by the end points of the line and a single control point. Freehand drawing gives greater scope for drawing complex curves, and would be the first choice for some types of drawing work. "Fine

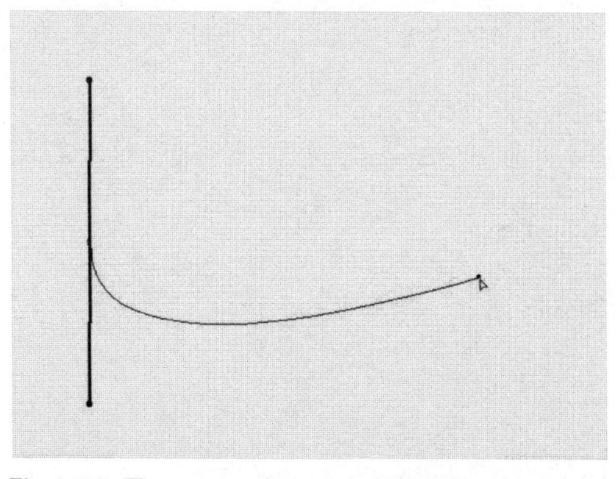

Fig.3.76 The second stage of drawing the curve

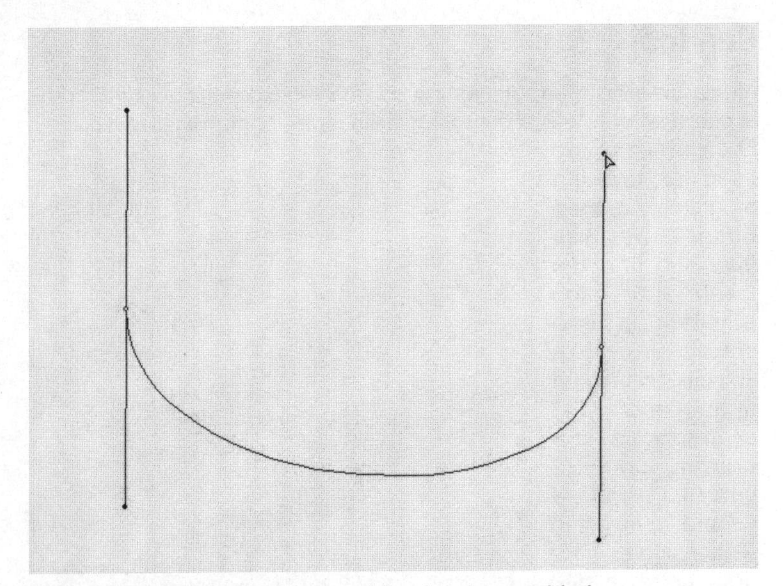

Fig.3.77 Here the second control line has been added

tuning" lines can be slow and awkward using this method though. Bezier curves enable a wide range of curves to be produced, and by using several control points it is possible alter the curve to suit your requirements.

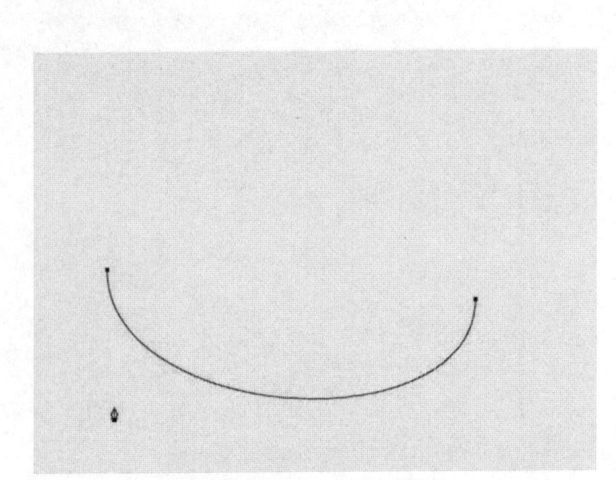

Fig.3.78 The finished Bezier curve

To try out the Pen tool left-click on its button in the tools palette and then drag a vertical line in the left-hand section of the work area (Figure 3.75). The Pen tool can be a bit confusing at first, because beginners tend to assume that this first line is the one that will become the curve. In fact this line is merely one set of controls for the curve. To produce the curve move the pointer across the screen and then press and hold down the left mouse button (Figure 3.76). Now try moving the pointer up the screen to drag a second control line (Figure 3.77), and the release the mouse button to complete the curve (Figure 3.78).

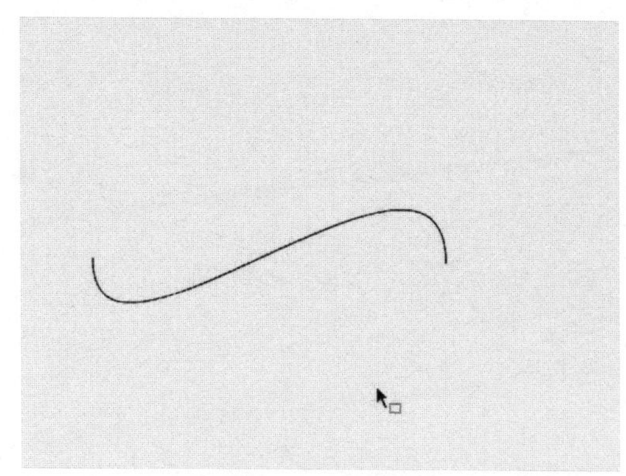

Fig.3.79 Reversing the direction of a control line gives an S-shaped curve

So how do the two lines control the Bezier curve? The direction of the first line sets the start direction of the curve, and the second line sets the finishing direction. Try repeating the previous exercise, but produce the second control line by moving the pointer down the screen instead of up the screen. This will produce a curve like the one in Figure 3.79. The second control line started at the top and finished at the bottom, so this is the direction for the end of the curve. The length of the two control lines also governs the curve obtained. In the example of Figure 3.80 there is a short control line at the left end of the curve, giving little curvature at that end. In contrast there is a much longer control line at the other end, and much greater curvature.

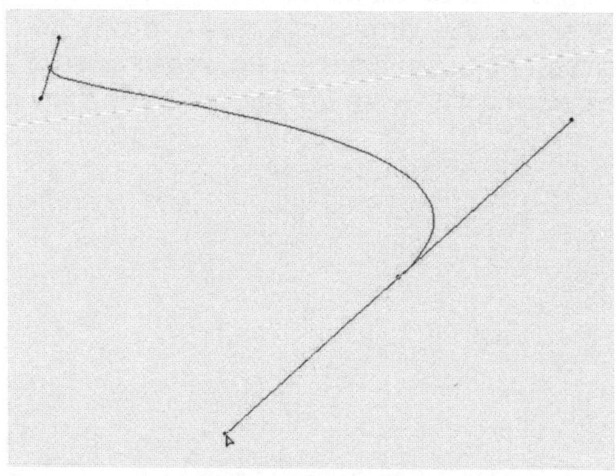

Fig.3.80 The length of the control lines determines the amount of curvature

Fig.3.81 The Arrow tool can be used to edit Bezier curves

Having drawn your curve it is set in position by selecting one of the tools other than the Pen tool. It is possible to do some fine adjustment to the curve. When the Arrow tool is placed close to any part of the curve an arc appears beneath the pointer, and the curve can then be dragged onto a new path (Figure 3.81). The Pen tool can be used to draw straight lines by left clicking on the screen. The first left-click sets the starting point, and further clicks add straight sections into the line. Double clicking on the final point leaves the shape open, like Figure 3.82. Going

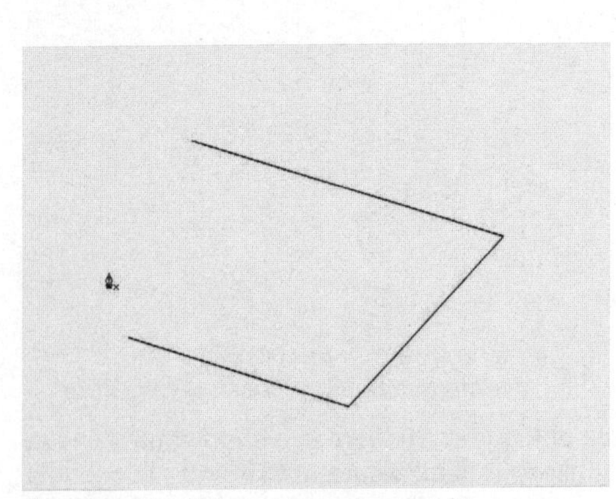

Fig.3.82 The Pen tool can be used to produce straight lines

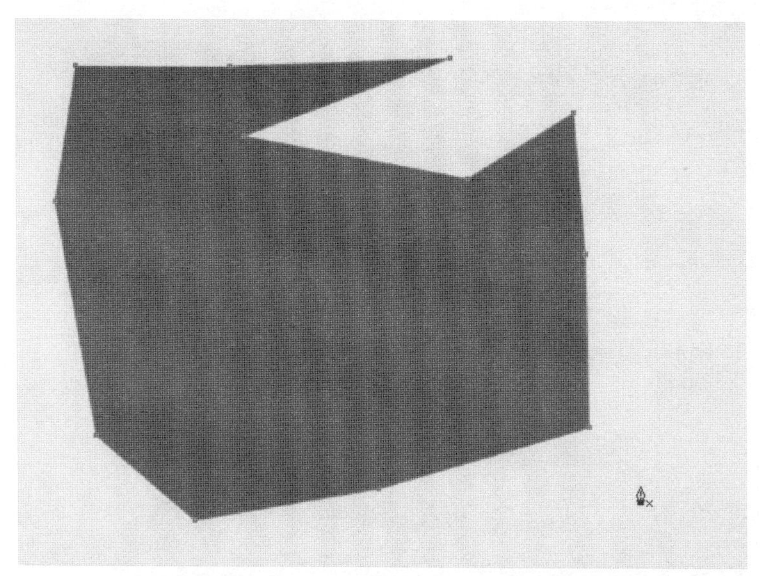

Fig.3.83 Enclosed outlines drawn with the Pen tool are automatically filled

back to the starting point closes the shape and the current fill colour is then applied to it, as in Figure 3.83. Shapes of both types can be edited in the usual way using the Arrow tool.

Pressure sensitive

Some graphics tablets are pressure sensitive, and with the right software this facility can be put to good use. In the case of Flash the Brush tool can be set to respond to a pressure sensitive stylus, and an extra button will appear in the Options section of the Tools palette when the Brush tool is selected. This button is the one in the top right-hand corner of the Options section (Figure 3.84), and it will only appear if your computer is

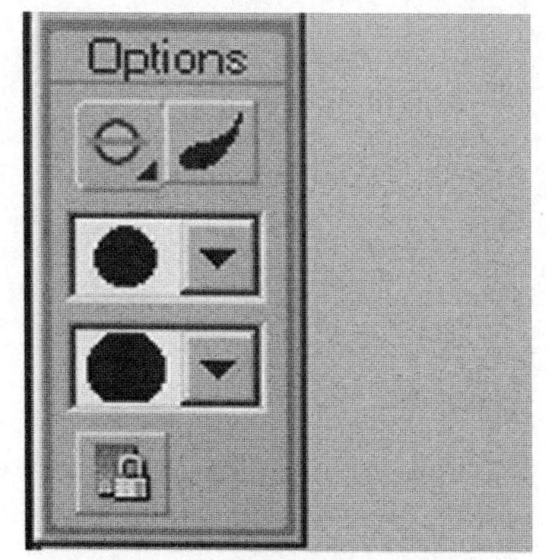

Fig.3.84 The pressure sensivity option button

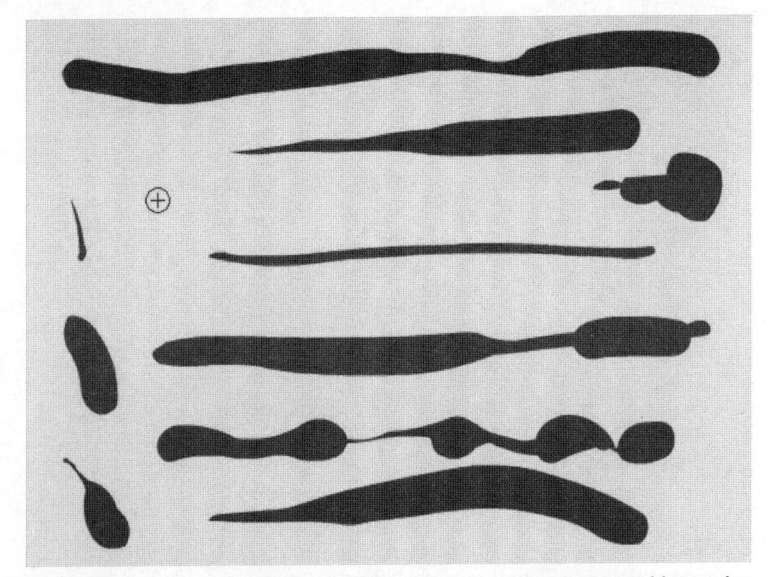

Fig.3.85 Varying line widths produced using a pressure sensitive stylus

equipped with a suitable graphics tablet. When this option is selected it is possible to vary the line width by altering the pressure on the tip of the stylus. Within the pressure range of the stylus, the harder you press the wider the line that is obtained. The Brush size sets the maximum stroke width that can be achieved.

The brush strokes in Figure 3.85 were all produced using the maximum brush size, with the variations in width produced by varying the pressure on the stylus. As pointed out previously, freehand drawing with a mouse is quite difficult, and even with experience most users never find it an easy or precise way to work. A graphics tablet and a stylus is a much better alternative for freehand drawing, and a pressure sensitive stylus gives even better control when used with the Brush tool.

Zoom

The Zoom control operates in standard fashion. With the "+" option selected, left clicking in the drawing area produces a zoom at a ratio of about 2 : 1 centred on the point that was clicked. The "–" option has the opposite effect, with the view zooming out at a ratio of about 2 : 1. Dragging a rectangle using the Zoom tool (Figure 3.86) results in that

Fig.3.86 Selecting the area for the program to zoom in on

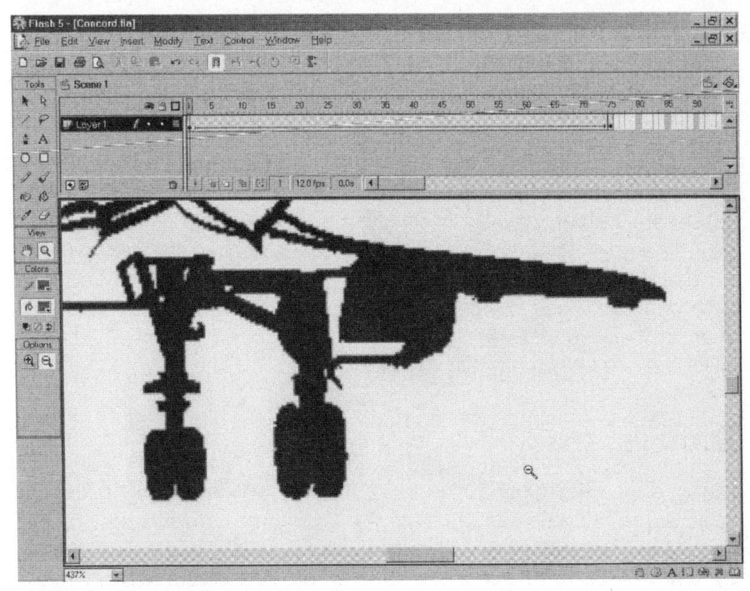

Fig.3.87 The zoomed view

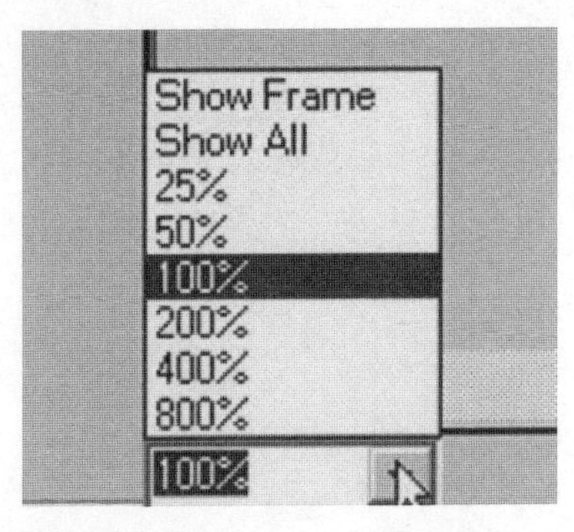

Fig.3.88 The popup zoom menu

area of the drawing being made as large as possible without anything within the rectangle going out of view (Figure 3.87).

There are several zoom levels available from the View menu, and they are also available from the popup menu near the bottom left-hand corner of the screen (Figure 3.88). The Show Frame option maximises the drawing area, and the Show All setting makes the used part of the drawing area as large as possible without any objects going off the edge of the screen. In fact a narrow margin is left around the objects, as in Figure 3.89, to allow some room to manoeuvre. Note that the 100 percent zoom level can be obtained by double clicking the Zoom tool button.

Fig.3.89 The Show All option zooms in as far as possible while keeping all objects visible on the screen

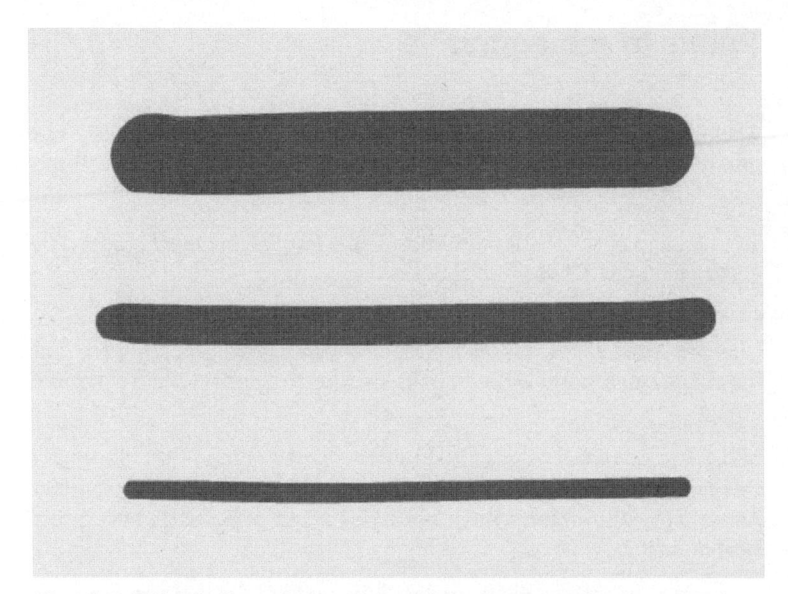

Fig.3.90 Different line widths produced by changing the zoom level and using the same brush size

One slight peculiarity of the Brush tool is that the width of the stroke depends on the zoom magnification used. The three strokes in Figure 3.90 were all made with the Brush tool at maximum size. The middle line was produced using a zoom level of 100 percent. Zooming in leaves the displayed brush width unchanged, but everything in the drawing area is enlarged. This makes brush strokes narrower. Zooming out has the opposite effect, with objects being displayed smaller but the brush staying the same size. Brushstrokes are therefore wider than at a 100 percent zoom level.

This is not really a drawback, and it does have its advantages. When you zoom in to make some fine adjustments, the brush size reduces to make "fine tuning" easier. It also increases the range of brush sizes, making it possible to have just about any required brush width. Note that it is only the Brush tool that operates in this way. Line widths and text sizes can not be adjusted using the same technique.

Points to remember

Enclosed shapes drawn with the line tool do not fill automatically, but can be filled with the Paint Bucket tool.

The nibbling effect occurs with lines, in the form of an object crossed by a line being cut in two.

Using the object snap facility it is easy to draw circles and squares. Get the shape close, and it will automatically snap to a perfect circle or square shape.

Lines, circles, rectangles, etc., can be pulled into new shapes using the Arrow tool. The objects must not be selected when undertaking this type of editing.

Freehand lines can be drawn using the Pencil tool. Use the Ink mode when the highest resolution is required. The Smooth mode will remove slight imperfections in lines and the Straight mode will largely remove curves.

The Editing Preferences dialogue box provides good control over the amount of tidying up (if any) Flash applies to freehand lines.

Although the Brush tool is superficially similar to its equivalent in paint programs, it is produces objects that can be edited in much the same way as circles, lines, etc. Flash does not produce bitmaps.

Various brush styles and sizes are available from the Options section of the Tools palette when using the Brush tool. There are also various painting modes that make it easier to paint the right objects while avoiding the wrong ones.

The Paint Bucket tool can be used to add a fill to enclosed shapes, or to alter existing fill colours. The Ink Bottle tool is used to change the colour of lines.

The Pen tool is used to produce complex curves known as Bezier curves.

The width of strokes produced using the Brush tool can be altered by changing the zoom level. This method does not work with lines, shapes, etc.

4

Editing and panels

Arrow tool

The Arrow tool in the top left-hand corner of the Tools palette is one that was encountered in earlier chapters, and it is used to select objects so that they can edited. As with any tool of this type, you have to be careful to select only the object or objects you wish to select and nothing else. Where appropriate, you also have to take care that you select the required objects in their entirety. As we have seen previously, a single object can be selected by left clicking on or very near it using the Arrow tool. If an

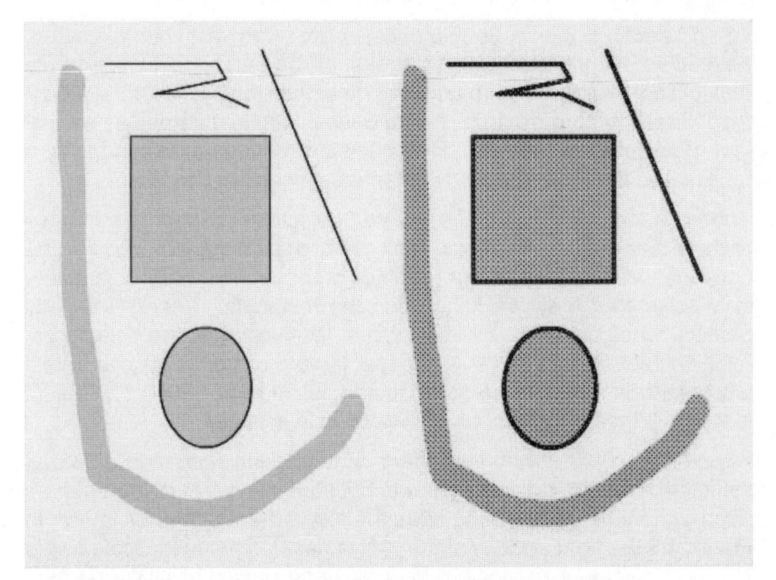

Fig.4.1 Selected objects (right) have a changed appearance

object is part of a group, selecting it with the Arrow tool will select the entire group.

Normally objects change in appearance when they have been selected so that you can see at a glance which item or items have been selected. Fills and lines both take on a patterned appearance, and thin lines appear wider in order to make the patterned appearance more obvious. Figure 4.1 shows some ordinary objects on the left of the drawing area, and selected versions on the right. When a group is selected its appearance remains unchanged but it is outlined in a blue rectangle.

Multiple selection

A number of objects can be selected simultaneously, and there is more than one way of tackling this. To select both the fill and outline of a filled object, simply double click on any part of the object. Double clicking selects all the segments in a complex line, whereas single clicking selects only the section that was clicked. A number of objects can be selected one by one, and it is just a matter of holding down the Shift key and left clicking on each object. The Windows convention is for the Control key to be held down while multiple selections are made, but this method does not work with Flash. It is the Shift key that must be used.

When selecting objects you sometimes get rather less than expected. As pointed out previously, single strokes of the Brush tool can generate multiple objects when using anything other than the Paint Normal mode. Also, what you consider to be a single line might be regarded as several individual sections by Flash. This multiple selection mode can be used to select all the individual parts when something like this occurs.

Another method is to select the required objects by dragging a rectangle around them using the Arrow tool. This does not work in quite the conventional way for a vector graphics program. Normally objects are only selected if they are fully within the rectangle. Alternatively any objects, whether partially or fully within the rectangle, are selected in their entirety. Flash has the unusual feature of being able to select whatever falls within the selection rectangle, and if only half of an object is within it, then only that half of the object is selected.

Figure 4.2 demonstrates this effect, with only the right side of image selected. This is a powerful feature, because the selected area can be used with all the usual editing while the rest of the image is left intact. In Figure 4.3 the right section of the image has been moved, scaled, and rotated while the left section has been left unprocessed. With this method

Fig.4.2 Only the right-hand side of the image has been selected

it is possible that you will sometimes select slightly more or less than intended, with some slightly disastrous editing resulting from this. However, the Undo facility enables things to be put back the way that they were so that another attempt can be made.

Lasso tool

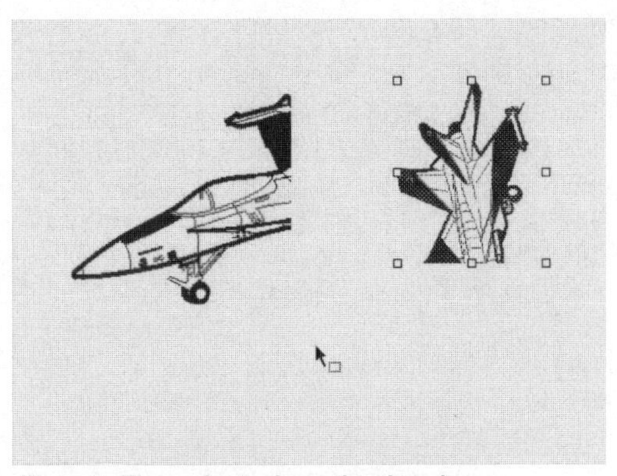

Fig.4.3 The selected section has been moved, scaled, and rotated

Although the rectangle method of selection, or marquee method as it is also known, is a powerful feature, its ability to cut objects in two can sometimes be a hindrance. The Lasso tool provides a useful alternative that enables a complex

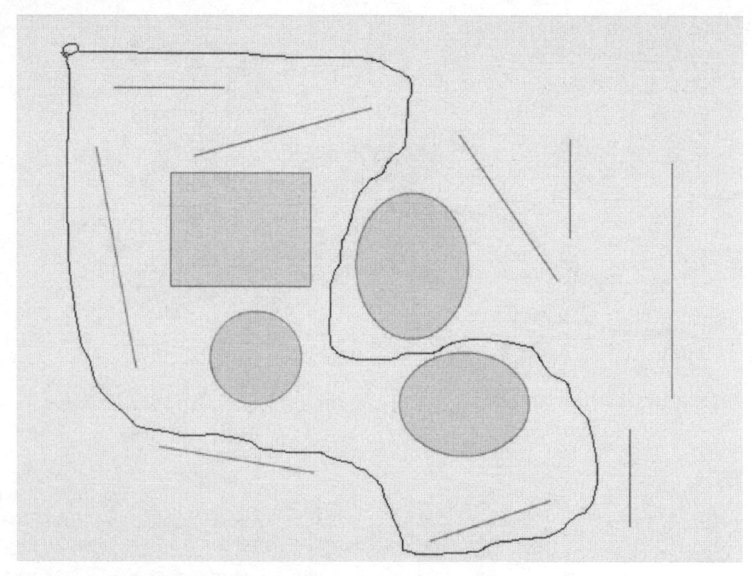

Fig.4.4. Selecting objects using the Lasso tool

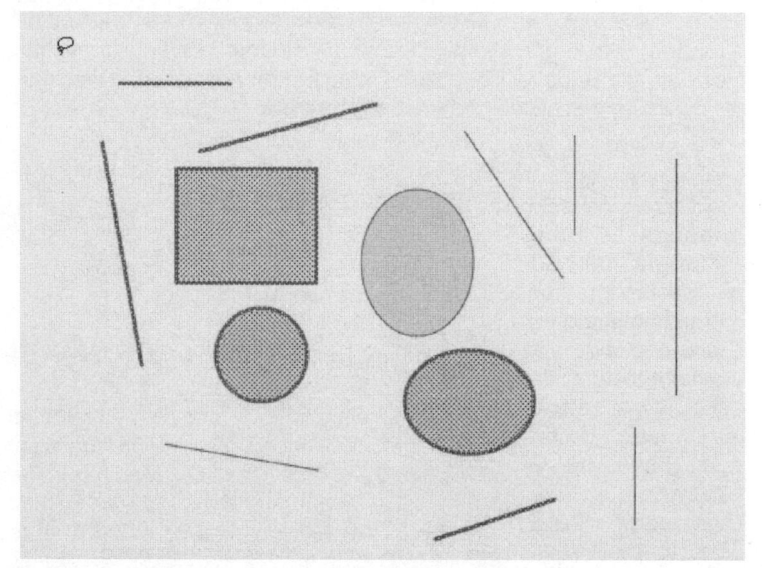

Fig.4.5 The result of the Lasso selection shown above

shape to be used for selection instead of a simple rectangle. Simply select the Lasso tool and then drag a line around the objects to be selected, like drawing with a freehand drawing tool (Figure 4.4). Any objects within the enclosed area will be selected when the mouse button is released (Figure 4.5).

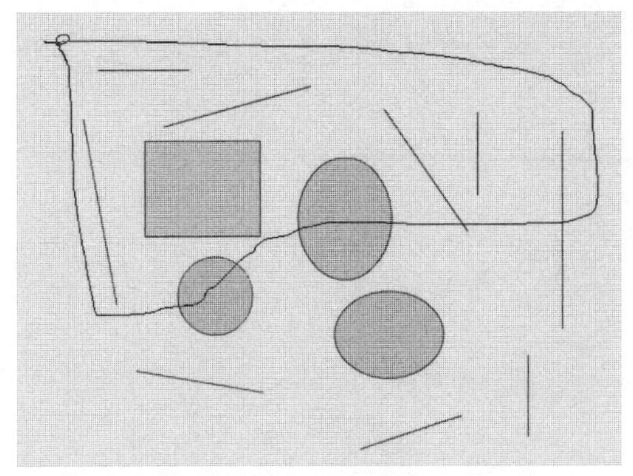

Fig.4.6 Only the parts of objects within the marquee are selected

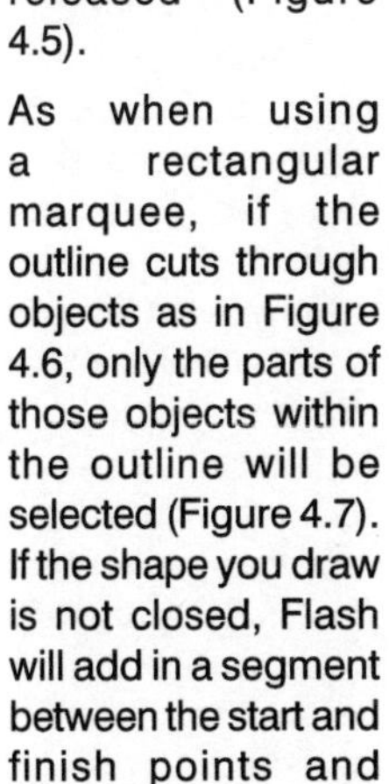

As when using a rectangular marquee, if the outline cuts through objects as in Figure 4.6, only the parts of those objects within the outline will be selected (Figure 4.7). If the shape you draw is not closed, Flash will add in a segment between the start and finish points and close the shape for you. It is best to close the shape yourself, as this avoids errors of judgement resulting in parts of your intended selection being left out (Figure 4.8 and 4.9).

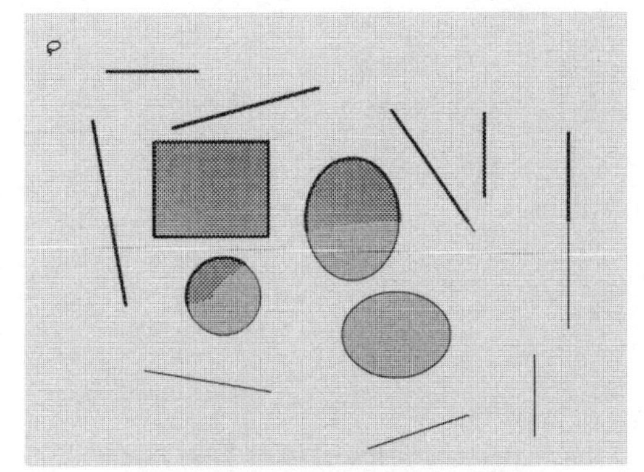

Fig.4.7 The result of the Lasso selection shown above

A selection can be made using the Lasso tool, and then further items can be added by holding down the Shift and using the Lasso tool again. It is also possible to make an initial selection using the Lasso tool, switch to the Arrow tool, and then make further selections with the Shift key held down. Things can also be done the other way round, with the Arrow tool being used first followed by the Lasso tool. By using a

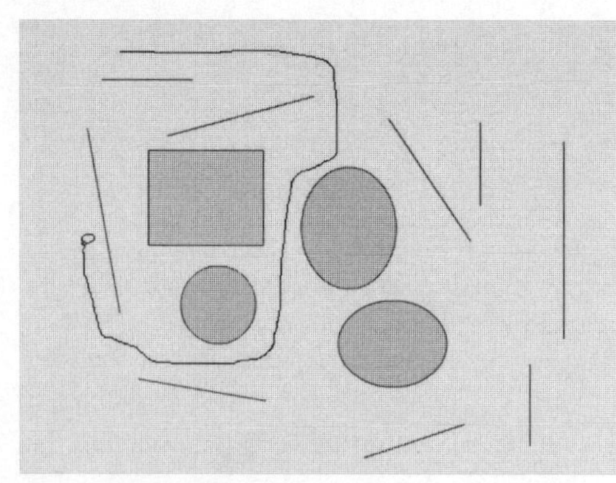

Fig.4.8 The line drawn using the Lasso tool has not been closed

combination of marquees and individual selections, making any desired selection using Flash should be quick and easy.

Deselect

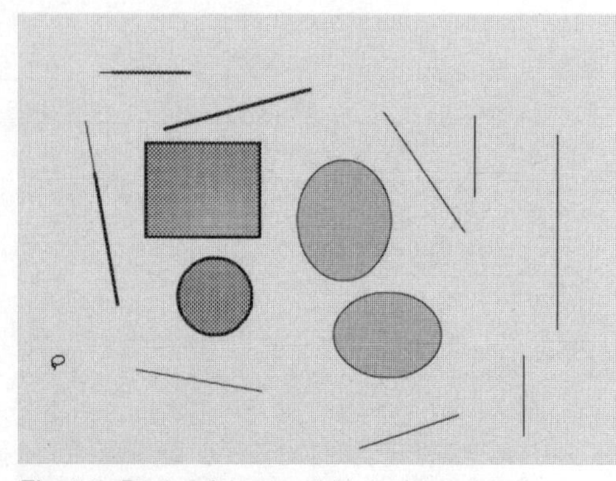

Fig.4.9 Parts of some objects have been left unselected

If you select something and then change your mind there are two methods of deselection available. If you have only selected a single item or wish to deselect all the selected objects, simply left-click on any blank area of the stage. In order to deselect one object in a multiple selection, hold down the Shift key and left-click on the object. In fact you can select and deselect objects at will with the Shift key held down. Left-click on an object to select it or left-click on a selected object to deselect it. This method is generally the quickest and easiest when multiple selections of complete objects are required. It is very easy to select the desired objects and deselect any that are chosen by mistake.

Basic editing

A number of basic editing tasks have been covered in previous chapters and will not be given detailed coverage here. When an object is not selected it is possible to use the Arrow tool to drag the ends of lines to new positions or drag the intermediate sections into arcs. Crossed arrows appear beneath the pointer when the Arrow tool is placed on an object, and the object can then be dragged to a new position on the screen. If multiple objects are selected, when the cross arrows appear these objects can be dragged in unison. Selected objects can be Cut and Copied, and having been Cut or Copied they can be used with the Paste command. Selected objects can be erased by operating the Delete key, but note that anything removed in this way is not usable with the Paste command. Any objects accidentally erased can of course be reinstated using the Undo facility.

Selected objects can be scaled and rotated using the facilities of the Modify menu, but do not overlook the Scale and Rotate buttons that appear in the Options section of the Tools palette when the Arrow tool is in use. These provide quick access to the Scale and Rotate functions.

Colour

The Stroke Color and Fill Color buttons in the Tools palette change to match the colours of any object that is selected. In many cases there will only be a line or a fill, and not both. Only one colour button or the other will then change. Where a filled object is selected in its entirety, both buttons will respond. For multiple selections, the buttons respond to the last object that was selected.

As explained previously, stroke and fill colours can be changed using the Ink Bottle and Paint Bucket tools respectively, but colour editing is sometimes easier using the colour buttons in the Tools palette. This method enables objects to be quickly set at any of the standard colours. Left-click on the appropriate colour button to bring up the colour chart and then choose a colour using the “eyedropper”. Any item that is currently selected will then use the new fill or stroke colour.

Of course, if the selected object only has a stroke colour and you change the fill colour, the object will remain unchanged. You have merely changed the current fill colour. Similarly, changing the stroke colour will have no effect on objects that have only fill colours. With this method of colour changing it is possible to select a number of objects and change them to the same fill or stroke colour simply by operating the appropriate colour button and selecting a new colour. Bear in mind that the Eyedropper tool will work with objects in the drawing area and is not only usable with the colour chart that appears. It is therefore possible to

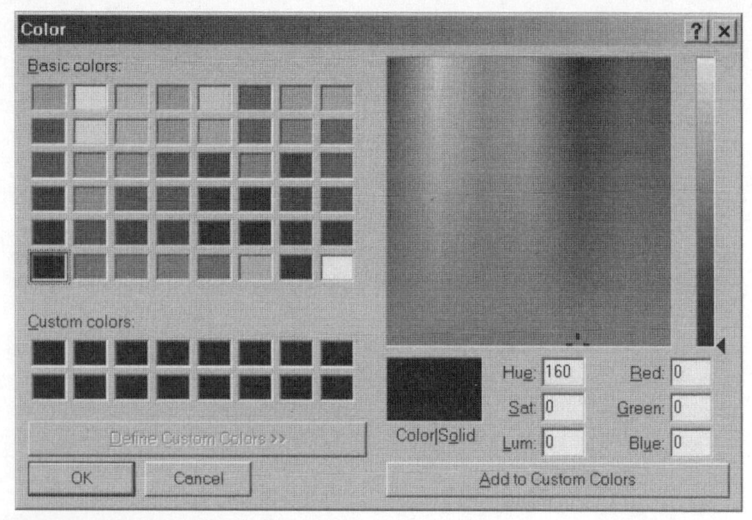

Fig.4.10 The colour Mixer panel

select a number of items and then set them to the same colour as any other object in the drawing area.

Colour mixing

In addition to the colour chart, a colour-mixing palette (Figure 4.10) can be produced by operating the button with the circular icon in the top left-hand corner of the chart. This makes it easy to produce any desired colour. Suppose that a strong but dark blue is required, similar to navy blue. The main part of the window on the right gives the colours of the rainbow at the top, and the same colours diluted with an increasing amount of mid-grey towards the bottom of the panel. In other words, there are saturated colours at the top and increasing unsaturated versions of these colours towards the bottom.

Nothing on this panel meets our requirements, but a strong blue colour can be selected by left clicking on a mid-blue colour towards the top of the panel. The cross-hairs sight moves to show the new colour selection. The slider to the right of the panel shows the selected colour in the middle, with increasing amounts of white towards the top, and black towards the bottom. In this example we require black added to the blue to darken it, and the slider is set towards the bottom of its range. If you

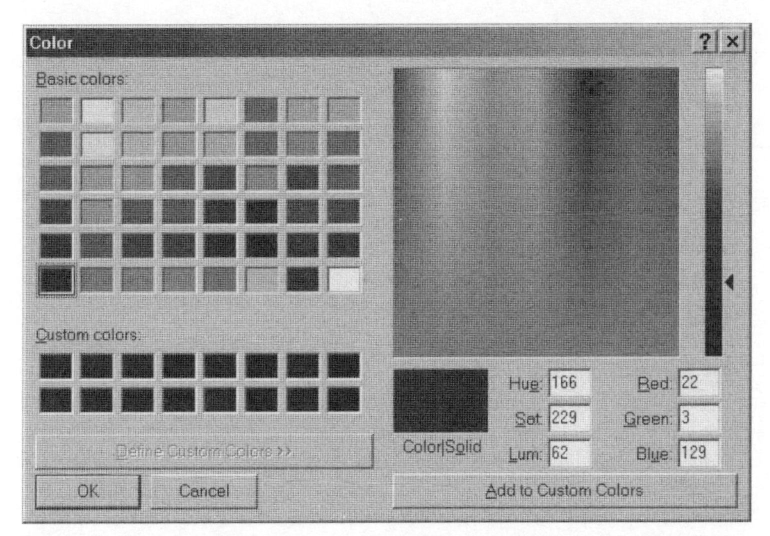

Fig.4.11 These settings have produced the required dark blue colour

try to approximate the settings shown in Figure 4.11 you should end up with a suitably dark blue colour.

The colour chart in the left-hand section of the window can be used as an alternative method of providing a basic colour that can then be adjusted using the slider control. The range of colours available here is relatively limited, but it will often provide a suitable basis for the required colour. Simply left-click on the required colour to select it and then adjust the slider control. In order to add a newly mixed colour to the custom colours beneath the main colour chart, first left-click on the rectangle you wish to contain the new colour. Then left-click on the Add to Custom Colours button to assign the new colour to the selected rectangle. Note that due to different conventions for PCs and Macintosh computers, colour selection using the Macintosh version of Flash is somewhat different to the method shown here.

Web safe

There is a slight problem in selecting web page colours. What looks just right on one computer may look somewhat different when displayed on another computer. One reason for this is simply that different monitors produce different colours from the same colour values. In actual fact, the same monitor will produce different colours depending on how it is set up.

A second problem is that not all computers have the same colour capabilities. Apart from differences between Macintosh computers and PCs, there can be differences between computers of the same general type. Some PCs have simple graphics cards offering relatively few colours, while others have graphics systems that can handle millions of different colours. A further complication is that the operating system and applications software might impose limits on the colours that can be used.

There is a set of so-called "browser safe" or "web safe" colours that can be reproduced by the popular Microsoft and Netscape browsers in both their Windows and Macintosh versions. Using these 200 or so colours does not guarantee that precisely the specified colour will be produced on every computer, but it does at least keep the inevitable divergences to a minimum. The "browser safe" colours are those that have 00, 33, 66, 99, CC, or FF as the hexadecimal values for each of the primary colours, but note that a few of the possible combinations are not guaranteed to always be spot on. If you operate one of the colour buttons in the Tools palette you will see these hexadecimal codes at the top of the colour chart. All the colours in the chart are of the browser friendly variety.

Of course, if you use the colour mixing facility to produce your own colours they will not be browser friendly, but this does not necessarily mean that they will not be displayed properly. It simply means there is a greater risk of things going slightly awry. Being realistic about matters, a slight lack of colour accuracy will not be the end of the world.

Gradient fills

In the version of the colour chart for fills (Figure 4.12) there are four circular entries along the bottom row of the chart. Selecting one of these produces a gradient fill. These are also known as graduated and fountain fills incidentally. Gradient fills can be used with any shape, but probably their most common use is with circles and ellipses to give a sort of three-dimensional effect, making a circle look like a sphere for example. Figure 4.13 shows a circle and an ellipse that have been given graduated fills, and both exhibit this three-dimensional quality. This type of gradient is known as a radial gradient fill, and there is also a linear variety.

A linear gradient fill is obtained by left clicking on the square in the bottom left-hand corner of the colour chart, and it produces fills like those in Figure 4.14. It again gives a sort of three-dimensional effect, with the objects seeming to be lit from the left side rather than from the front. There are actually two more linear gradient fills at the right-hand end of the bottom row, and these give very colourful results. The greyscale reproduction of Figure 4.15 does not do them justice.

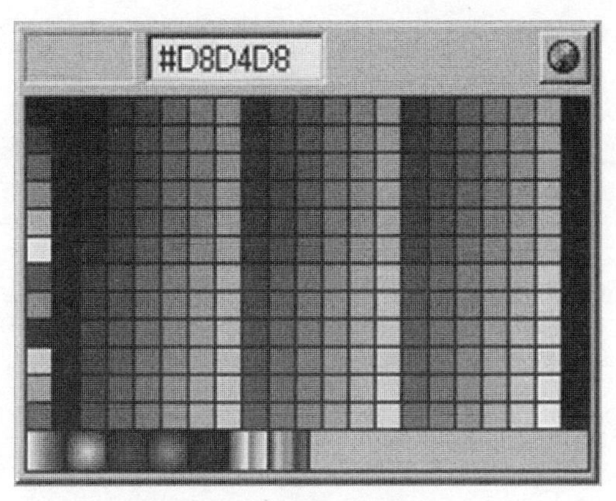

Fig.4.12 The Fills colour swatch

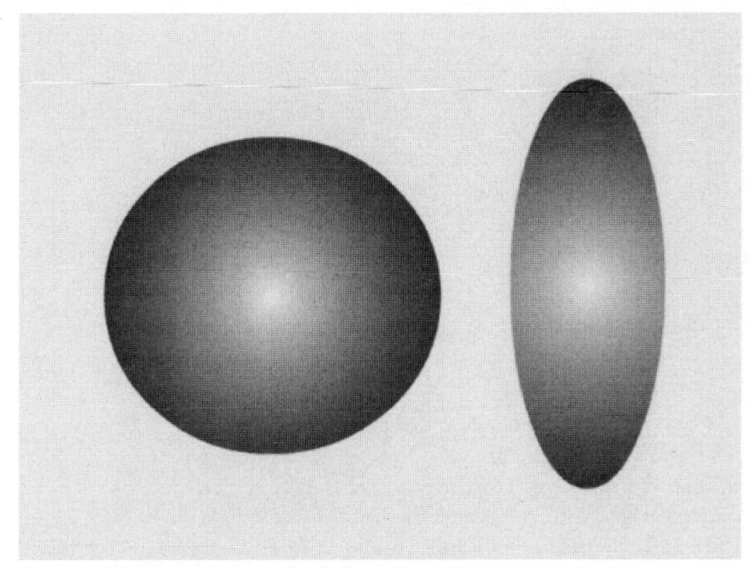

Fig.4.13 Two examples of radial gradient fills

Fig.4.14 Four objects having linear gradient fills

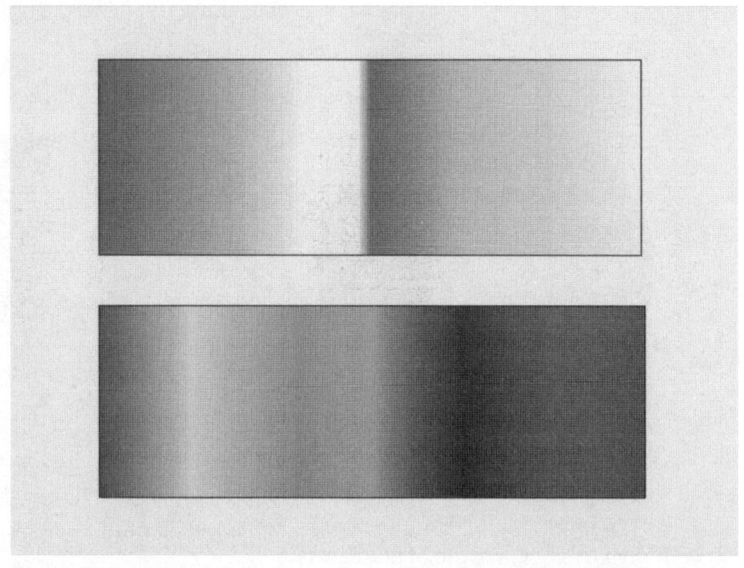

Fig.4.15 Two examples of complex mutil-coloured linear fills (honest)

Panels

Most of the facilities described so far in this book have been available without using the various panels. To some extent the panels duplicate facilities that are available via other parts of the user interface, but in order to get the best results from gradient fills, and some other features, it is essential to resort to the panels. Select Panels from the Window menu, and then choose Swatches from the submenu that appears. This will produce the panel of Figure 4.16, which is obviously very similar to the pop-up colour chart that appears when one of the colour buttons in the Tools palette is operated. Although similar it is definitely not the same. This panel can be used to select the stroke or fill colours,

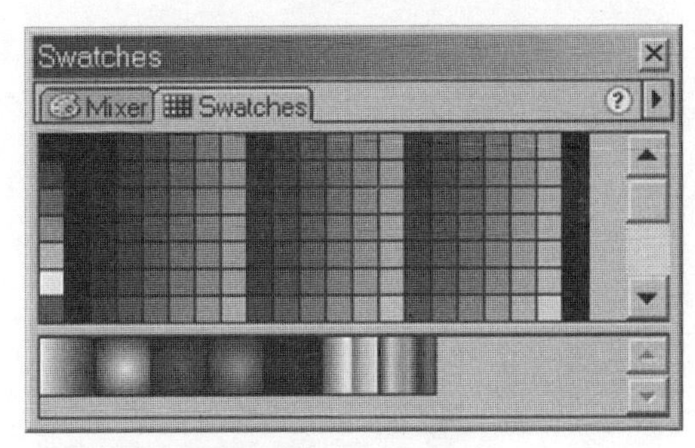

Fig.4.16 The Swatch panel

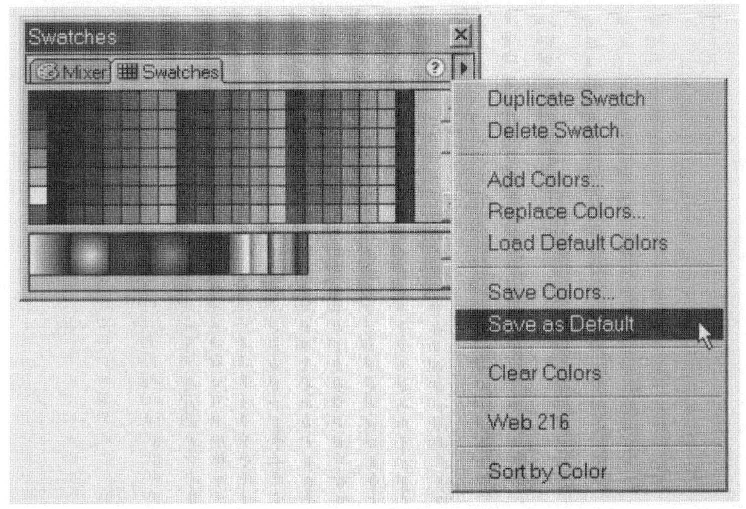

Fig.4.17 The popup menu of the Swatch panel

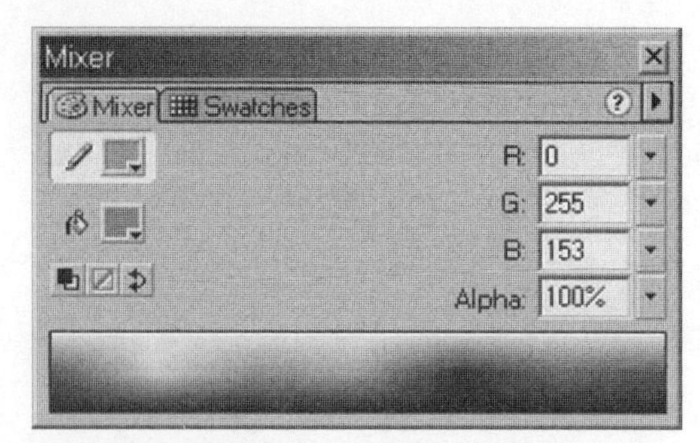

Fig.4.18 The Mixer is simple but effective

and the colour buttons in the Tools palette control it. Whichever of these buttons is active, that is the type of colour that the panel will select. If it is not already selected, the Fill button will be operated automatically when a gradient fill colour is selected in the Swatch panel.

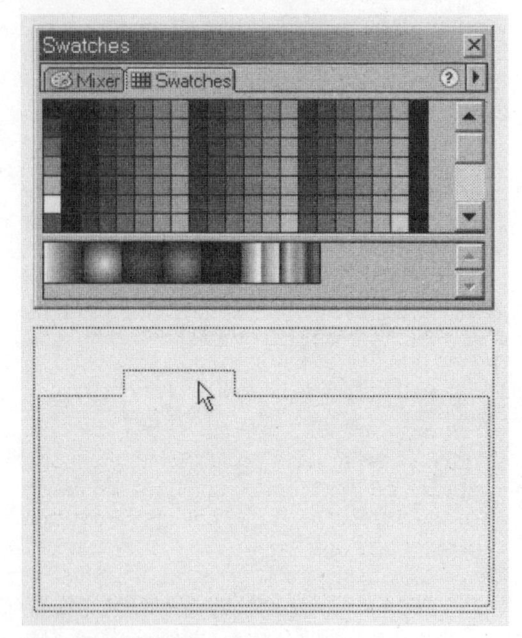

Fig.4.19 Dragging a panel from a group

Panel organisation

The Swatch panel has an additional featured compared to the standard colour chart, and this is a pop-up menu that can be activated by left clicking the arrowhead near the top right-hand corner of the screen (Figure 4.17). This enables new colour sets to be saved, the default colour set to be reloaded, and things of this type. There is a sort of simplified version of the colour mixer grouped with the Swatch panel (Figure 4.18), and this is selected by operating the Mixer tab.

For the benefit of those who are not familiar with control panels it should perhaps be explained that they are usually organised in groups, with the desired panel being obtained by operating its tab. In this way you have rapid access to a number of panels without huge expanses of screen area being occupied by panels that are not currently in use. However, a panel can be dragged from a group (Figure 4.19), and when the mouse button is released it will be independent of the group (Figure 4.20). The panel can be dragged back into the group again, or into another group if preferred.

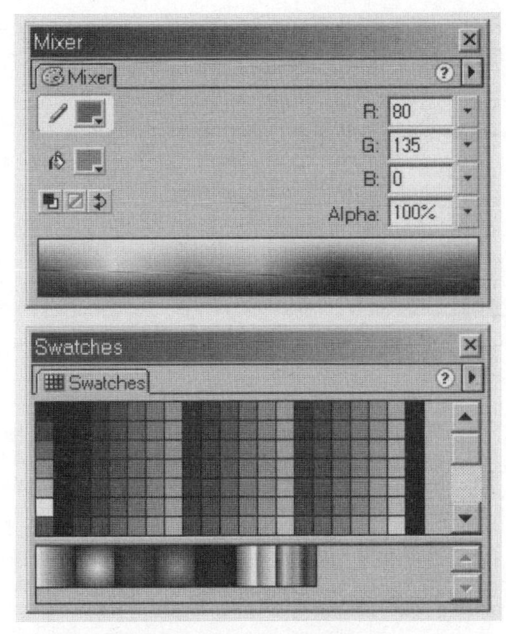

Fig.4.20 The two panels separated

Mixer panel

To select a new colour using the Mixer, operate the stroke or fill button, as appropriate, and then left click on the required colour in the lower part of the screen. There is a spectrum of saturated colours across the middle of the colour bar, with paler versions towards the top and darker versions towards the bottom. Although the colour bar is quite small it nevertheless gives access to a huge range of colours. Another way of selecting colours is to type in values for the three primary colours in the upper three text boxes. Note that in this case decimal values from 0 to 255 are used and not hexadecimal numbers from 00 to FF.

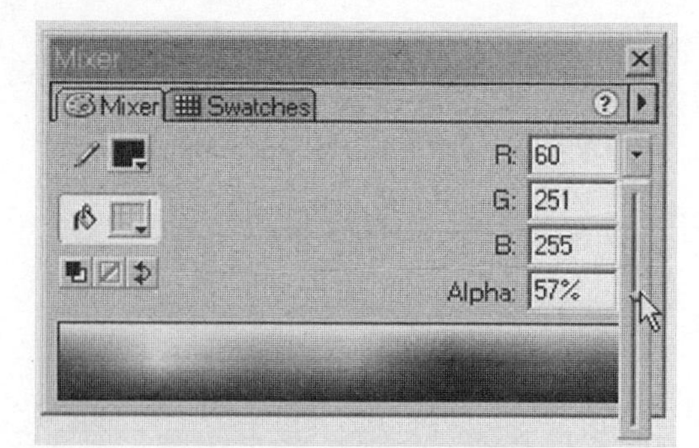

Fig.4.21 Adjusting the Alpha setting

Transparency

In the Mixer panel there is a useful extra in the form of the Alpha setting, which is the bottom of the four text boxes on the right-hand side of the window. The Alpha settings control the transparency of colours. A value from 0 to 100 percent can be typed in here, or left clicking on the arrowhead beside the box permits the value to be adjusted by means of a scrollbar (Figure 4.21). The same method of adjustment is also available for the primary colour values incidentally.

As one would expect, transparency governs how much or how little of any background object shows through the fill. In Figure 4.22 there is an

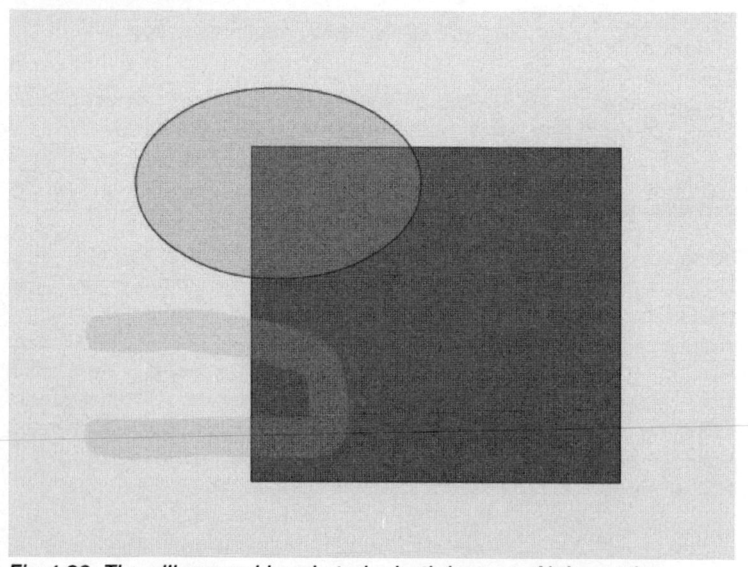

Fig.4.22 The ellipse and brushstroke both have an Alpha setting of 34 percent

opaque rectangle that is overlapped by two objects having the transparency set at 34 percent. These two objects have been grouped so that they appear in front of the rectangle, but due to their transparency the rectangle is still visible. The effect is to some extent lost in a greyscale image, where the mixing of the foreground and background colours is lost. However, if you try a few examples of your own you will soon see how this mixing works. Objects are given a sort of coloured glass effect by using a suitably low Alpha setting.

Custom gradients

The gradient fills in the default colour set are a bit limiting, and you will probably wish to define your own. Start by selecting Panels from the Window menu, followed by Fill. This produces the window of Figure 4.23, and this permits a simple fill to be selected by operating the colour button and picking a colour from the popup chart. The menu (Figure 4.24) allows other types of fill to be selected, or no fill to be used. There are two types of gradient fill available, and we will start with the linear variety. A window like Figure 4.25 is produced when this option is selected.

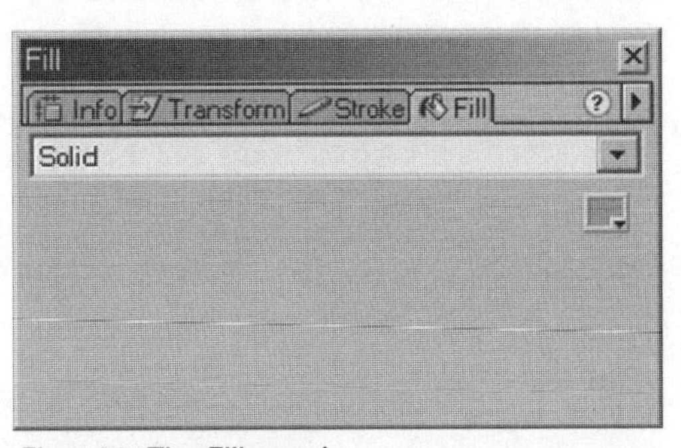

Fig.4.23 The Fill panel

There is a form of scrollbar beneath the menu, with a colour button to its right and a small preview area to the left. If you left-click on one of the slider controls, the colour button will assume the colour of that control. Left

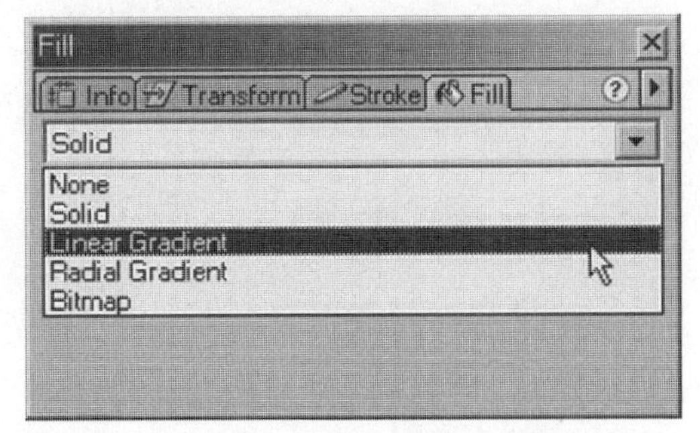

Fig.4.24 The Fill panel's pop-down menu

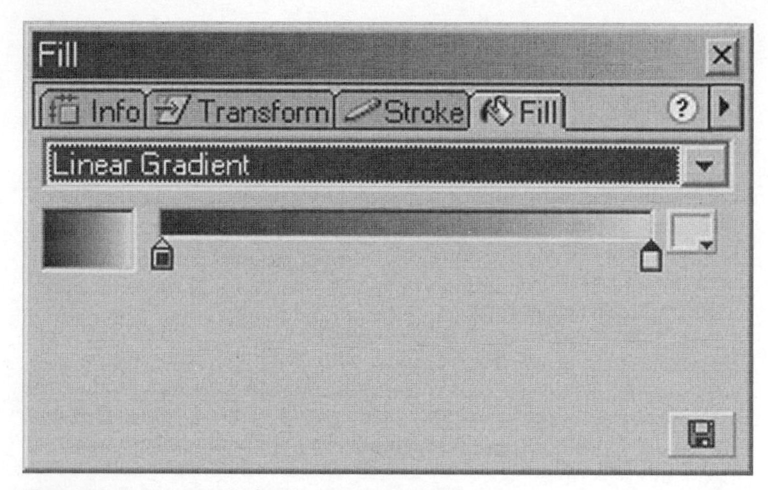

Fig.4.25 The controls for linear gradient fills

clicking on the colour button then brings up the usual colour swatch, and any of the available colours can then be selected. That colour is then used for the slider control and its end of the gradient. You can therefore have any desired start and finish colours by clicking on one slider and selecting a colour, and then clicking on the other slider and choosing another colour.

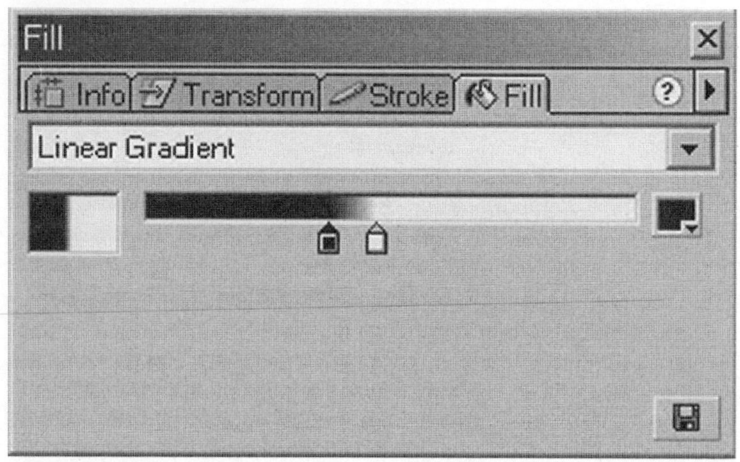

Fig.4.26 The gradient is controlled via the sliders

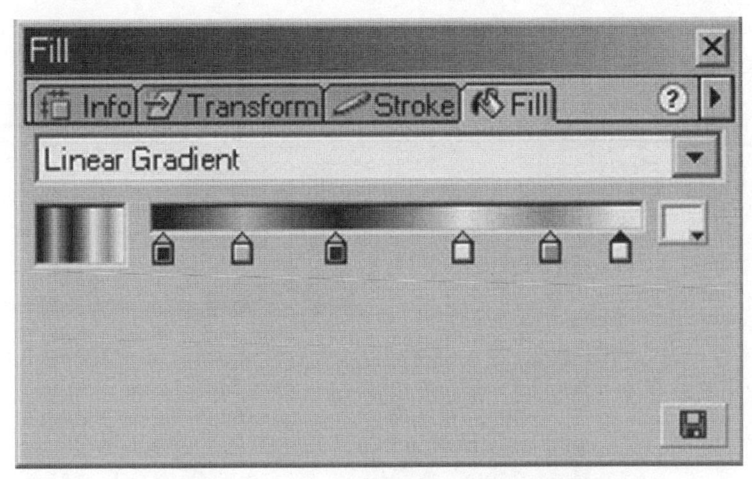

Fig.4.27 Complex fills can be produced by adding more sliders

Complex gradients

By default the sliders are at the end of the gradient bar, and there is a steady transition from one colour to the other. The gradient occurs between the two sliders, so it is possible to have the gradient cover a small section of the fill by moving the sliders close together, as in Figure 4.26. The possibilities do not end here, because there can be more than two sliders. To add a new slider just left-click in an empty area beneath the gradient bar and a new slider will appear.

Remember that the colour assigned to each slider can be altered by left clicking on the slider and then using the colour button in the usual way. Figure 4.27 shows six slider controls in use and in Figure 4.28 there are three objects that use this fill. Using complex linear gradients can produce some psychedelic effects, and they are also good for producing shiny metallic effects. Should you decide that a gradient fill is too complex, unwanted sliders can be removed by dragging them beyond the ends of the gradient bar and into oblivion. Dragging them downwards has the same effect.

On the face of it, the linear gradient fill is a bit limiting because it only provides horizontal graduation. What if you require a vertical gradient or one at an odd angle. It is not possible to set the gradient at a different angle, but the same effect can be obtained by filling an object and rotating

Fig.4.28 Three objects having linear radial fills

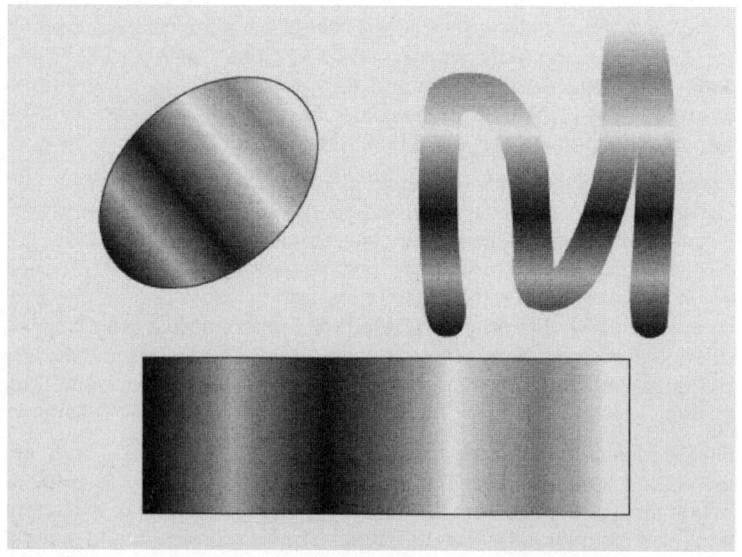

Fig.4.29 Linear radial fills are rotated with the objects they fill

it. Figure 4.29 shows the same objects as Figure 4.28, but one has been turned through 45 degrees and the other has been rotated by 90 degrees. In both cases the gradient fill has been rotated with the object. Other methods of controlling gradient fills are covered later in this chapter.

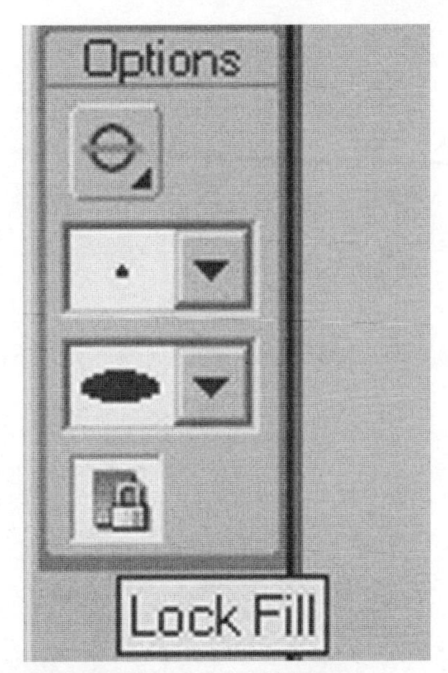

Fig.4.30 The Lock Fill button

Lock Fill

When using the Brush tool, one of the buttons in the Options section of the Tools palette is the Lock Fill button (Figure 4.30). When this is operated, a linear gradient is spread across the whole stage, rather than being adjusted to fit objects that are

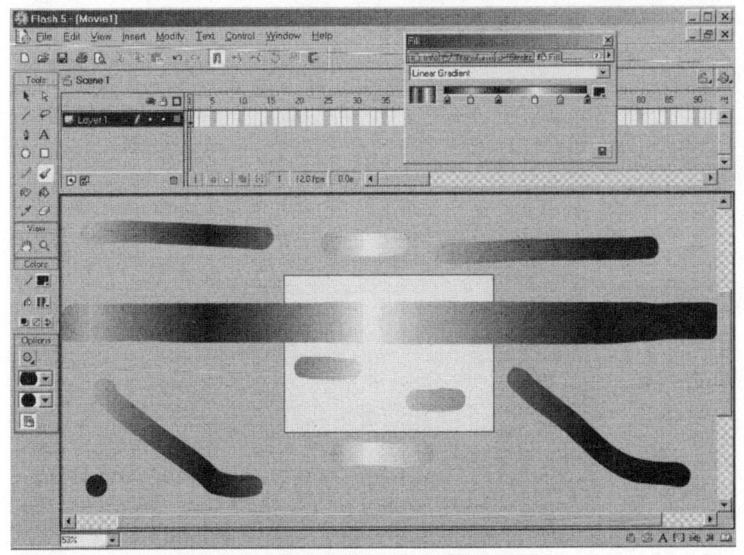

Fig.4.31 The spreading effect of the Lock Fill button

Fig.4.32 The top object was added before operating the Lock Fill button

Fig.4.33 An object being painted

Fig.4.34 The fill apears on the compled object

painted with the brush tool. Figure 4.31 shows this effect quite clearly. This is probably not of much practical use, but there is another way of using the Lock Fill facility. If an object is painted on the drawing area without using locking, as in the top stroke of Figure 4.32, and then further objects are painted using the Lock Fill facility, the additional objects will use the same gradient fill. This effect can be seen in the lower two objects of Figure 4.32. Note that the gradient fill does not appear when an object is being painted (Figure 4.33), but it is shown as soon as the object has been completed (Figure 4.34).

A gradient can be added to the colour chart and Swatch panel by left clicking on the arrowhead near the top right-hand corner of the Fill panel and then selecting the Add Gradient option from what is effectively a single item menu (Figure 4.35). The gradient is only used with the current document, and will be saved and loaded with that document.

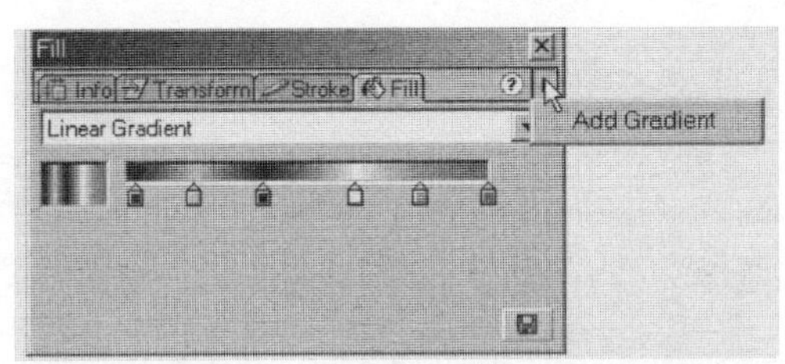

Fig.4.35 Adding a gradient fill to the swatch

Radial fill

The method of control for radial fills is much the same as for the linear variety (Figure 4.36). There are the same slider controls, gradient bar, etc., and more sliders can be added if required. Figure 4.37 shows some objects that use

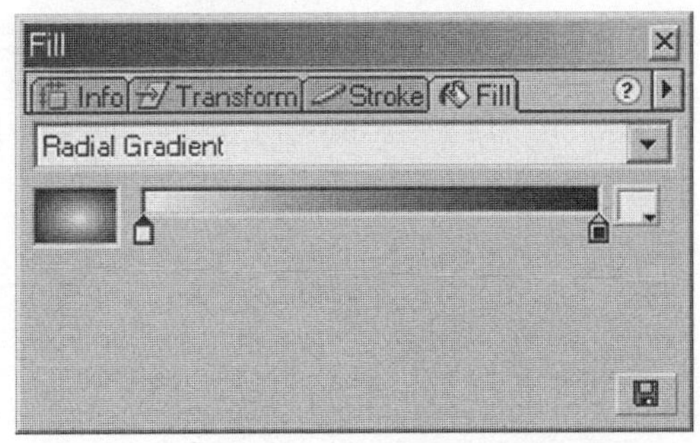

Fig.4.36 The Fill panel for radial gradients

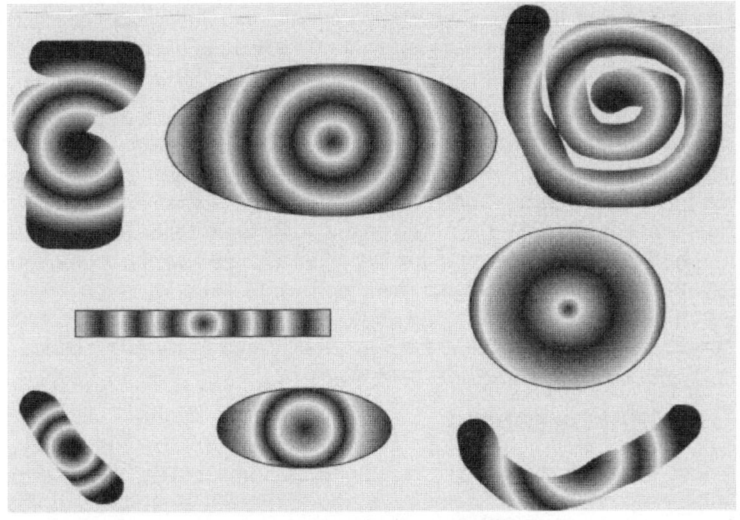

Fig.4.37 Some objects using a complex radial fill

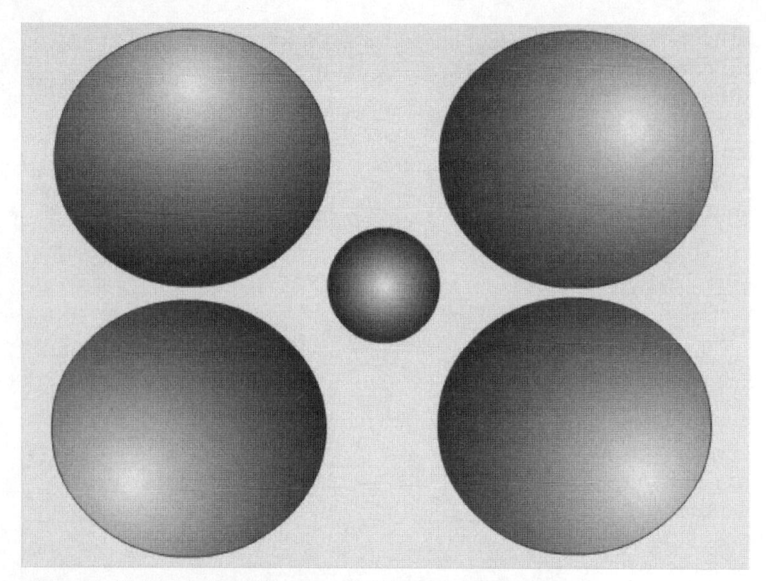

Fig.4.38 Using radial fills with the Paint Bucket tool

complex radial fills. As pointed out previously, one of the main uses of a radial fill is to make a circle look like a sphere. This is done using a simple radial fill that is light in the centre and increasing dark towards the edges. Moving the centre of the fill off centre can alter the apparent position of the light source.

On the face of it, there is no way of doing this using Flash, and it would appear that the centre of the fill will always be at the centre of the circle. In fact it is possible to move the centre of the fill if the fill is added using the Paint Bucket tool. The centre of a radial fill is wherever the Paint Bucket tool is left clicked within an object. In Figure 4.38 the Paint Bucket tool has been used to move the highlight off centre in the four larger circles. The three-dimensional effect tends to be much more convincing with the centre of the fill moved off centre. Objects are mostly lit from above, and moving the centre of fills towards the top gives this effect.

Gradient tweening

Gradient fills can be used to good effect with tweening, giving more convincing movement. Start a new movie, draw a circle towards the bottom left-hand corner of the screen, and then use the Paint Bucket

Fig.4.39 The first frame of the tween

tool to give it a radial fill so that you have something like Figure 4.39. Select the circle and the radial fill and then choose the Shape option from the Tweening menu in the Frame panel. Next left-click on frame 30 in the Timeline and select the Keyframe option from the Insert menu. Finally, move the circle and fill to the right-hand side of the drawing area and use the Paint Bucket tool to move the highlight of the radial fill over to the left. This should give something like Figure 4.40.

Fig.4.40 The final frame of the tween

Fig.4.41 A frame near the middle of the sequence

If you press Enter to run the movie the circle will of course move across the bottom of the drawing area, taking a little over one second to complete the trip. Although shape tweening is being used, strictly speaking there is no change in the shape of the circle. What actually changes is the radial fill, with the highlighted area moving across the circle as the circle moves across the screen. Figure 4.41 shows Frame 15 of the sequence, with the highlight at a roughly central position. The effect obtained is that of a sphere moving across the screen, with a fixed light source slightly above and in front of the sphere.

Try another shape tween, but this time use something like Figure 4.42 and 4.43 as the start and finish frames. The tweening with gradually move the highlight across the circle, giving a frame like Figure 4.44 at the half way stage. There are two ways that your brain can interpret this movie when it is run. Either the "sphere" seems to have a light patch and to be rotating, or the "sphere" seems to be stationary with the light source moving across and in front of it. In this simple example there is nothing else in the picture to help resolve this matter, but in a proper animation there would be other elements to make matters clear to the user. Shadows are often an important factor in getting the right animation effect.

Fig.4.42 The first frame in a tween where the ball does not move. The viewer gets the impression of the ball rotating or the light source moving

Linear and gradient fills are very useful tools that can greatly enhance what would otherwise be some rather unconvincing animation. However, bear in mind that gradient fills increase file sizes and can generally slow things down. They are great when used wisely, but should not be used just for the sake of it.

Fig.4.43 The final frame of the sequence

Fig.4.44 A frame from the middle of the tweening sequence

Bitmap fills

If a really complex fill is required it is necessary to resort to the Bitmap option in the Fill panel. A bitmap file created with a paint program, or even using a digital camera or scanner, can then be used as a fill. When used as fills, small versions of bitmaps are used to "tile" the filled object. In order to use a bitmap it is necessary to import the bitmap first. Select the Import option from the File menu, which will bring up the usual file browser (Figure 4.45). A range of file types can be imported, including the popular Jpeg and Png bitmap types. However, some types of bitmap will have to be converted to one of the compatible file types before they can be imported into Flash. Once imported, the bitmap will appear in the drawing area. If you wish to add several bitmaps to the Fill panel they must all be imported. Figure 4.46 shows three imported bitmaps, which can also be seen in the Fill panel in Figure 4.47.

The required bitmap is selected by left clicking on its thumbnail picture in the bitmap section of the Fill panel. The bitmap will then appear in shapes or brushstrokes that are drawn in the work area, or existing shapes or strokes that are filled using the Paint Bucket tool. Figure 4.48

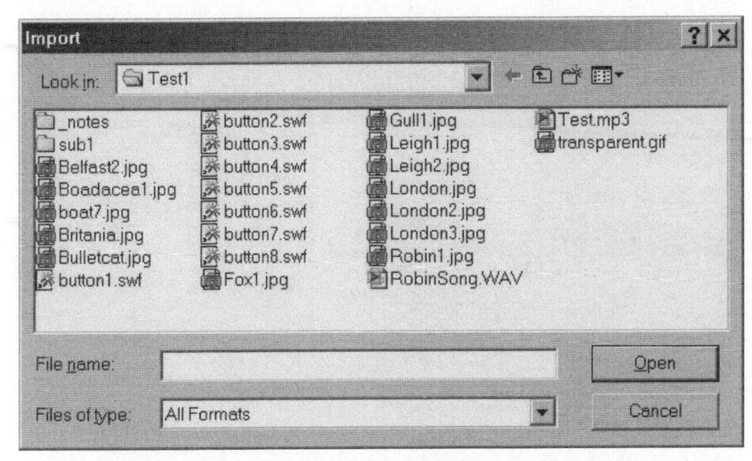

Fig.4.45 Selecting the Import function brings up the usual file browser that enables the required file to be selected and opened

Fig.4.46 Three bitmap images loaded onto the drawing area. Only a limited range of editing can be undertaken with bitmaps and they can not be tweened

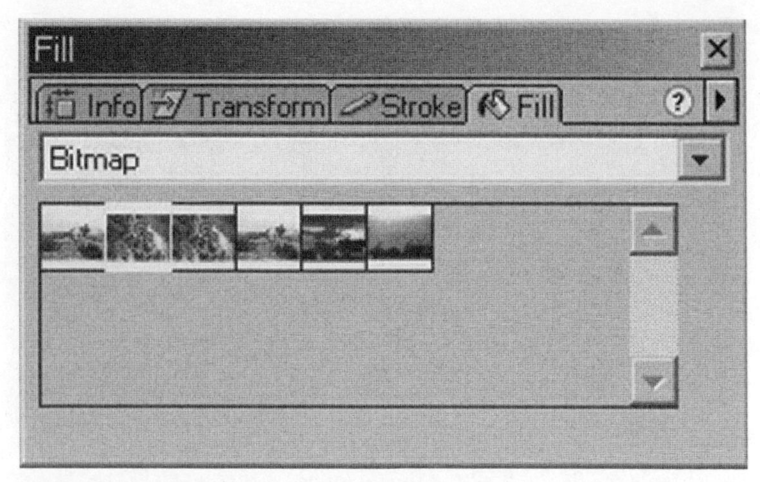

Fig.4.47 Six bitmaps loaded into the Fill panel

Fig.4.48 A bitmap loaded onto the Stage and the same image used as a bitmap fill on the right

shows an imported bitmap (left) and the same image used as a bitmap fill (right). The tiling effect is clearly visible in the filled shape. Although small, the tiled images are accurate miniatures of the original image, as can be seen from the zoomed view of Figure 4.49.

Fig.4.49 A close-up view of the bitmap fill

Transform

There are several useful tricks that can be used with gradient and bitmap fills. As pointed out previously, a linear fill can be rotated, but it is also possible to change its angle using the Paint Bucket tool. This method is the easier option in many circumstances. Figure 4.50 shows a linear radial fill in its normal version. In Figure 4.51 the same linear fill has been selected, and the Paint Bucket tool has then been dragged diagonally across the rectangle from the top right to bottom left. This produces the fill shown in Figure 4.52, where the angle of the fill is the same as the line that was dragged across the rectangle.

Fig.4.50 The original version of the fill

Fig.4.51 Dragging a line using the Paint Bucket tool

Fig.4.52 The angle of the fill matches that of the line above

Fig.4.53 The inverted version of the fill

Dragging the Paint Bucket tool from bottom left to top right produced the modified fill of Figure 4.53. Reversing the direction in which the Paint Bucket tool was dragged has reversed the direction of the linear fill, with the lightest part of the fill now in the top left-hand corner instead of the bottom right-hand corner.

Fig.4.54 The Transform Fill button

With the Paint Bucket tool selected there is a Transform Fill button in the bottom left-hand corner of the Options section in the Tools palette (Figure 4.54). This provides some useful features with gradient and bitmap fills. Try drawing an object on the screen and then giving it a simple linear gradient fill. Then select the Paint Bucket tool and operate the Transform Fill button.

The first thing you will notice is that the pointer is not the usual "bucket", but is a version of the Arrow tool. Left-click on the gradient fill to select it, and three handles will appear (Figure 4.55). It is possible to move the fill off centre by dragging the handle at the middle of the fill (Figure 4.56). The handle on middle right-hand side enables the gradient to be compressed or expanded (Figure 4.57), and the one in the top right-hand corner enables the fill to be rotated (Figure 4.58). These facilities can be achieved via other means, but you might find it more convenient to make adjustment to linear gradient fills using this method.

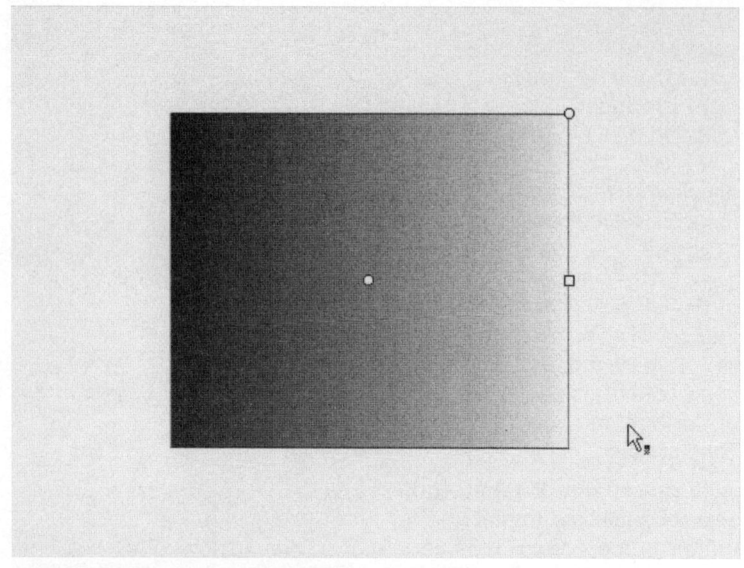

Fig.4.55 Selecting the rectangle causes three handles to appear

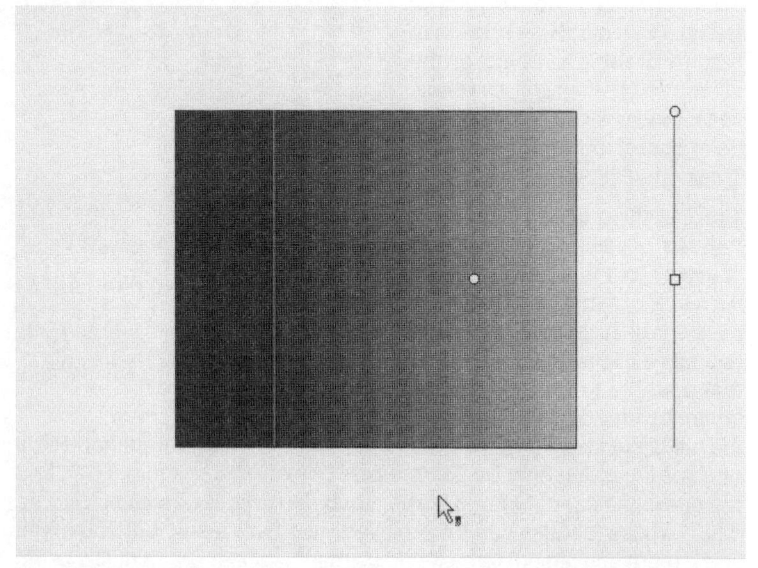

Fig.4.56 One of the handles enables the centre of the fill to be moved

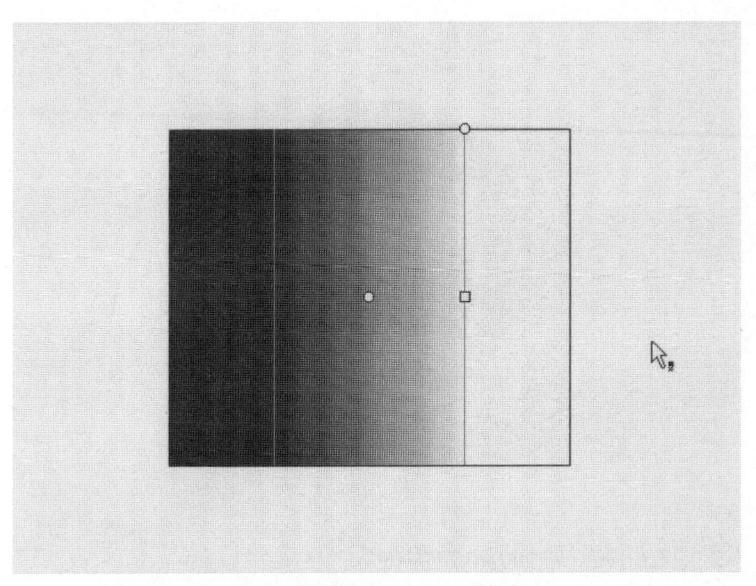

Fig.4.57 Another handle permits the gradient fill to be compressed (as in this example) or stretched

The Paint Bucket tool and Transform Fill button also work with radial gradient fills, but in a slightly modified fashion. As before, the fill can be stretched, compressed and rotated. The third handle enables the fill to be distorted into a sort of elliptical version of a radial fill. This could obviously be useful when using a radial fill with an ellipse, but it can also be used to good effect with other shapes (Figure 4.59).

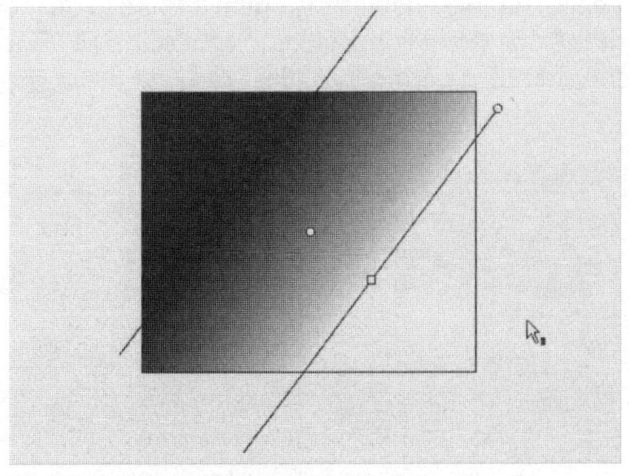

Fig.4.58 The third handle enables the fill to be rotated

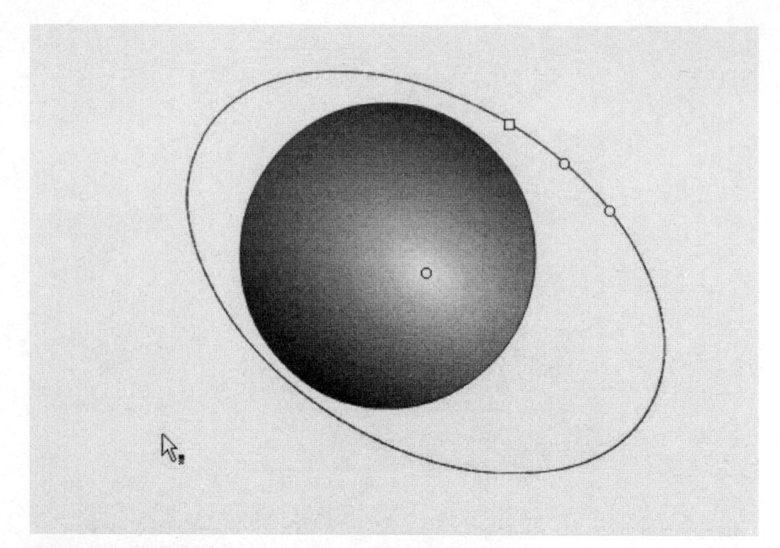

Fig.4.59 Radial fills can be stretched into ellipses

It is also possible to use the Transform Fill button with bitmap fills. Nine handles appear on the selected "tile" in the bitmap (Figure 4.60). The central handle enables the entire bitmap to be moved. Using the handles in the corners it is possible to rotate the fill (Figure 4.61), and the other four handles permit the "tiles" to be skewed (Figure 4.62).

Fig.4.60 Nine handles appear when editing a bitmap fill

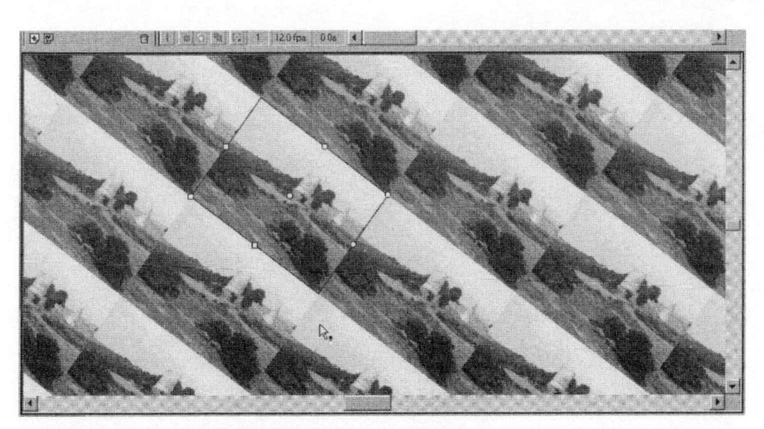

Fig.4.61 Here a bitmap fill has been rotated

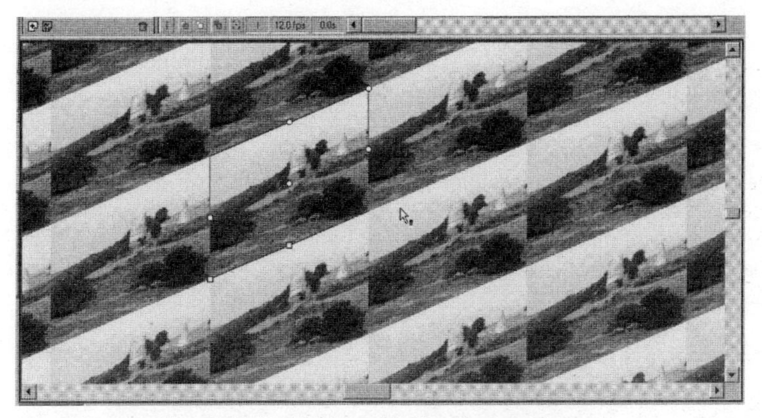

Fig.4.62 Here skewing has been added to the rotation

Tracing

When a bitmap is imported into Flash it is possible to edit it, but only in fairly limited ways. A bitmap can be scaled and rotated, and flipped for example, but not much else is possible. A greater range of editing effects can be used if a bitmap is converted into a vector graphic, and this can be done using the tracing facility. This can also produce some interesting arty effects from digital photographs or scans.

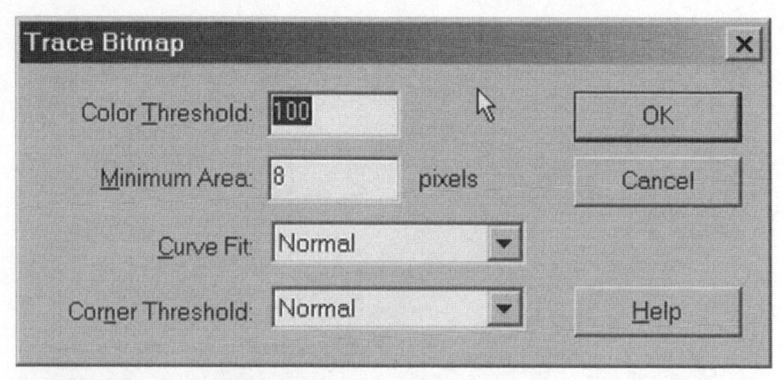

Fig.4.63 The Trace Bitmap dialogue box

To try out the tracing facility, import a bitmap, select it using the Arrow tool, and then choose the Trace Bitmap option from the Modify menu. This will produce the dialogue box of Figure 4.63. When first experimenting with this feature just accept the defaults and operate the OK button. After some processing the bitmap will be converted to a vector graphic. I used the picture of Figure 4.64, which looked like

Fig.4.64 The bitmap image in its "raw" form

Fig.4.65 The minimalist version of the traced bitmap

Fig.4.66 This version is closer to the original, but still loses some detail

Fig.4.67 This zoomed view shows some of the shapes that make up the image

Fig.4.68 The shapes in the image can be selected, as in this example

Figure 4.65 after processing. The end result is clearly a minimalist version of the original with the detail largely lost, but some interesting results are often produced.

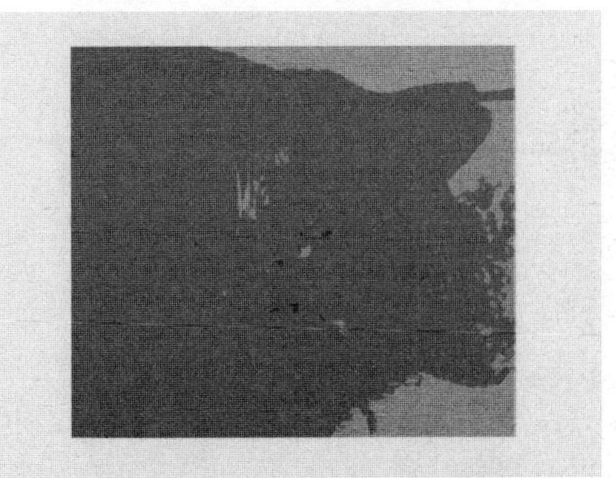

Fig.4.69 Going too far with the minimalism produces an unrecognisable image

By altering the settings in the Trace Bitmap dialogue box it is possible to obtain a more detailed image. Figure 4.66 shows the result obtained using the same bitmap as in the previous example, but with a Colour Threshold setting of 50 instead of 100. This is much closer to the original, although the shapes that make up the image are clearly visible in a slightly zoomed version (Figure 4.67). With the bitmap it is only possible to select the whole image, but with the traced version the image is a vector graphic, and each element can be selected individually. In Figure 4.68 one of the larger shapes has been selected to demonstrate this point.

Fig.4.70 An image produced using a Colour Threshold of 75

Using the right settings it is possible to obtain a vector image that gives a good imitation of the original bitmap, but it is also possible to go the other way and produce an image that is minimalist to the point of being barely recognisable. Figure 4.69 shows the result of using a Color Threshold value of 200 with the same bitmap used in earlier examples. In most cases an intermediate value gives the best results. Figure 4.70

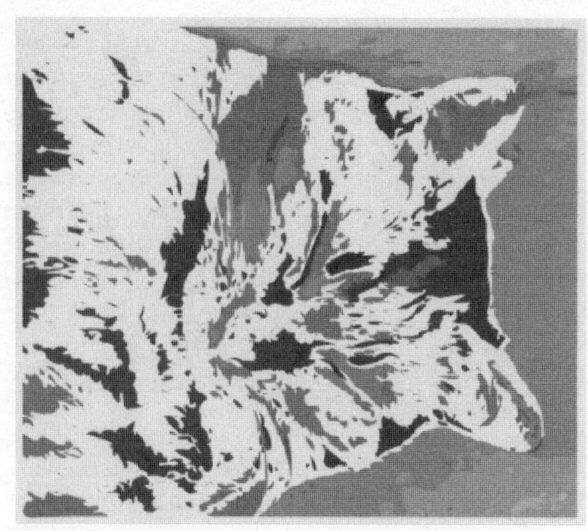

Fig.4.71 In this version the main shape has been erased

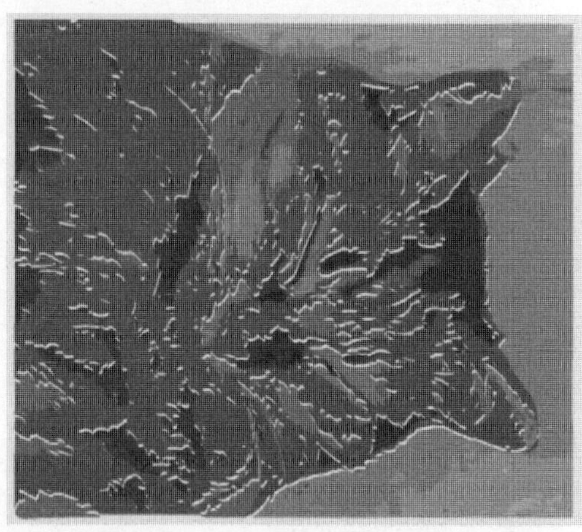

Fig.4.72 In this version the main shape has been moved up slightly

shows the image obtained using a Color Threshold value of 75. This gives quite good results but also produces a reasonably simple image that does not produce huge files.

Do not forget that the traced image can be edited in the usual ways, with colours being altered, lines being dragged into new shapes, and so on. Often quite simple editing will produce quite dramatic changes. The image of Figure 4.71 differs from the image of Figure 4.70 only in that the main shape has been selected and deleted. In the version of Figure 4.72 the main shape has been selected and moved slightly.

For the record, these are the functions of the four parameters that can be set by way of the Trace Bitmap dialogue box:

Color Threshold

Adjacent pixels of slightly different colour are grouped together in the traced version of the image. The value used here determines how close (or otherwise) the colours have to be before they are grouped together. As the examples already provided demonstrate, the lower the number used, the less readily pixels are grouped together. Low numbers therefore give more detailed and accurate results, but also produce much larger file sizes. In fact the file size can be larger than that of the bitmap used as the source of the image. This value must be in the range 1 to 500. Note that it can take a very long time for the processing to be completed if low values are used. Also, if you computer lacks the necessary computing power the process may simply grind to a halt.

Minimum Area

This parameter requires a value between 1 and 1000. It sets the number of surrounding pixels used when determining the colour used for a pixel.

Curve Fit

The Curve Fit setting determines how closely outlines are traced. A menu provides six options from Pixels to Very Smooth, with the latter being the least accurate.

Corner Threshold

There are three options that provide sharp corners, rounded corners, or something between the two.

In practice it is necessary to experiment a little with various settings to find the ones that give the best results for your purposes. A click on the Undo button will reverse the tracing process so that you can try again with different settings.

Tweening a tracing

One huge advantage of converting a bitmap into a vector graphic is that tweening can be used on the converted version, but not on the original bitmap. Some quite interesting effects can be obtained using shape tweening with a converted bitmap. Figure 4.73 shows the first frame in a 25-frame movie. The image has been compressed vertically using the Scale function but has been left at the original width. The image is used in its unaltered state in the final frame, and running the movie results in the image dropping down from the top of the screen until it reaches full size. However, this does not work quite as one might expect.

Figure 4.74 shows frame 12, and although the movie is at roughly the halfway point, the image is still not recognisable. Even at frame 20 (Figure 4.75) it is still far from obvious what the image will eventually be, and this method keeps your audience guessing. Finally, at frame 25 (Figure 4.76) the image is completed, and it is obviously a picture of a cat. The scrambling of the picture until it has almost totally expanded seems to be due to the individual elements of the picture being compressed, rather than the picture as a whole being compressed. Anyway, it gives interesting results that have creative possibilities.

Fig.4.73 The first frame of the tween

Fig.4.74 Frame 12

Fig.4.75 Frame 20

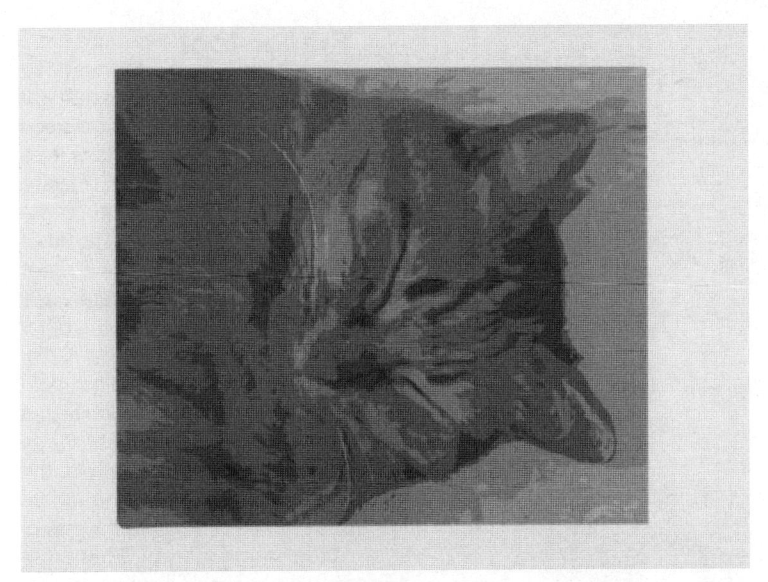

Fig.4.76 The final frame of the tween

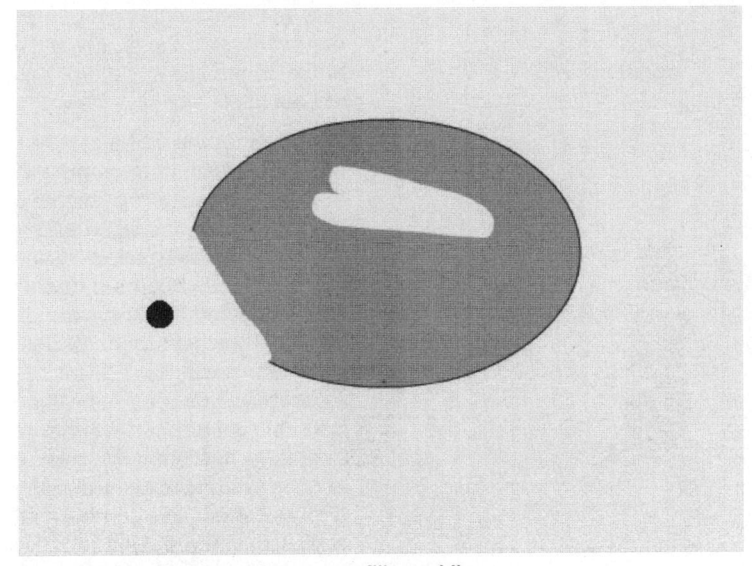

Fig.4.77 The Eraser tool removes fills and lines

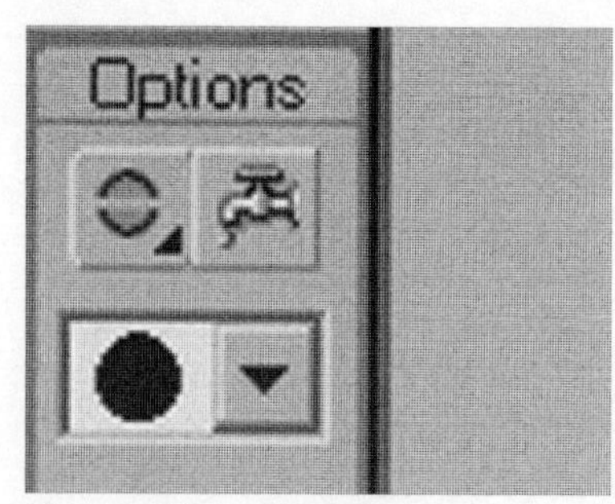

Fig.4.78 The eraser size menu

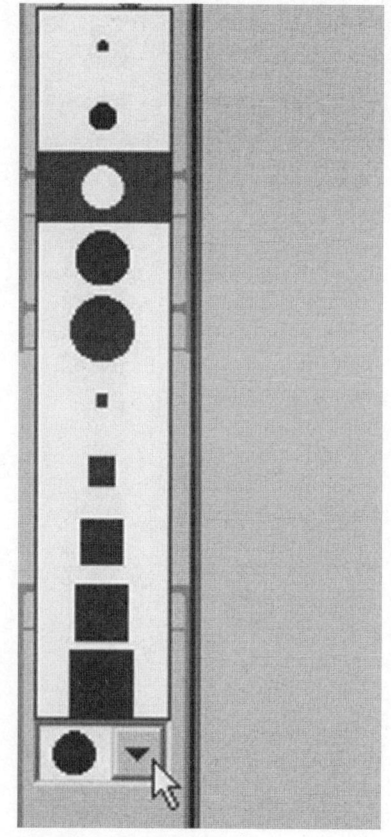

Fig.4.79 The 10 shapes and sizes

Eraser tool

The Eraser tool does what you would expect, and can be used to remove parts of objects or lines (but not normal text) (Figure 4.77). The Options section of the Tools palette has several facilities to make it easier to remove the appropriate parts of the drawing while leaving other parts untouched (Figure 4.78). Several sizes are available in both round and square versions (Figure 4.79). The Eraser Mode button (Figure 4.80) offers the standard mode plus selective ones where only certain types of object are erased. There are options to erase only lines, fills, and fills that have been selected using the Arrow tool. There is also an Erase Inside option. This only works with the fill where the erase command is started, and will not affect anything else.

When using one of the selective erasure modes it can appear as though things are not working properly. In Figure 4.81 the fill of the ellipse has been selected, and the eraser has been set to only erase selected fills. However, it has clearly erased parts of both outlines and the fill of the rectangle. However, everything is as it should be once the erasure operation has been completed and the mouse button is released (Figure 4.82). This can be a bit confusing at first, but the selective modes are quite easy to use once you have gained some experience with them. If things should go slightly awry from time to time it is just a matter of operating the Undo button so that you can try again.

As with the Brush tool, the effective size of the Eraser tool changes when the zoom magnification is changed. Zooming-in effectively makes the Eraser tool smaller, and zooming-out enlarges it. This is

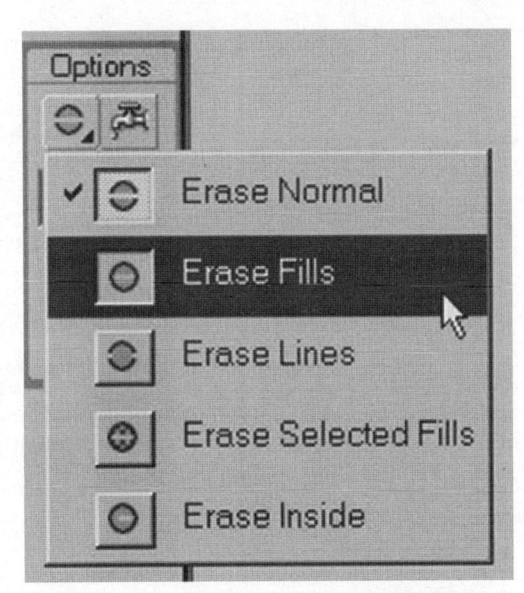

Fig.4.80 Five eraser modes are available

Fig.4.81 At first a selective mode might not seem to be working

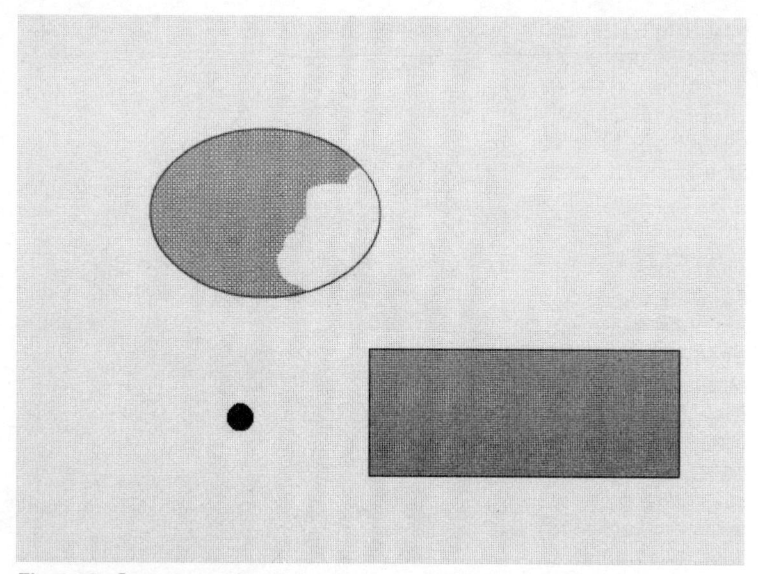

Fig.4.82 Once completed the erase operation has provided the desired result

generally advantageous, since the size of the tool reduces when you zoom-in to make detailed adjustments. This makes it easier to undertake any "fine tuning" of objects.

Faucet tool

In the options for the Eraser tool there is a Faucet button. The Eraser tool operates in a totally different way when this option is selected, and the pointer changes to a "tap" to remind you that this mode is in operation. When used with fills the Faucet tool works much like the Paint Bucket tool, but it fills enclosed shapes with nothing. Looking at it another way, left clicking on a fill using the Faucet tool erases the fill. The Faucet tool does not only work with fills though. Left clicking on a line using this tool instantly removes the line.

The Faucet tool is obviously a lot quicker and easier to use than the normal Eraser tool when it is necessary to remove complete objects. The Eraser tool is more versatile in that it enables parts of objects to be trimmed away. It would be a mistake to think of the Eraser tool as something that is only suitable for correcting errors. Sometimes the easiest way of doing things is to draw an object and then trim away the parts that are not needed.

Subselect tool

The Subselect tool, like the Arrow tool, is for selecting and editing objects, but it is primarily for editing points rather than complete objects. It is at its most simple when used with straight lines or shapes that have outlines constructed from straight lines. The outline of the filled rectangle in Figure 4.83 has been selected using the Subselect tool, and a handle has appeared at each corner. Handles that give control over individual points in lines are often called "nodes" incidentally. The Subselect tool is not used to edit fills, although changes to an outline will give corresponding changes to any fill that it contains.

Fig.4.83 The outline has been selected using the Subselect tool

A small filled square appears near the pointer when it is placed near the selected line. It is then possible to drag the line, complete with any fill, to a new position. However, this is not the primary purpose of this tool, which is really intended for moving points. In this case

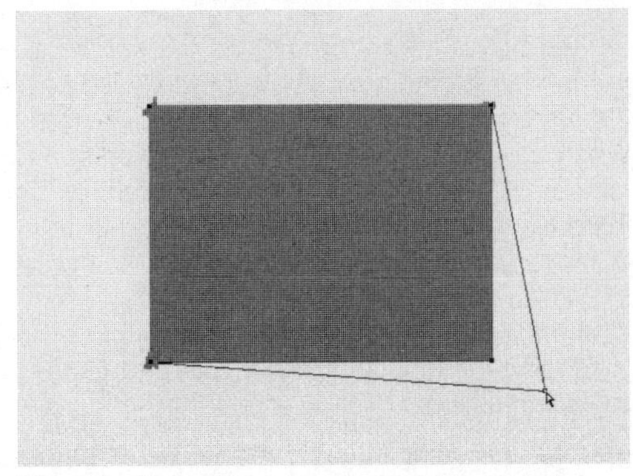

Fig.4.84 Dragging a corner of the rectangle

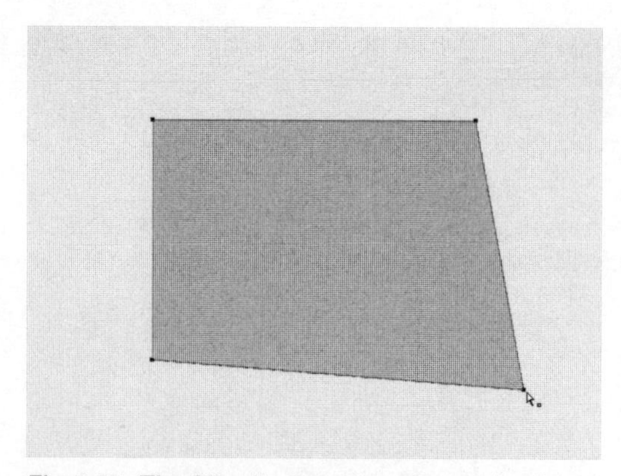

Fig.4.85 The fill adjusts to the change in shape

any of the four handles can be dragged to a new position, and the outline will be rubber-banded to indicate the new shape that will be obtained (Figure 4.84). A small non-filled square appears just beneath the pointer when it is close enough to a handle to drag it. When the mouse button is released the outline is redrawn and the fill is adjusted to fit the new shape (Figure 4.85). Obviously it is very useful to be able to adjust shapes and lines in this way, and some interesting perspective effects can also be obtained by altering shapes using this method.

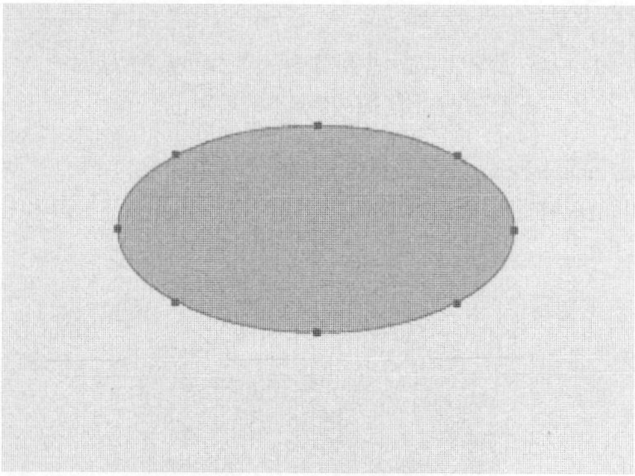

Fig.4.86 The control points and nodes produced on an ellipse

The Subselect tool operates in a different manner when used with curved lines or shapes. Left clicking on the outline of the ellipse in Figure 4.86 has produced a number of handles on the outline. A handle can be dragged to a new position, and the revised outline of the shape will be rubber-banded as in Figure 4.87. Releasing the mouse button results in the new outline being drawn and the fill adjusting to fit it (Figure 4.88).

You will also notice that three lines have appeared in Figure 4.87. One on the handle that has been dragged, and the other two on the handles

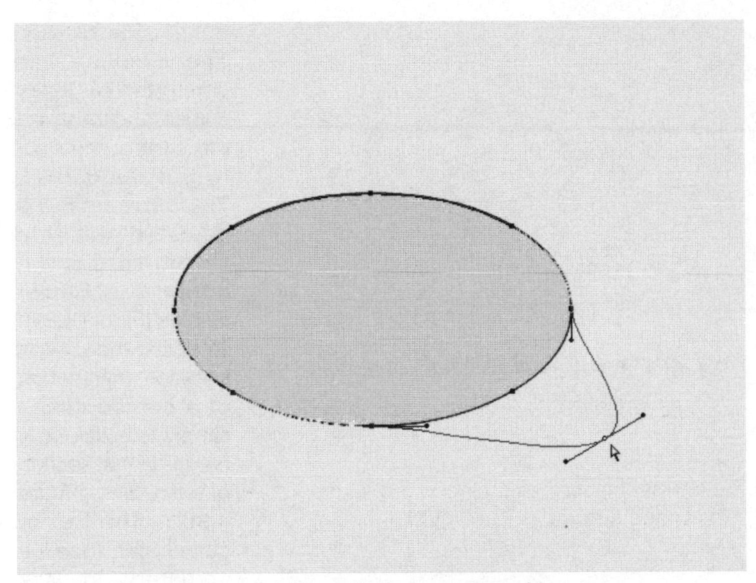

Fig.4.87 Dragging one of the nodes to a new position

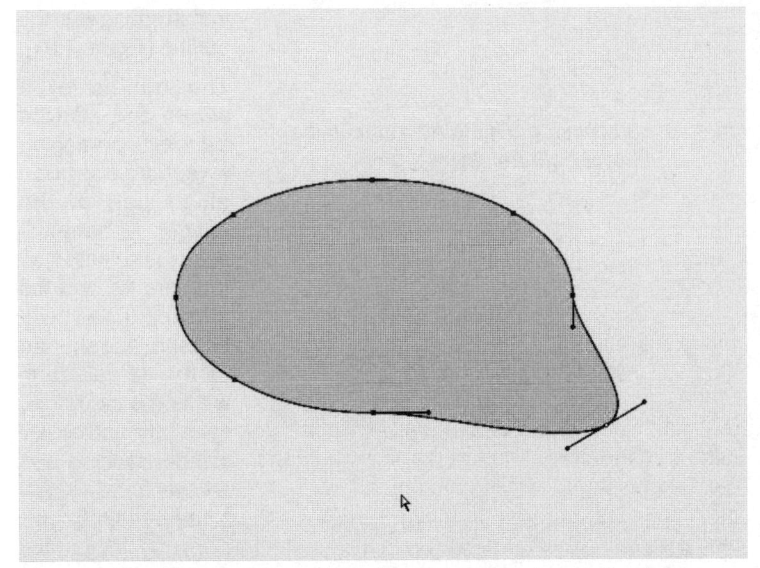

Fig.4.88 The fill has again adjusted to match the change in shape

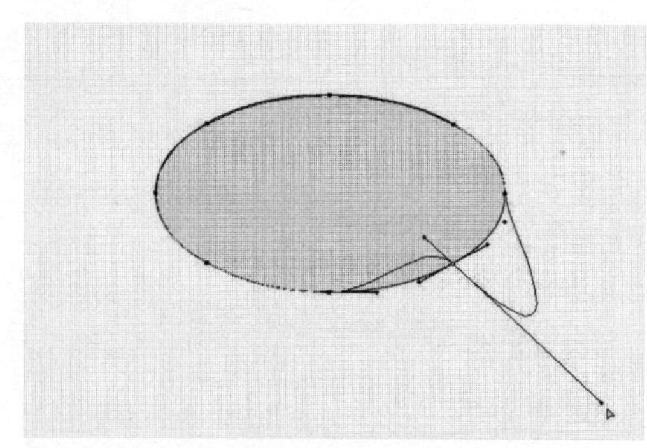

Fig.4.89 The outline of an elipse consists of Bezier curves

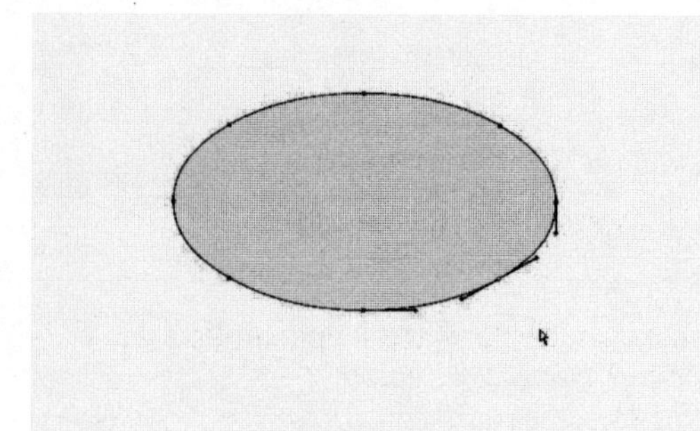

Fig.4.90 Left clicking a handle produces the relevant control lines

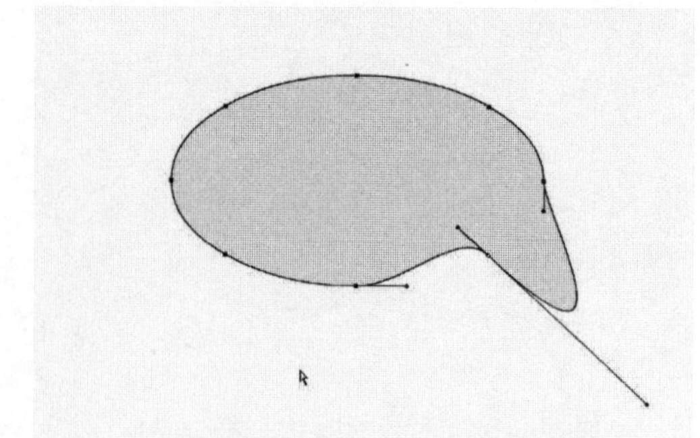

Fig.4.91 The curves are adjusted in the normal way

either side of this. The outline is comprised of Bezier curves, and these are the control lines for two of the curves. The curves can be adjusted via the control lines in the normal Bezier fashion (Figure 4.89). To obtain the control lines for any section of a curved shape simply left-click on a handle in that section of the outline (Figure 4.90). The Bezier curves can then be adjusted in the normal way, and the fill will adjust to match changes in the outline (Figure 4.91).

The outline of a shape can also be selected by dragging a rectangle around all or part of the shape. If the entire shape is selected, all the handles and the control lines will appear. If only part of the shape falls within the rectangle, the entire outline will still be selected and all the handles will appear. Only the control lines for sections of the shape

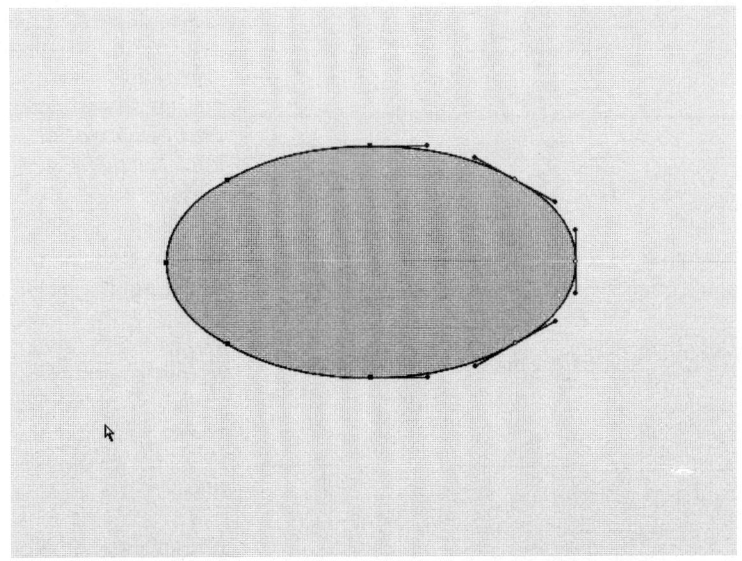

Fig.4.92 The control lines appear for the part of the ellipse that was selected

at least partially within the selection rectangle will appear though. In Figure 4.92 the right half of the ellipse was selected.

Curve editing

Editing curved lines using the Subselect tool is much like editing curved shapes. In Figure 4.93 the line has been selected using the Subselect tool and numerous handles have appeared on the line. These can be dragged to new positions (Figure 4.94). The control

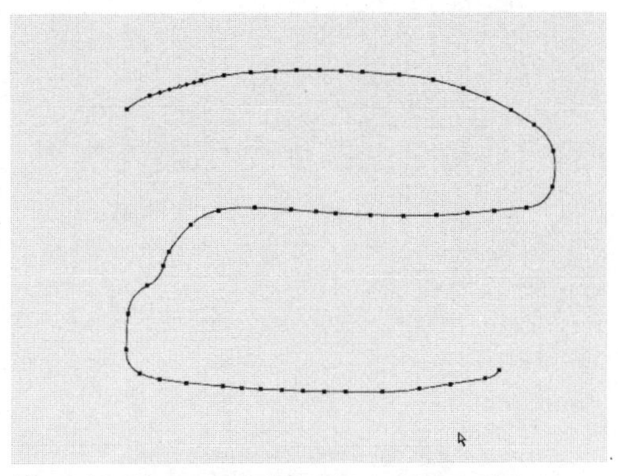

Fig.4.93 Numerous handles appear when a complex curve is selected

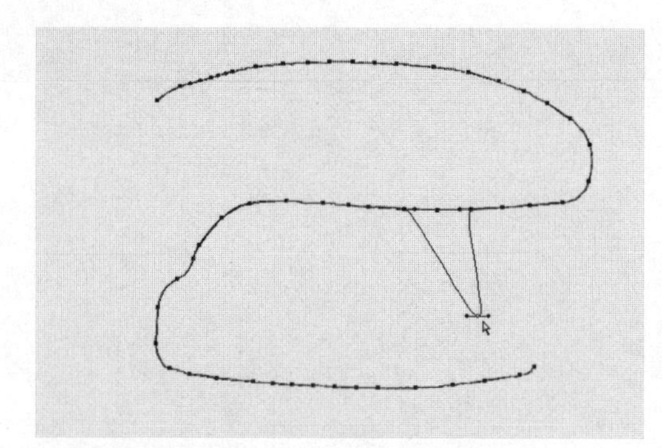

Fig.4.94 Dragging a node on a curve

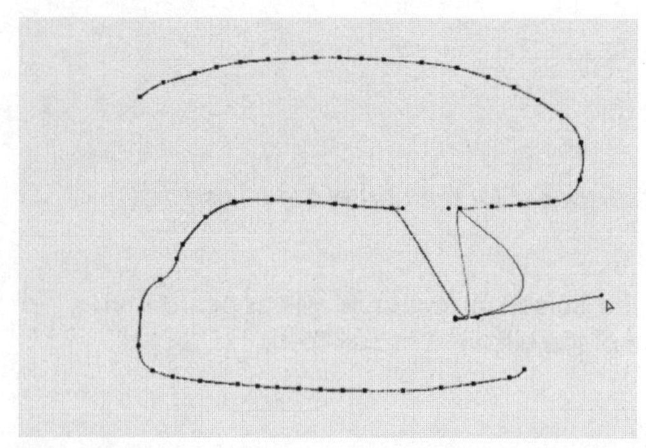

Fig.4.95 The usual Bezier controls are available

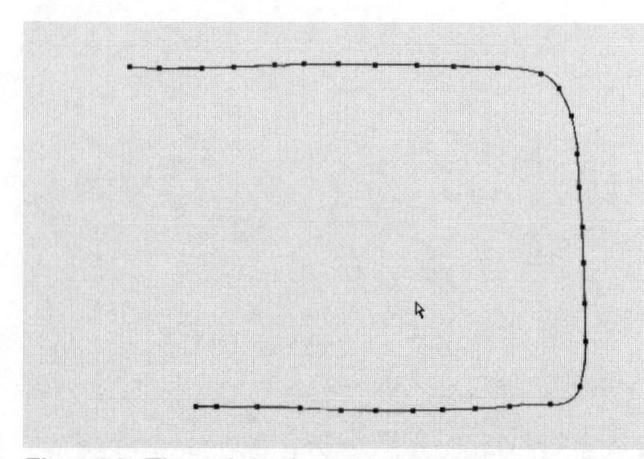

Fig.4.96 The original control points on the line

lines can be produced in the same ways as for curved shapes, and they are adjusted in the usual way (Figure 4.95).

Normally if an object is selected using the Subselect tool, operating the Delete key or selecting Cut from the Edit menu deletes the entire object including any fill. The situation is different if a node is left clicked to produce the control lines. Using the Delete key or the Cut function then deletes the selected node, but otherwise leaves the object untouched. Figure 4.96 shows a line that has been selected using the Subselect tool, and Figure 4.97 shows this line after a node has been deleted from the bottom right-hand corner.

A number of nodes can be selected using the rectangle method or by holding down the Shift key and selecting the nodes

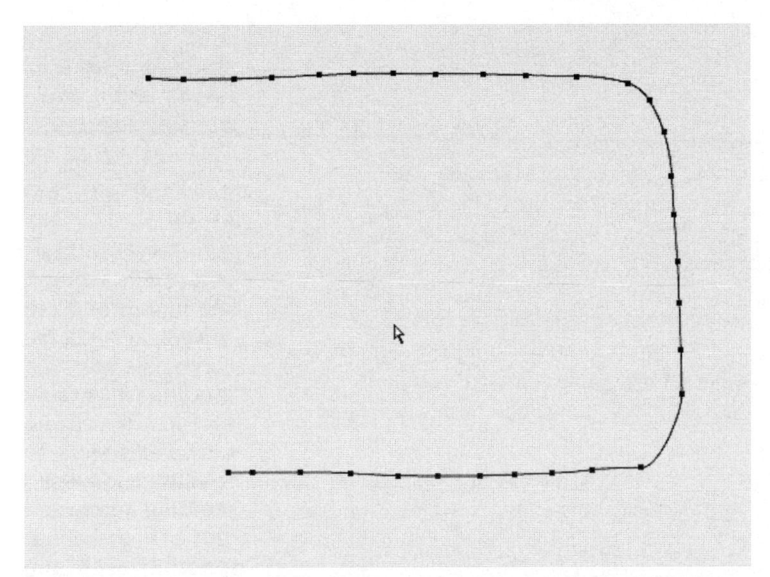

Fig.4.97 A node in the bottom right-hand corner has been deleted

individually. If consecutive nodes are selected and the delete key is operated, the nodes are removed but the line is otherwise left intact (Figure 4.98). Using the Cut facility will still delete the whole line incidentally. Selecting non-consecutive nodes and operating the delete key results in sections of the line being erased. Usually the best way of cutting pieces out of lines is to draw two straight lines across the existing line at the points where it must be cut (Figure 4.99). This is one large object if the Subselect tool is

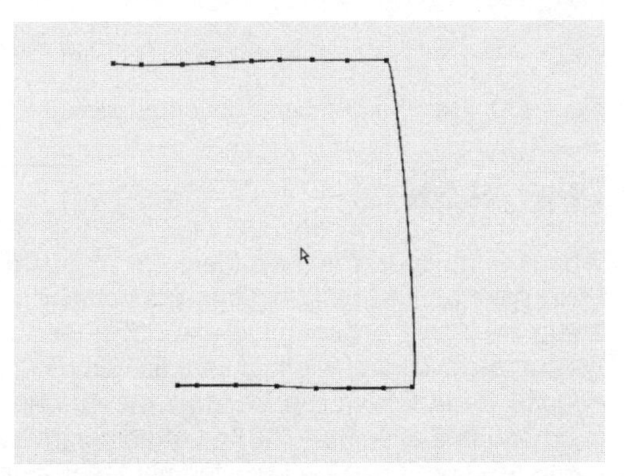

Fig.4.98 A large number of consecutive nodes have been erased

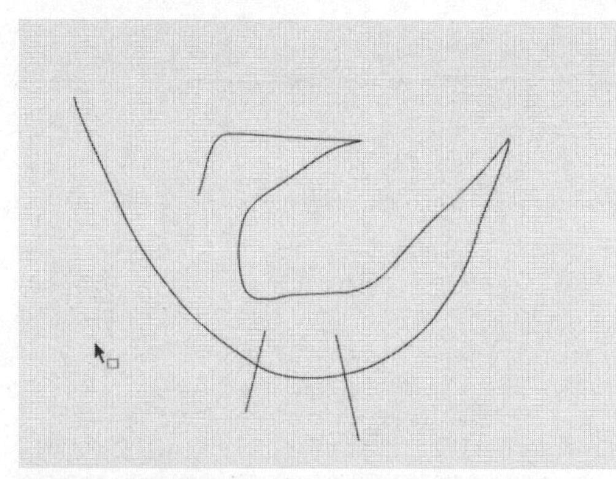

Fig.4.99 Adding the two construction lines

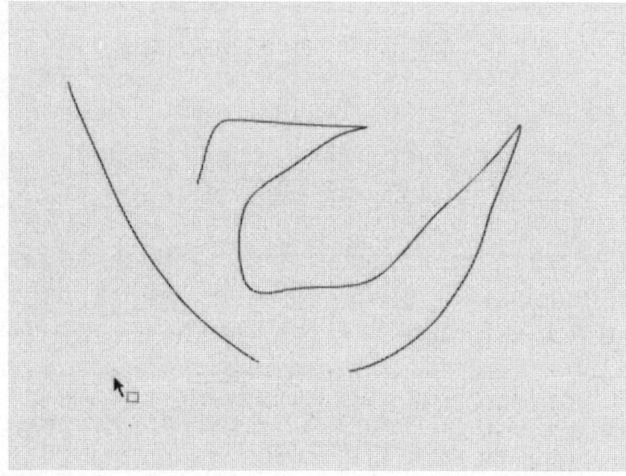

Fig.4.100 The line has been cut successfully

used, and selecting any of the three lines results in the whole lot being selected.

The situation is different with the Arrow tool. The curved line effectively cuts each straight line in two and the straight lines cut the curved line into three sections. The middle section of the curved line can therefore be selected and erased separately from the rest of the line, together with the straight lines that are no longer needed (Figure 4.100). Of course, the Eraser tool can be used to remove unwanted sections of lines, but with some types of drawing this method is more precise.

Line width

When the brush tool is used there are various options available via the Tools palette, but similar facilities are not available when drawing lines. There are some options available using Stroke panel, which enables the colour, style, and width to be adjusted. To launch this control panel choose Panels from the Window menu, and then Stroke from the submenu that appears. The line width parameter must be in the range 0.1 to 10, and it can be adjusted via the popup slider control (Figure 4.101). The pop-down menu offers a range of line types (Figure 4.102) and the colour is controlled using the usual colour button and chart.

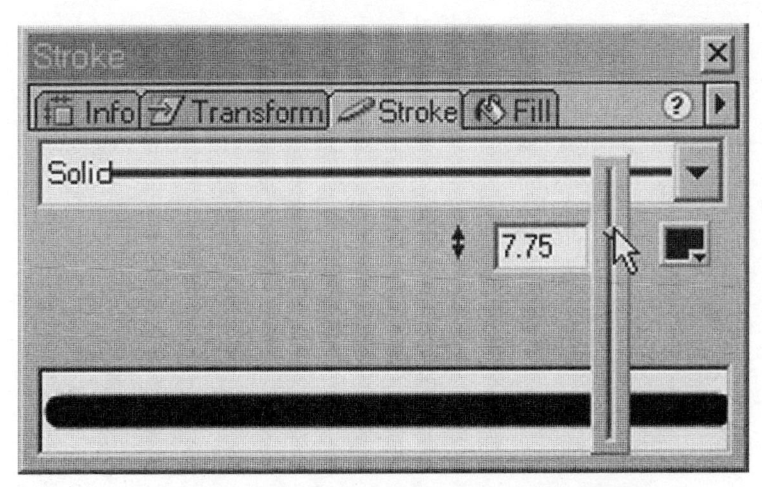

Fig.4.101 The Stroke panel enables line widths to be adjusted

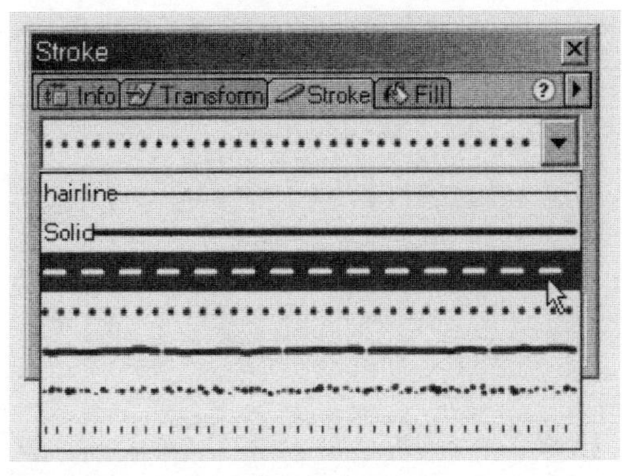

Fig.4.102 Various line styles are available

The preview box at the bottom of the window enables you to see what a given set of parameters will look like before you start drawing.

The settings in the Stroke panel are used as the current ones and will be used for any new lines that are drawn. If a line is selected, the parameters in the panel will change to those of the selected line. Any changes made in the Stroke panel while the line is selected will be applied to that line immediately. The settings in the Stroke panel are used for lines drawn using the Pen, Pencil, and Line tools, plus the outlines of rectangles and ellipses (Figure 4.103). They are not used for the Brush tool, which is controlled by the options in the Tools palette and the Fill panel.

Fig.4.103 The Stroke panel controls the widths of lines drawn using the Line tool, Oval tool, etc., but not the Brush tool

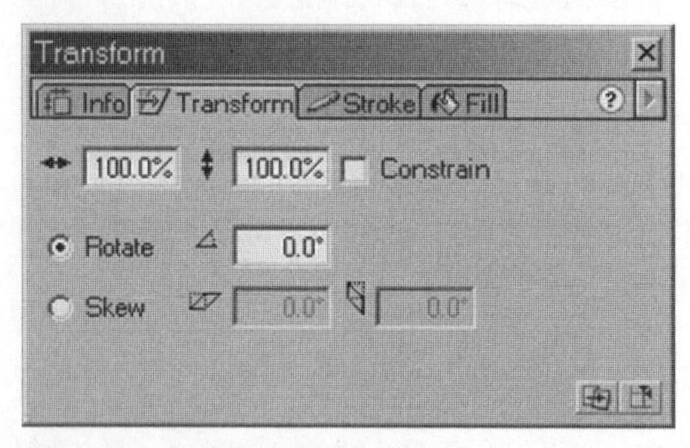

Fig.4.104 The Transform panel

It is worth looking at some of the other panels, and in an editing context the Transform panel (Figure 4.104) is a useful one. It permits precise rotation, separate x and y scaling, and skewing. Type new values into the text boxes and operate the Return key to make them take effect on the selected object or objects. Use the left-hand button at the bottom of the window to make a copy of the selection with the transformations applied.

Points to remember

Drawing a rectangular marquee using the Arrow tool will select whatever falls within the rectangle, even if it contains parts of objects. By holding down the Shift key, objects can be selected and deselected by left clicking on them. Double clicking selects complete objects, such as all parts of a line having multiple segments, or an outline and its fill.

A marquee of any desired shape can be drawn using the Lasso tool. If parts of objects fall within the marquee, only those parts will be selected.

The usual editing facilities of the Edit menu (Cut, Copy, and Paste) operate on selected objects.

The colours of selected objects can be altered using the Color buttons in the Tools palette, the Swatch panel, or the Mixer panel. This enables large numbers of objects to be changed simultaneously.

Colour accuracy is likely to be best on users' monitors if the browser friendly colours are used, but Flash can handle a full range of several million colours.

Gradient fills are useful for three-dimensional effects, amongst other things. The Fill panel gives good control over radial and linear fills, and further control is available via special facilities of the Paint Bucket tool. Some dynamic effects are possible using gradient fills in conjunction with tweening.

For complex fill patterns a bitmap can be used. A limited but useful range of editing is possible to help obtain the required effect.

An imported bit map can be traced, which effectively means that it can be converted into a piece of line art. Minimalist versions of the original, accurate conversions, or anything in between can be produced. Bear in mind that accurate conversions can produce very large file sizes and long download times.

The Eraser tool can be used to tidy up minor errors or as a creative tool. It can remove all or parts of fills and lines, but does not work with normal text. It will work with bitmap fills but not with bitmaps.

In its Faucet guise the Eraser tool provides a quick means of erasing complete objects. Like the regular Eraser tool, the Faucet version does not work with normal text or bitmaps.

The Subselect tool is similar to the Arrow tool, but it is primarily for editing points rather than complete objects. It can be used to adjust individual points in a line or shape, and adjust Bezier curves for example.

Line width, colour, and type can be controlled via the Stroke panel. Existing lines can be altered by selecting them and then changing the settings in the panel. A number of lines can be selected and edited en masse.

5

Layers and tweening

Transparently obvious

Layers mimic a traditional method of producing animations that uses transparent film and opaque inks or paints. In its most simple form the background is drawn on one piece of film and a character, car, or whatever is drawn on a second piece that is placed over the background film. The item in the foreground can be moved slightly from one frame to the next, and when the movie is run it will move around in front of the background. The point of this system is that it is not necessary to make any changes to the background, which is the same for every shot.

In some cases it is only necessary to slide the foreground film slightly from one frame to the next in order to obtain the required animation effect. In other cases the foreground item has to be altered slightly from one frame to another, to make the legs move when a character walks for example. In either case the background can remain the same. The situation would be very different if the background and the foreground were placed on the same sheet of film, with each frame having to be drawn "from scratch".

In practice it would be normal for each element in an animation to be drawn on a separate sheet of film. Suppose that there has to be a background plus three characters in the foreground. If one of the characters has to dance while the other two stand and watch, it is only necessary to alter the character that dances. If the dancing character then has to walk off stage in front of the other two characters, it is still only necessary to alter the character that walks. It would be placed on the top layer of film, and would obscure the other two characters as it passed in front them, much as if it were a real actor walking in front of two more actors.

It could be made to walk between the two characters by moving its film back one in the layering process. The layering process would again make sure that you saw the bits of each character that you were supposed to see, and that any parts that should be obscured would be covered over.

However simple or complex the animation, this layering method ensures that only parts that are actually moving have to change from one frame to the next. Everything else can stay the same. It also avoids having to carefully draw backgrounds so that they do not overlap the edges of items in the foreground, or leave gaps. With traditional animation this helps to keep down the amount of time taken to produce each frame, which can easily become excessive.

When applied to computing and the frame by frame approach, the advantages are exactly the same. The layered approach does not necessarily reduce the amount of calculations the computer has to perform in order to bring the animation to life. It takes a lot of computing power to work out which bits should be visible and which parts of each layer should be hidden. In most practical animations though, it probably helps to keep down the amount of calculation required.

Layers or groups

There is clearly some similarity between layers and groups, with both offering the ability to hide one object behind another. So how do you know which one to use in a given situation. In some cases it would probably be possible to use either method effectively, but the two methods have their separate uses. In general, if an object will be animated it is better if that object is given its own layer. This gives the greatest versatility, and leaves your options open.

Grouping is mainly used on layers where there will be no animation, but you may wish to change your mind about the position of individual elements. For example, there could be a background scene containing a house and two trees. It is unlikely that it would be necessary to animate the house or the trees, but you might decide it was better if they were moved slightly. With the house and trees as three groups there is no problem. Each element can be individually selected and moved to a new position without leaving holes in the background. The same effect could be obtained using layers, but the situation does not really warrant the generation of three additional layers since it can be handled perfectly well by other means. Using lots of layers provides versatility, but using them just for the sake of it can simply confuse matters.

Making layers

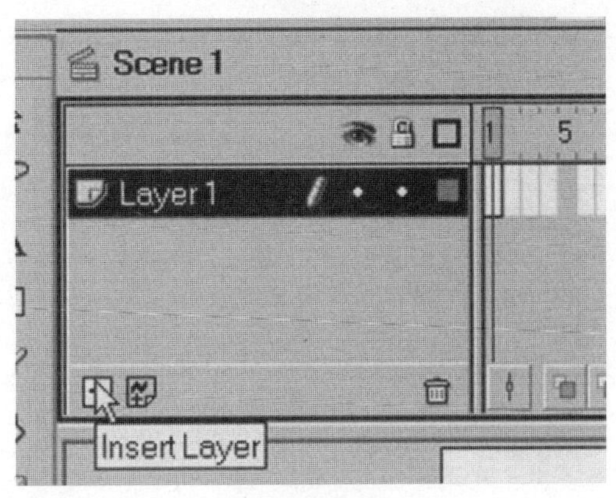

Fig.5.1 The Insert Layer button

Flash automatically generates one layer when a new movie is started, and by default this is called "Layer 1". The names of layers are shown towards the left end of the Timeline. There are two ways of adding a new layer, and one of these is to select the Layer option from the Insert menu. The other is to operate the Insert Layer button in the bottom left-hand corner of the Timeline (Figure 5.1).

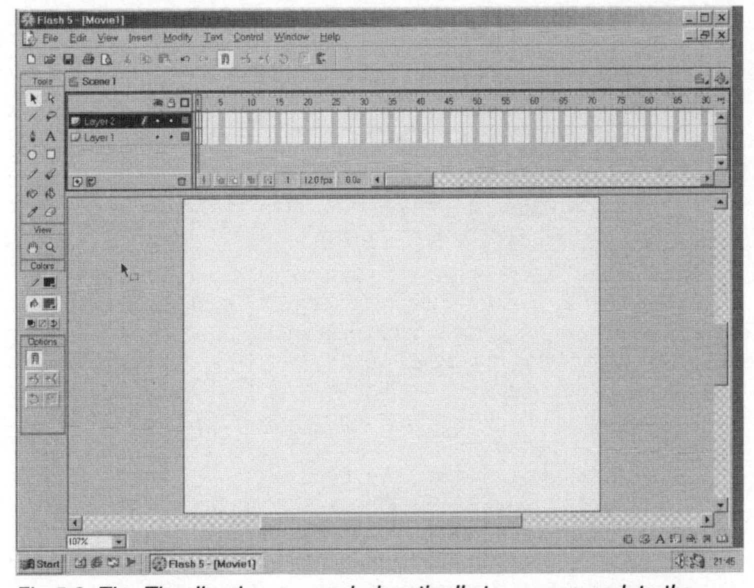

Fig.5.2 The Timeline has expanded vertically to accommodate the new layer

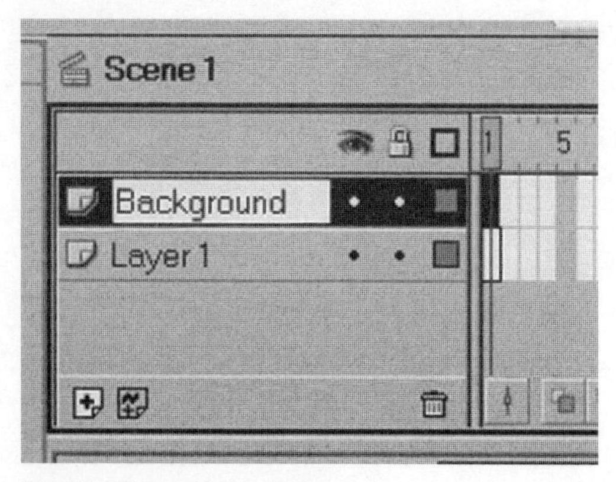

Fig.5.3 Renaming a layer

Either way, a new Layer is added into the Timeline, and it is called "Layer 2" (Figure 5.2). It is advisable to rename layers to something more meaningful, such as "Bkground", "Girl1", or whatever that the layer will contain.

A layer's name can be altered by double clicking on the name in the Timeline, which opens a text box so that a new name can be typed in (Figure 5.3). Operate the button beside the name when the change has been completed. An alternative method of changing the name is to double-click on the button just to the left of the name. This brings up the Layer

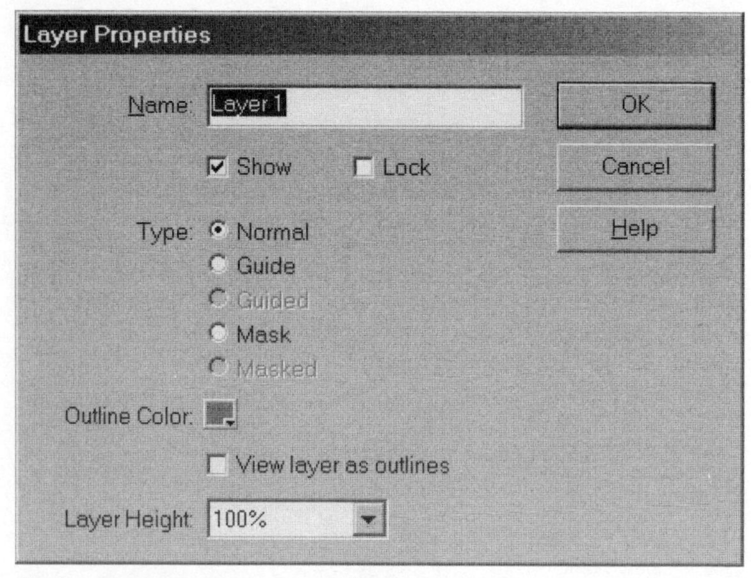

Fig.5.4 The Layer Properties dialogue box

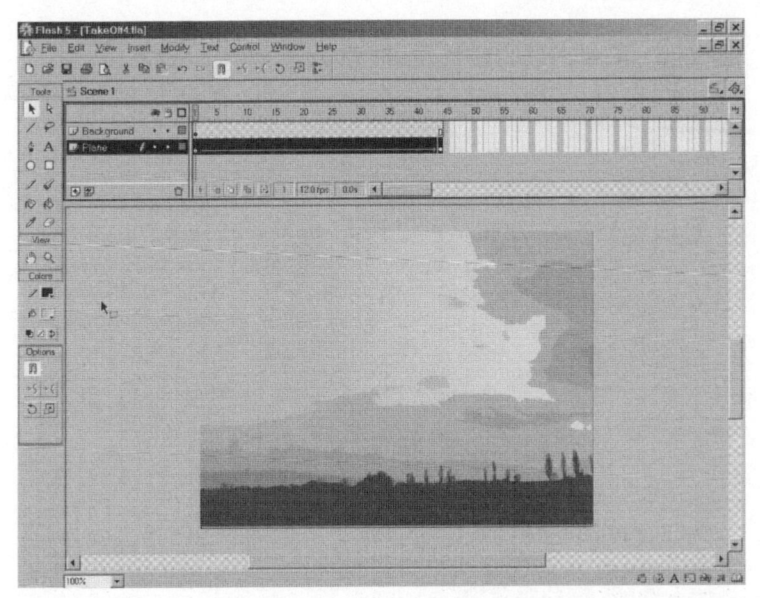

Fig.5.5 The foreground object is hidden behind the background layer

Properties window for the appropriate layer (Figure 5.4). The name can be changed using the text box at the top of the window. Operate the OK button when the changes to the text have been completed.

To select a layer, simply left-click on its name in the Timeline. When you switch to a new layer, any objects in the current frame of that layer are selected. Only objects in the current layer can be edited, and any new objects that are added will, of course, be added to the current layer. If an object is selected using the Arrow or Subselect tools, the current layer will become whatever layer the object happens to be on. This avoids having to keep changing the current layer as you move from one object to another, but you have to pay attention in order to keep track of which layer is currently in use.

By default all layers are visible, but obviously layers at the front can obscure those at the rear. The layer at the top of the Timeline is the one at the front, running through to the back layer at the bottom of the list. In Figure 5.5 things are round the wrong way, with a sketched background on top and a jet plane hidden behind. The idea of this animation is to have the background fixed on one layer with the jet plane flying up, up, and away into the sunset on the other layer.

Swapping the layers is easy, and it is just a matter of dragging the background layer down beneath the other layer (Figure 5.6). Note that you must drag the part of the Timeline that contains the layer's name and nowhere else. Swapping the layers has produced the desired effect, with the plane appearing in front of the background (Figure 5.7). In this example there are only two layers, but the same dragging technique can be used with three or more layers.

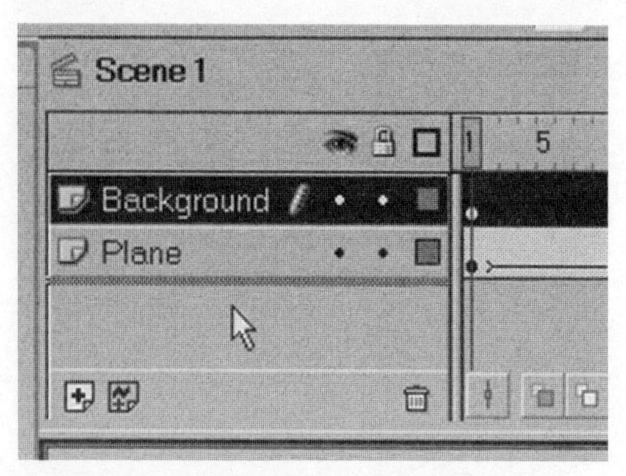

Fig.5.6 Dragging one layer beneath another

Fig.5.7 Reversing the layers in the Timeline has brought the Plane layer to the fore, and the plane is now visible

Fig.5.8

Fig.5.9

Fig.5.10 The final frame in the motion tweening sequence

With the two layers in place it is then just a matter of applying the normal motion tweening technique to get the plane to fly off into the sunset. Figures 5.8 to 5.10 show the animation about one third and two thirds of the way through, plus the final frame. As these frames clearly show, there are no problems with the background bleeding onto the plane, holes in the background where the plane used to be, or anything of this nature. Like the traditional approach using layers of transparent film, the background takes care of itself and you only have to manipulate the bits that move.

You can easily try a simplified version of this animation yourself. Draw a rectangle to completely cover the drawing area and add an interesting fill, such as a linear gradient. Create a new layer and make it the front layer if it is not already at the front. With the front layer selected, add a circle near the bottom left-hand corner of the drawing area and give it a radial fill so that a sphere effect is obtained. Rename the front layer to "Sphere" and the rear layer to "Background". This should give you something like Figure 5.11. Select frame 1 in the Sphere section of the Timeline and then choose the Create Motion Tween option from Insert menu. Then select frame 50 in the same section of the Timeline and choose the Keyframe option from the Insert menu. Frames 1 to 50 in the Sphere section of the Timeline should now be blue - violet in colour.

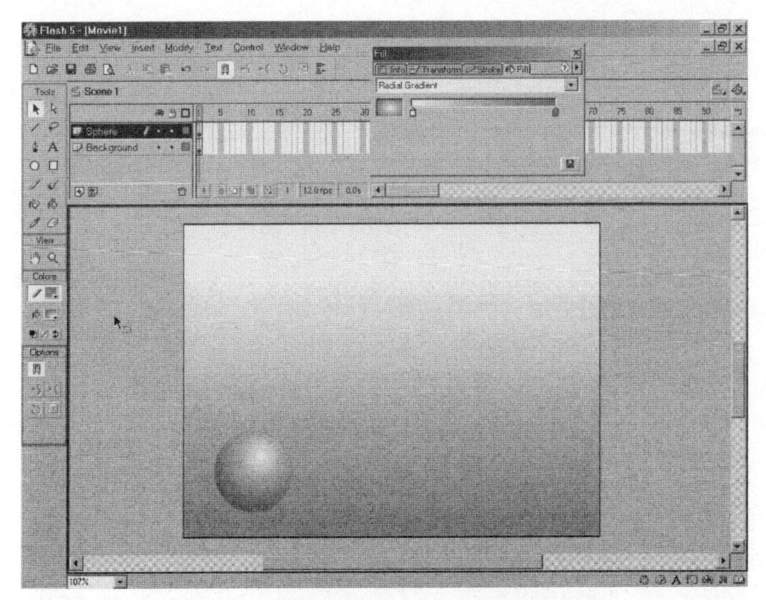

Fig.5.11 The first frame of the two-layer tweening exercise

Now you see it

On the face of it the only task now is to change the circle in frame 50 so that some movement is obtained when the animation is run. If you try moving the circle into the top right-hand corner of the drawing area in frame 50, and reduce its size as well, the "sphere" will fly off into the distance when the animation is run. However, the background will disappear as soon as the animation moves on to frame 2, and it will be absent for the rest of the movie. This happens because the background has been placed in frame 1 and has not been copied into any of the other frames.

One way around the problem would be to select frame 1 in the Background section of the Timeline, and then choose the Create Motion Tween option from the Inset menu. Then select frame 50 in the Background section of the Timeline and choose the Keyframe option from the Insert menu. As no tweening of the Background layer is required, this would be doing it the hard way, but it would work. All that is needed is to select frame 50 in the Background layer and then select Keyframe from the Insert menu. This will add the background image into all 50

Fig.5.12

Fig.5.13

frames and the desired effect will be obtained when the movie is run. Figures 5.12 and 5.13 show the middle and end frames of the sequence.

Layer visibility

There are a number of icons and buttons on the Timeline that have not been covered so far. Left clicking on the eye icon renders all layers invisible, unless all of the layers are already switched off. If they are all switched off already, operating this icon switches them all on. Beneath this icon there is either a black dot or

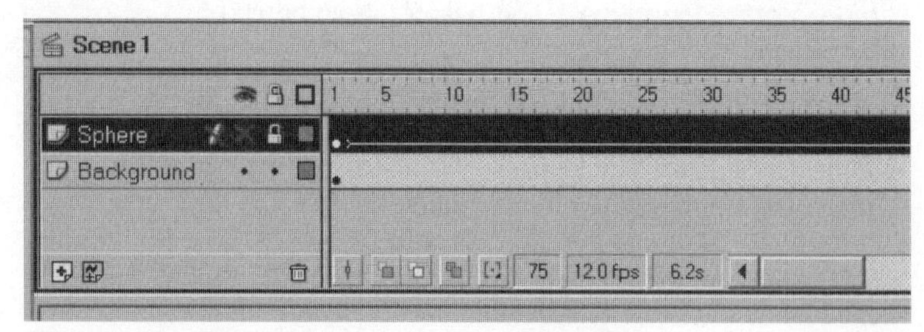

Fig.5.14 The Sphere layer has been switched off

a red cross for each layer. There is a dot if a layer is switched on, or a cross if it is hidden. In Figure 5.14 the Sphere layer is switched off and the Background layer is switched on. Simply left-click on a dot or cross to toggle a layer from one state to the other. Switching off a foreground layer is often helpful when editing a layer where some objects are partially obscured. In fact it is often easiest to edit objects with everything on other layers banished from the screen.

Locking layers

There is an icon that looks like a padlock next to the eye icon. Left clicking on this icon locks all layers unless they are already locked, in which case it unlocks all layers. Individual control over the locking of layers is achieved in much the same way as setting the visibility. A dot is shown if a layer is unlocked, and a padlock icon is shown if it is locked. The point of locking a layer is that it prevents any accidental changes from being made. Existing objects can not be edited because the usual methods of selecting them will fail to work. Trying to add new material to a locked layer produces the error message of Figure 5.15, and nothing can be added.

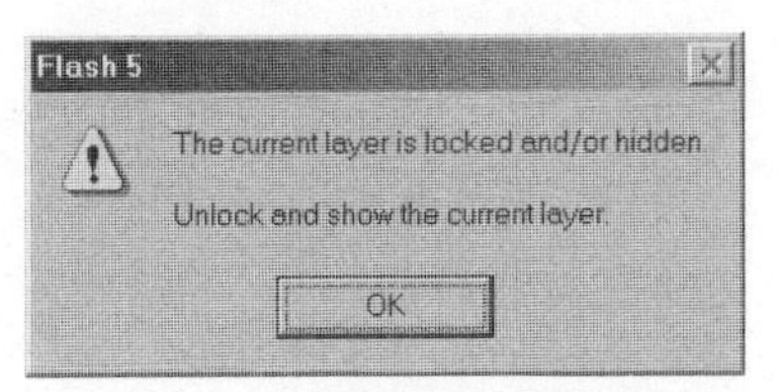

Fig.5.15 The warning message

This avoids accidental changes to one layer while working on another layer, and inadvertent shifts from one layer to another by selecting something in the other layer. Remember that selecting one layer in the Timeline does not normally prevent editing of another layer. Selecting an object results in its layer being automatically set as the current one. Where there is a mixture of objects on locked and unlocked layers, the objects on unlocked layers can be edited as if the

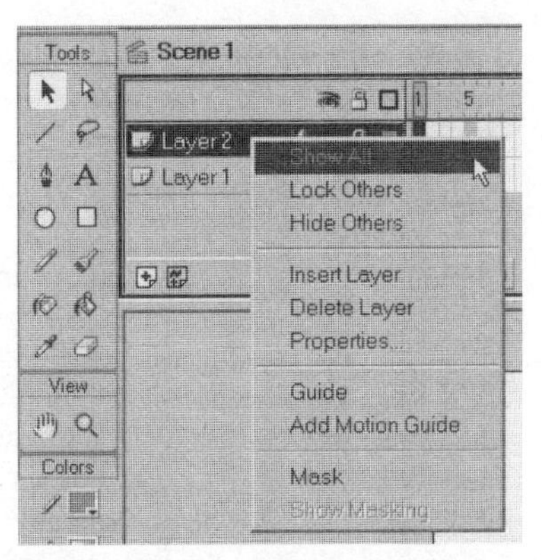

Fig.5.16 The Layer popup menu

Fig.5.17 The jet plane opening frame in outline view

locked layers were not there. For example, left clicking on a locked object using the Arrow tool will actually select any unlocked object hidden beneath the locked object.

Right clicking on the name of a layer in the Timeline produces the popup menu of Figure 5.16, and one of the options enables the layer to be deleted. The fact that a layer is locked will not prevent it from being deleted, but it can be restored again using the Undo function.

Outline view

The third icon in the row selects an outline view. Operating this icon sets all layers to outline view unless they are already shown as outlines. It then sets all layers to normal view. Figure 5.17 shows the previous jet plane example in outline view. Individual layers are controlled by their respective square icons, which are shown filled for layers in normal view, or as outlines for layers that are in outline view. Left-click on an icon to toggle its layer from one state to the other. The colour of the icon is the colour that is used for the outlines in that layer. This colour can be changed by selecting the layer in the Timeline and then Choosing Layer from the Modify menu. The Outline Color button brings up the usual colour chart so that a new colour can be selected.

On the face of it there is no point in using the outline mode, which gives a rather sketchy and often confusing version of a movie. The advantage of this mode is that is requires a lot less memory than normal, which can be important if a number of complex objects using gradient fills and a number of layers are in use. If your computer has the latest microprocessor and masses of memory there is probably no point in bothering with the outline mode.

Selecting layers

It is possible to have more than one layer at a time selected, and it is just a matter of holding down the Shift key and selecting the required layers by left clicking on their names in the Timeline. However, only contiguous layers (layers next to each other) can be selected. If there are five layers and you select the ones at the front and the rear, the three in between will also be selected. You might need to edit across layers from time to time. In most cases this involves copying an object or group from one layer to another. First select and copy the object or group in the usual way. Then select the other layer in the Timeline and use the Paste option in the Edit menu to copy the object or group to the second layer.

Fig.5.18 The smaller plane is a copy of the one on the left

Figure 5.18 shows the earlier jet plane example, but the plane has been copied onto a layer positioned between the two original layers. It has then been flipped horizontally and reduced in size to push it further back than the other plane. Finally, a bit of motion tweening has been used to move it across the screen. Figures 5.19 to 5.21 show three frames from the sequence. Notice how the correct layering effect is

Fig.5.19

Fig.5.20

Fig.5.21

obtained in Figure 5.20 where the two planes overlap. The larger plane is on the front layer and correctly passes in front of the smaller plane, proving that the copied version has been correctly moved to the new layer. If you try out an animation of this type you should find that it gives a much more dynamic effect than having a single object in motion, and it also tends to give a more convincing effect.

Fig.5.22 The onion skin effect applied to the jet plane animation

Onion Skin

There is a row of four control buttons below the main section of the timeline. Working from left to right, the first of these buttons is the Center Frame button. This moves the play head to the centre frame of the movie. The next button provides the onion skin effect, which simply means that movement over several frames is shown as a single image. Figure 5.22 shows this effect applied to the twin jet plane movie. The idea of this is that it lets you see how much change there is from one frame to the next. The frames covered by the onion skin effect are shown in mid-grey on the Timeline (Figure 5.23), and there are handles at each end of this area that enable the frame coverage to be adjusted. Figure 5.24 shows a much wider frame range in use.

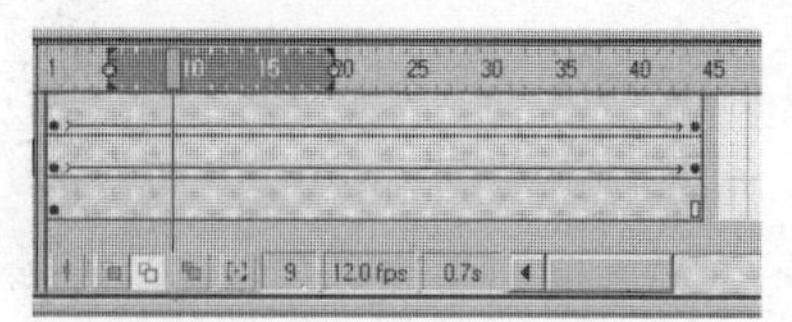

Fig.5.23 The grey area shows the onion skin frames

The next button is the Onion Skin Outlines button. This gives the onion skin effect, but the tweened objects are only shown in outline form (Figure 5.25). All layers that are tweened are shown in outline form, not just the layer or layers that are selected. Other layers are shown normally, and the background in Figure 5.25 is therefore shown in full.

Fig.5.24 The onion skin effect applied to a large number of frames

Fig.5.25 The outline version of the onion skin effect

Multiple frames

The fourth button enables multiple frames to be edited. The frame range is adjusted in the same manner as for the onion skin effects. This feature is used with frame by frame animations, and it enables the selected range of frames to be viewed simultaneously. In Figure 5.26 a simple seven-frame bouncing ball animation is shown using this method. If anything is seriously out of position it should become obvious when this option is used. Any object can be selected and

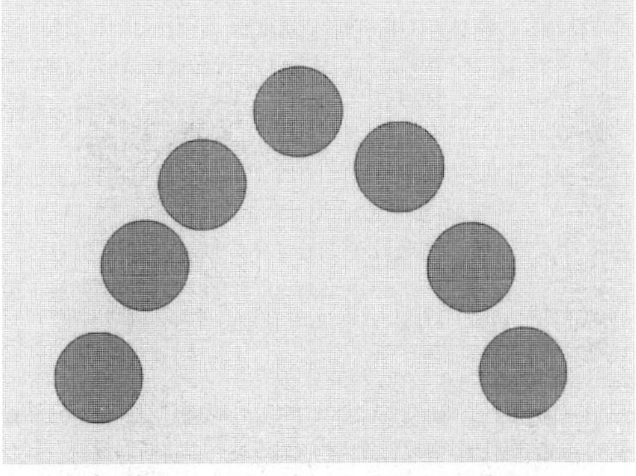

Fig.5.26 All seven frames of the animation

dragged to a new position. It is perhaps worth mentioning that by dragging the play head it is possible to move backwards and forwards through any movie as fast or as slow as you like, and this is often helpful in locating glitches in the action.

Modify markers

Finally, the fifth button produces the popup menu of Figure 5.27. With the Always Show Markers option ticked the onion skin markers are always shown, but are in a sort of outline form when the onion skin modes are not in use. Selecting the Anchor Onion option locks the onion skin markers in place, but the onion skin effect will only be displayed if the play head is within one of the selected frames and one of the onion skin modes is switched on. The Onion 2 and Onion 5 options respectively apply the onion skin effect two and five frames either side of the selected frame. The Onion All option is used to apply the effect to all the frames in a movie.

Fig.5.27 The popup menu

Frame rate

Next to the set of five control buttons there are three digital displays. The first of these simply shows the number of the frame that is currently selected, and the one at the opposite end shows how far into the movie this frame is in terms of time. The current frame rate is shown on the middle display, and Flash defaults to 12 frames per second. This is much lower than the frame rate for television and professional film production, which normally use a rate of 24 per second or more. However, 12 frames per second is considered a good compromise value for Web use where high frame rates could give excessive download times.

In order to change the frame rate double-click on the display to bring up the Movie Properties window (Figure 5.28). Note that with a high frame rate set it is possible that this rate will not always be obtained in practice due to the limitations of the hardware used to display the movie. If you

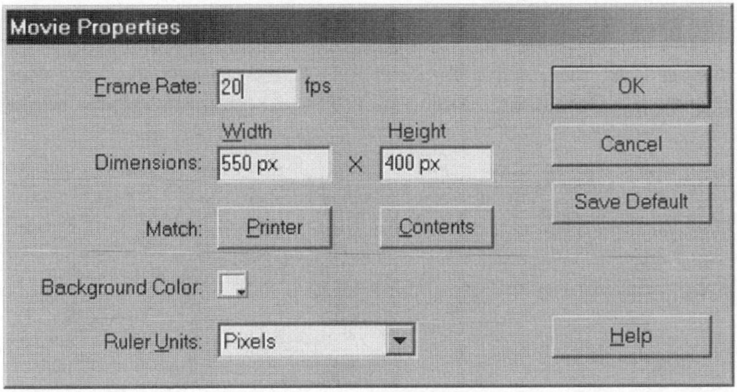

Fig.5.28 The Movie Properties dialogue box

wish to make the new rate the default, operate the Save Default button in the Movie Properties dialogue box. Operate the OK button if the new rate is only to be used in the current movie.

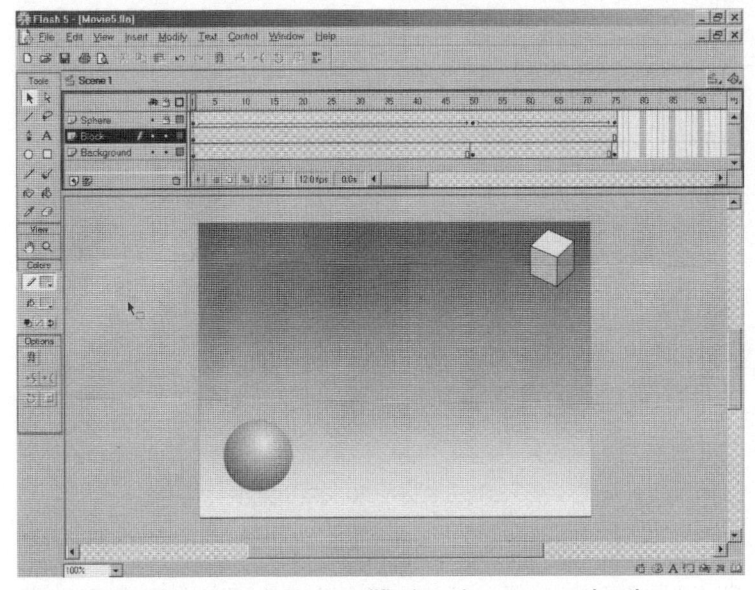

Fig.5.29 The first frame in the modified motion tween animation

Multi-tween

The demonstration animations used so far have featured either one tween operation or two of them running in parallel on separate layers. However, it is perfectly acceptable to string two or more sets of tweening together to get more elaborate results. Figure 5.29 shows the first frame in an extended version of the animation that has the ball flying off into the distance. A cube has been placed on a new layer that goes between the ball and the background. Initially things are exactly as before, with the ball flying off to the top right-hand corner of the drawing area. Here it seems to hit the cube (Figure 5.30) and bounce off down to the bottom right-hand corner of the screen (Figures 5.31 and 5.32).

Fig.5.30

In order to add the extra section of motion tweening, first left click on frame 50 (the final frame of the movie) in the Sphere layer. Then select Create Motion Tween from the Insert menu. To make the second tween (say) 25 frames long, left-click 25 frames further down the Sphere section of the Timeline, or at frame 75 in other words. Finally, select Keyframe from the Insert menu, and the new

Fig.5.31

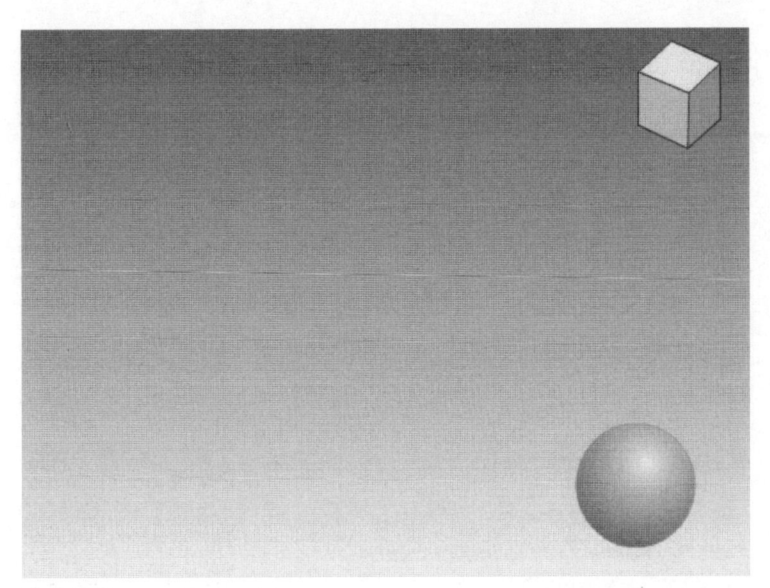

Fig.5.32

motion tween section has been added. Frames 51 to 75 should then go a blue - violet colour to show that they contain a motion tween.

Of course, there are still a few jobs to do in order to complete the movie. First, with frame 75 still selected, the ball should be dragged down towards the bottom of the drawing area and scaled up. The new intermediate layer is then added and the cube is drawn in. With this type of thing it is best to draw it in any convenient part of the screen and then drag it into place behind the ball. The movie should be set at frame 50 when this is done, so that the ball is at the end of its first tween. The movie will then work after a fashion, but the background will disappear after frame 50. The easiest way of rectifying this is to drag the keyframe at frame 50 on the background layer along to frame 75. The movie should then run properly.

Being able to drag keyframes is extremely useful. Suppose that you find the additional 25 frames to be inadequate, with the ball falling too fast. Dragging the keyframes at frame 75 along to frame 80 or 85 will add another five or 10 frames and slow the rate of descent. The keyframe at frame 50 on the Sphere layer can be dragged to a new position as well, perhaps to make the ball hit the cube at an earlier frame. Although we have added two sets of motion tweening together in this example, you can use any combination of motion tweening, shape tweening, and frame by frame animation.

Frame panel

Fig.5.33 Frame 1 of the motion tween

The Frame panel provides some options that govern the way motion tweening operates. To demonstrate the rotation options I created a simple motion tween having the object shown in Figure 5.33. Over 50 frames this is moved and rotated to the position shown in Figure 5.34. The default method of rotation is Auto, and this gradually moves the tweened group from the original position and orientation to the final position and orientation. In this example the object is therefore at an angle of about 45 degrees at frame 25 (Figure 5.35). This is a feature that has been exploited in some of the example movies discussed previously.

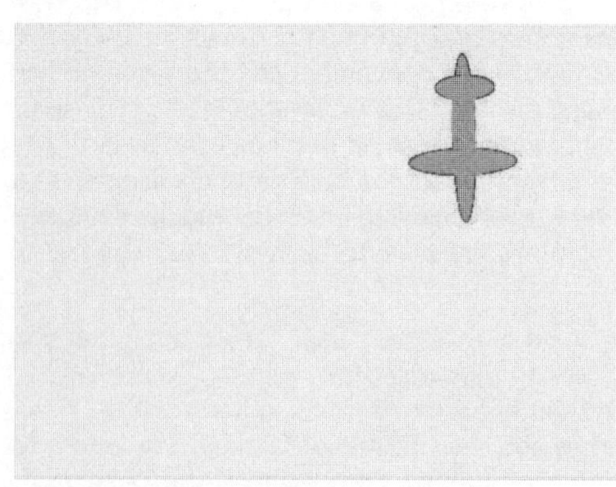

Fig.5.34 The final frame of the tween

To bring up the Frame panel select Panels from the Window menu followed by Frame from the submenu that appears. Make sure that the play head is at the first frame of the sequence and that the group being tweened is selected. Activating the Rotation menu gives three options in addition to the Auto mode (Figure 5.36). If None is selected, the group is not rotated at all. It moves across into place, but does not rotate in the process.

When the final frame of the sequence is reached, the group suddenly takes on any rotation that has been applied. Figure 5.37 shows the penultimate frame using the None option. The group has moved across the screen but the rotation has not been applied. You effectively have a 49 frame motion tween followed by a frame by frame animation having just one frame. If the Scale checkbox is not ticked, any change in scale will only be applied in the final frame using any rotation mode, so make sure this box is ticked if you wish to use a smooth change in scale.

Fig.5.35 The middle produced using the Auto rotation setting

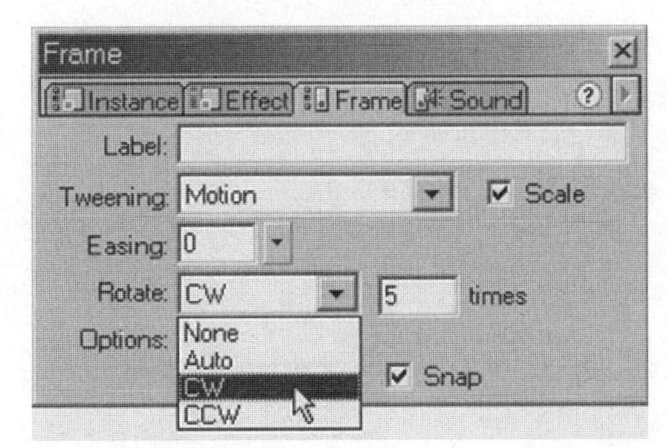

Fig.5.36 The Rotation menu

Fig.5.37 The final frame using no rotation

Adding spin

The other two options enable the group to be rotated a certain number of times in a clockwise (CW) or counter clockwise (CCW) direction. The required number of rotations is typed into the small textbox next to the rotate menu. This can produce some spectacular results and it is well worth giving it a try. Note that with this method the tweening will work towards the orientation in the final frame, and it will also gradually apply any change in scale. You can therefore use this method to have something hurtle off into the distance or hurtle towards the viewer. Figures 5.38 and 5.39 show the middle and last frames using clockwise rotation and a reduction in scale in the final frame. Note that any rotation you use between the first and last frames will be added to the number of rotations specified using the Frame panel.

Fig.5.38 The middle frame

Fig.5.39 The final frame

Easing

The easing value controls the relative rate of change at the beginning and end of the movie. Using a value of 0 there is a linear rate of change throughout the movie. A negative value gives a slow initial change and faster movement towards the end. The lower the value used, the more this effect is emphasised. A positive value has the opposite effect, with the action running fast initially and gradually slowing down as the tween progresses. The valid range is from –100 to +100. Values can be typed into the text box or the popup slider control can be used to adjust the value.

This feature can be useful with something like the jet plane animations featured previously in this chapter. One plane starts close to the viewer and moves off into the distance. The apparent speed tends to be higher when an object is close to the viewer and reduces as it gets further away. Using a positive easing value for this plane would give this type of motion. The change in scale will also be applied more strongly initially, but this is again the way things would look in real life. Note that each layer has its own set of tweening values, so it is possible to use different easing values, etc., for each layer.

Guide layer

In the motion tweening examples provided so far the tweened groups go straight from point A to point B. It would be more than a little useful to be able to use complex paths without having to resort to the frame by

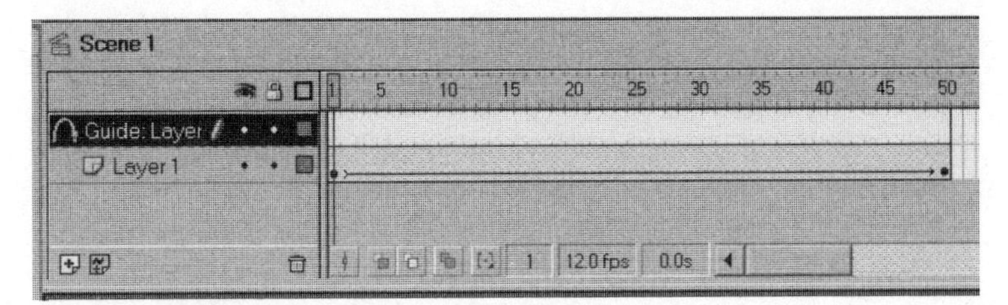

Fig.5.40 A guide layer added to the Timeline

frame approach or stringing together multiple tweens. This can in fact be achieved by using a guide layer to make a tweened group follow the required path. To try out a guide layer first make a simple motion tween

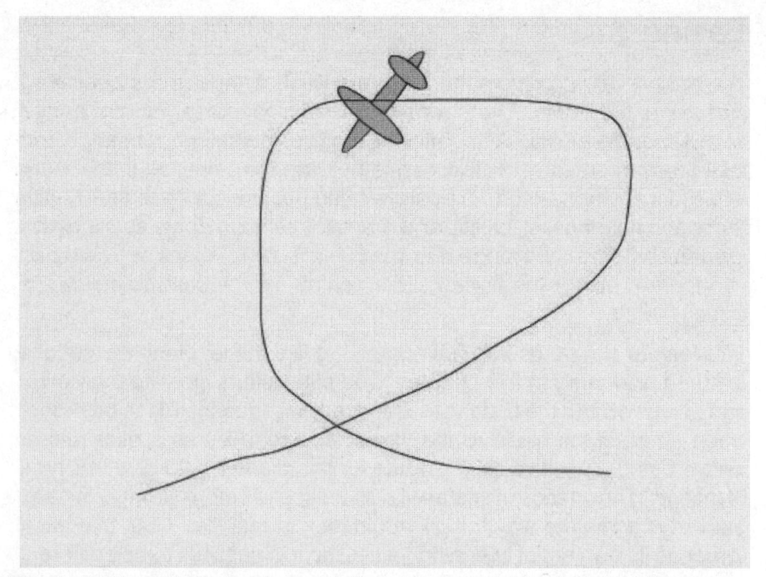

Fig.5.41 About half way through the tween, and the object is still following the line correctly

in the normal way. Then select Motion Guide from the Insert menu, and a new layer called Guide Layer will appear in the Timeline (Figure 5.40).

With this layer selected a guideline can then be drawn using any of the normal drawing tools, but for most purposes the Pencil tool in the Smooth mode is the best choice. Where a neat curve is required, dragging a straight line into an arc is often the easiest way good results. When you are happy with the line drag the group to one end in frame 1, and then drag it to the opposite end of the line in the final frame.

The movie is then ready for testing, and the group should accurately follow the line. Figure 5.41 shows a frame from the middle of a simple demonstration animation using this facility, and the object is hugging the line correctly. The guideline is visible when running a movie in Flash, but it is not displayed when a movie is run in the Flash Player program. Try running a simple movie using the Test Movie option of the Control menu and the guideline will be conspicuously absent. Of course, it can be hidden in the Flash drawing area by switching off visibility for the Guide layer.

There are a couple of useful options available in the Frame panel when using a guideline. The first of these is the Snap option, and when selected this causes the group to snap to the guideline, as in the previous example. If the snap option is not used it is necessary to position the registration point of the object quite accurately or it will not follow the guideline. If the group does not follow the line but instead goes straight from point A to point B, it has not been "attached" to the guideline properly. Note that the group being tweened does not have to start and finish at the ends of the guideline. Any two points can be used. If the guideline is a closed shape the group will take the shortest route between the start and finish points.

Registration point

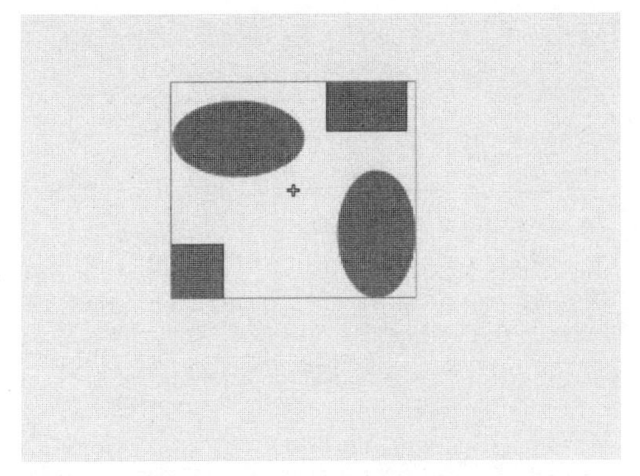

Fig.5.42 The cross is the registration point

The registration point of a group or bitmap is placed at its centre by default, but it can be moved. Select the group or bitmap and then chose the Transform option from the Modify menu, followed by Move Center from the submenu that appears. A small cross then appears at the middle of the group or bitmap (Figure 5.42), and this can be dragged to a new location, as in Figure 5.43. In the majority of cases it will probably be best to have the registration point within the group, but it can be placed outside it if

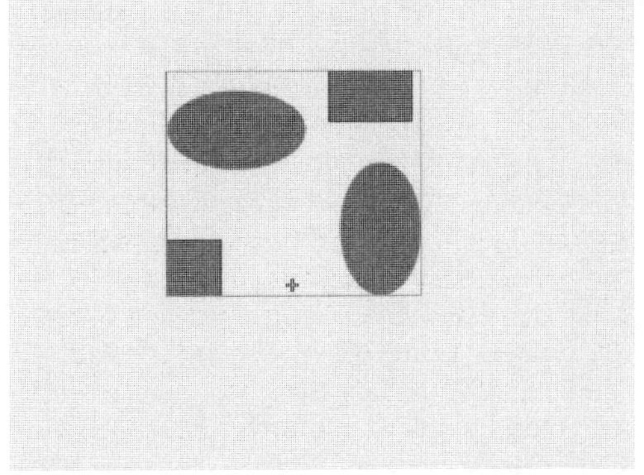

Fig.5.43 The registration point has been moved

necessary. If you change the registration point when using motion tweening with a guideline, make sure it is changed for the group in both the first and final frames. There might otherwise be a sudden jump in position when the final frame is reached.

Orient to path

With this option selected in the Frame panel the orientation of the tweened group follows the guideline. This can be seen in Figures 5.44 and 5.45, which shows two frames from a simple motion tweening animation. This uses the same group of objects that was utilized in the previous tweening exercise. Rather than maintaining the same orientation, as in the previous exercise, this time the orientation changes so that the group is always aligned with the guideline.

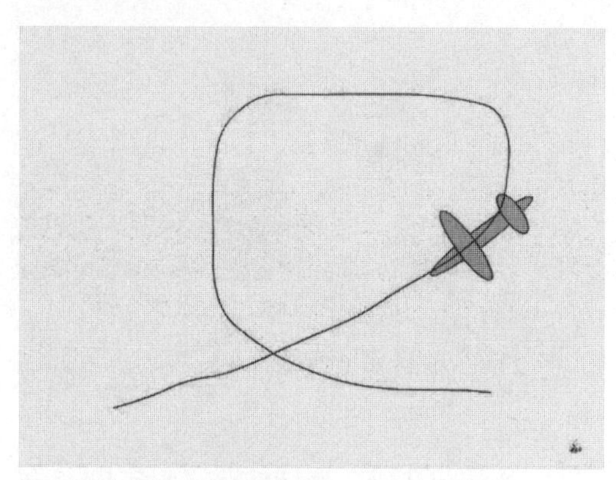

Fig.5.44 The orientation is governed by the guide path

This option can be used to good effect in many practical applications of motion tweening. Figures 5.46 to 5.48 show frames from the beginning, middle, and end of an animation based on the one featured previously where the jet plane took off. Here the idea is to produce something more dramatic. With the plane having just

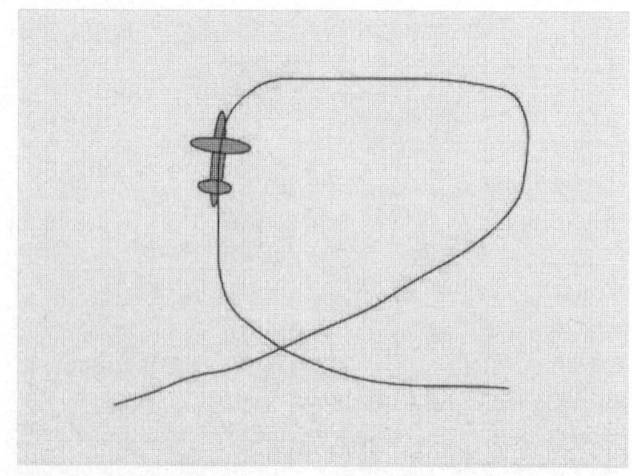

Fig.5.45 The orientation still matches the line

Fig.5.46 The orientation of the plane should follow the guide path

Fig.5.47 About half way through the tween and still on track

Fig.5.48 The plane's orientation has followed the guide path correctly right to the end

swooped down it now pulls up and away into the wide blue yonder. The guideline gives the plane a suitable path and by orienting the plane to the guideline it is always pointing in precisely the right direction.

Multiple paths

There is no difficulty in having two or more layers using motion tweening with separate guidelines. First set up both layers for basic motion tweening. Then select the first layer and choose Motion Guide from the Insert menu. This produces a guide layer to which the first guideline can be added. Then select the second layer and repeat the process for that layer. The Timeline should then look something like the one in Figure 5.49. Make any final adjustments and the movie is then ready for testing. Figures 5.50 to 5.52 show three frames from a modified version of the animation featuring two jet planes that was shown previously. As can be seem from these, the two planes correctly follow their separate guide paths.

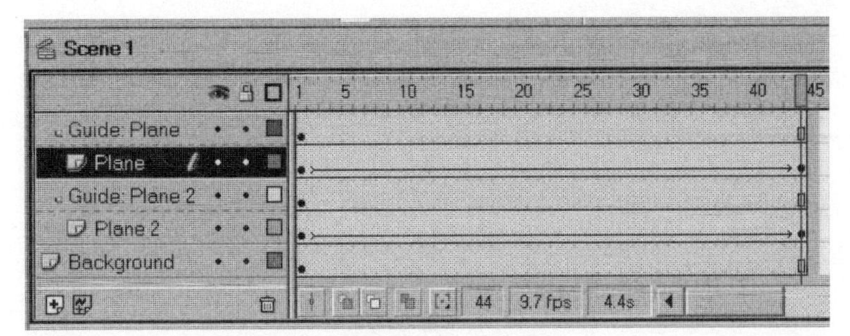

Fig.5.49 Two guide layers added to the Timeline

Shape tweening

Motion tweening is used where the same objects are used throughout the tweening process. The objects might undergo some rotation or scaling during the tweening process, but they are essentially the same objects at the beginning and end of the movie, and therefore during the intermediate frames as well. There is sometimes a choice of using shape or motion tweening. There can be some shape changing in motion

Fig.5.50 The first frame of a tween using two guide paths

Fig.5.51

Fig.5.52

tweens, and motion is possible in shape tweens. However, shape tweening is generally reserved for use when one object turns into another during the tweening process. This can not be achieved using motion tweening.

Fig.5.53 The frowning face

To try out shape tweening, draw a simple frowning face in frame 1. Like the one in Figure 5.53 it does not have to be very convincing, and it just needs to have a mouth that droops at the sides. Now create a keyframe a short way down the Timeline, at frame 12 perhaps. Invert the mouth by selecting it, choosing Transform from the Modify menu, and then selecting Flip Vertical from the submenu that appears. If a fill has been used for the face this will probably need to be redone in order to fill in the holes left by changing the shape of the mouth. This should produce something like Figure 5.54. You now have the start and finish versions for the face, but no in between steps. If you run the movie there will be the same face for frames 1 to 9 followed by a sudden change to the smiling face at frame 10. The shape tweening must now be added to get a gradual change from one face to the other.

Fig.5.54 The smiling face

Start by left clicking on the Timeline at around the middle of the sequence. Left-click on the Timeline itself and not on the numbered scale above it, and frames 1 to 9 should then be selected. Launch the Frame

Fig.5.55 The mid-way version

Fig.5.56 The final eye positions

Fig.5.57 The mid-point frame

Fig.5.58 The semi-faded nose

panel by selecting Panel from the Window menu, and then Frame from the submenu. Select shape tweening from the Tweening menu of the Frame panel, and the face displayed on the screen should then assume an intermediate state (Figure 5.55). Also, frames 1 to 9 will change to a pale green colour to indicate that shape tweening is in use over these frames.

Running the movie now produces the desired effect, with the frown gradually turning into a smile. Try moving the face slightly in the final frame and running the movie again. In addition to the change in expression the face will steadily move across the screen. Basic motion tweening can be achieved using shape tweening.

Groups of objects have not been used in this exercise, and groups can not be shape tweened. An error message will always appear if you try to do this. If you should try to tween something that is giving Flash problems, the usual solid line across the tweened section of the Timeline will change to a broken line. The problem with groups is that Flash needs to identify each element in the first and last frames and match them up. Even with no groups in use it is possible that things will occasionally get confused with some odd looking results being produced.

Fading out

As a further experiment, select each eye in turn and rotate it through 180 degrees using the Scale and Rotate option in the Transform submenu. This will give something like Figure 5.56 as the first frame, and Figure 5.57 about half way through. The eyes gradually look downwards as the movie progresses.

Fig.5.59 The failed tween

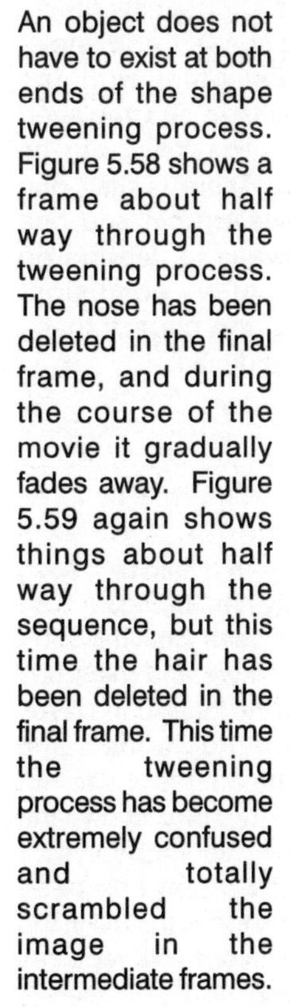

An object does not have to exist at both ends of the shape tweening process. Figure 5.58 shows a frame about half way through the tweening process. The nose has been deleted in the final frame, and during the course of the movie it gradually fades away. Figure 5.59 again shows things about half way through the sequence, but this time the hair has been deleted in the final frame. This time the tweening process has become extremely confused and totally scrambled the image in the intermediate frames.

Fig.5.60 The first frame of the shape tween

Fig.5.61 The final frame of the shape tween

Fig.5.62 The the half-way point

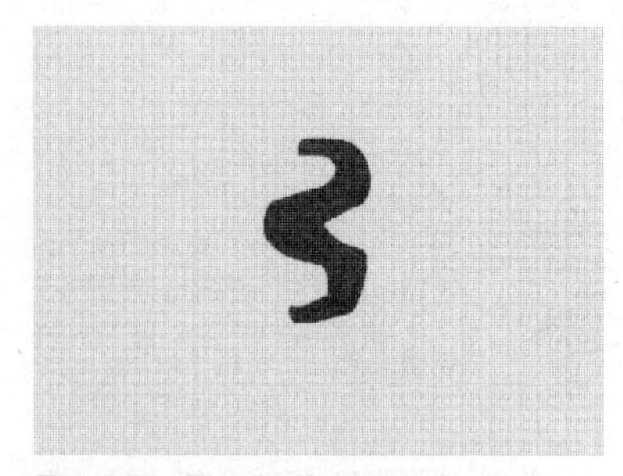

Fig.5.63 The half-way point in the modified movie

The safest way to tween is to work on the basis of one object per layer, so that there is no chance of any confusion occurring. The black ellipse of Figure 5.60 was replaced with the green rectangle of Figure 5.61. The image of Figure 5.62 is produced at the half-way point. The shape is half way between the ellipse and rectangle, and you will have to take my word for it that the colour is a dark green. Figure 5.63 shows the image at the half-way point with the rectangle erased and replaced by a squiggly line drawn with the Brush tool. There is only one object to tween from and one object to tween to, leaving no chance of confusion. Accordingly, the correct shape has been produced.

Easy come, easy go

Shape tweening is good for making things appear "out of thin air", such as the classic rabbit being produced from an empty hat. In Figure 5.64 the hat has been drawn on the background layer and there is a small dot on the foreground layer. However, the dot is the same colour as the hat, so it can not be seen. Figure 5.65 shows the final frame in the shape tween, and a clipart rabbit has been positioned on top of the hat in the foreground layer. This replaces the dot, which has been deleted.

Fig.5.64 The hat but no rabbit

Fig.5.65 The final frame, with fully formed clipart rabbit

When the animation is run the rabbit grows and rises out of the hat. Figures 5.66 and 5.67 show two intermediate frames of the movie, and these show the effect. Although there is a complex object in the final frame of the tween, there is only one simple object in the first frame. This keeps things simple and reasonably free from odd effects as the rabbit emerges.

Of course, you may prefer to deliberately "throw a spanner in the works" to get a more complex effect as the change occurs. Figure 5.68 shows an intermediate frame produced by adding two extra dots in frame 1. This gives some multiple imaging effects with

Fig.5.66 The rabbit starts to emerge

Fig.5.67 The rabbit has nearly grown to full-size

Fig.5.68 The multi-image effect produced by using three sources

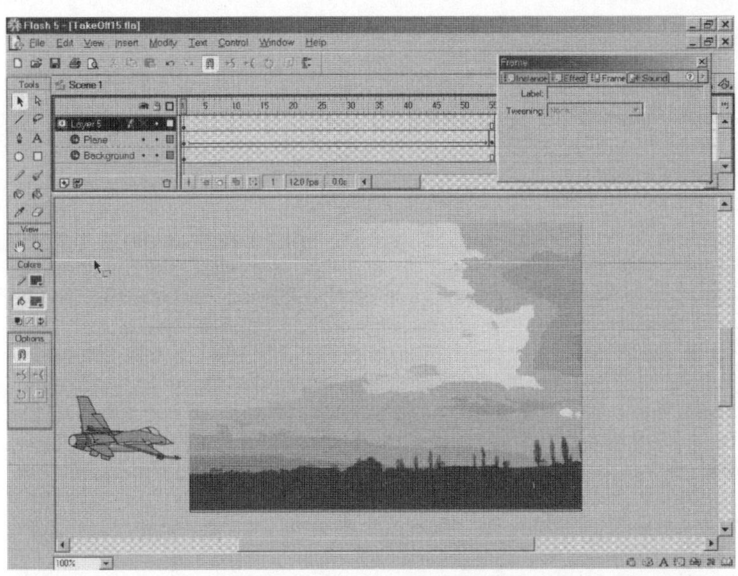

Fig.5.69 The start position for the plane, outside the background area

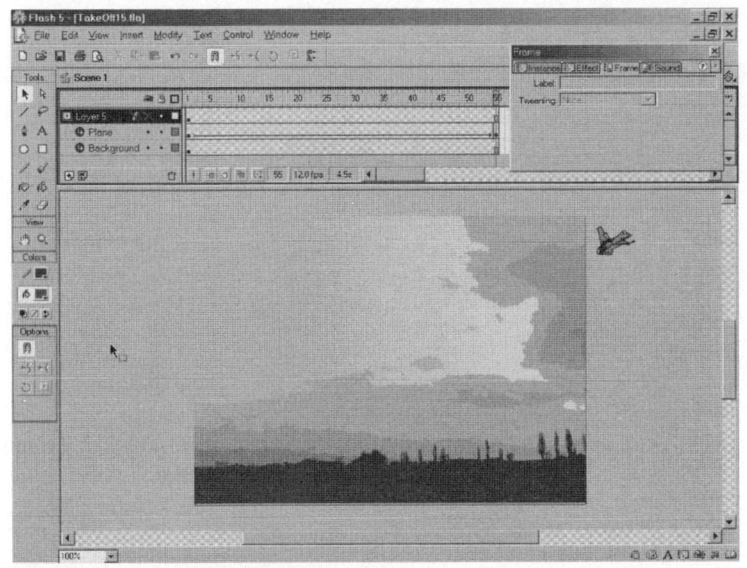

Fig.5.70 The final position of the plane

the rabbit finally coming together in the final frame. In order to make something disappear it is just a matter of reversing the process. Start with the complex image and finish with one simple object hidden in a background layer.

Masking layer

A masking layer, as its name suggests, is used to hide things that you do not wish the viewer to see. As a simple example, take the set-up of Figure 5.69 where the plane starts off the left-hand side of the drawing area. It then goes across the background and off the other side, ending up in the position shown in Figure 5.70. The idea is that the viewer should only see the background area when the movie is first played. The plane swoops in from the left and out again on the right. At the beginning and end of the movie the plane is not visible. Unfortunately, you can not rely on the player program to clip the viewing area to precisely match the background area. When the movie is viewed it is quite likely that rather more than the background area will be visible, ruining the effect.

It is possible to overcome this problem using a masking layer to hide everything outside the background area. The first task is to make an ordinary layer and then move this above any layers that must be masked. With the new layer selected, choose Layer from the Modify menu to bring up the dialogue box of Figure 5.71. Left-click the Mask radio button and then operate the OK button. The icon next to the layer's name should have changed to a downward pointing arrow. Next any layers that must be masked have to be set to the correct operating mode. Select the first layer to be masked and then choose the Layer option from the Modify

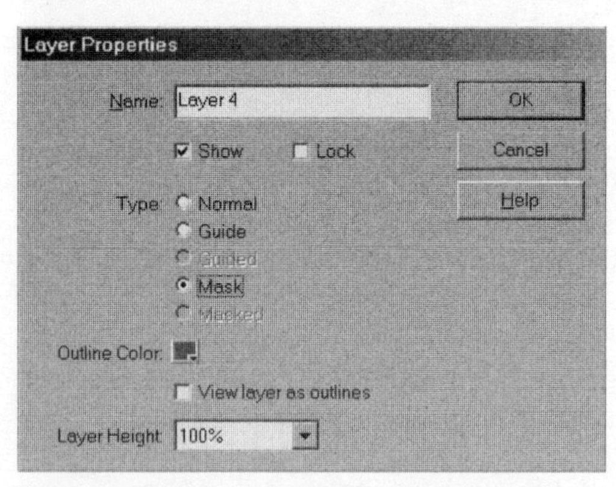

Fig.5.71 The Layer Properties dialogue box

menu. This produces the Layer Properties dialogue box, and this time the Masked radio button is operated. Left-click the OK button to implement the change.

Note that it is not possible to use guide path and masking on the same layer. In this example it means that the plane has to fly straight across the screen if motion tweening is used, and no guideline can be used. Of course, a more elaborate path can be used with the frame by frame approach. All the layers that are to be masked are processed in the same way, and the Timeline should then look something like Figure 5.72. The icons beside the masked layers change to right-angled arrows to show that the masking layer above masks them.

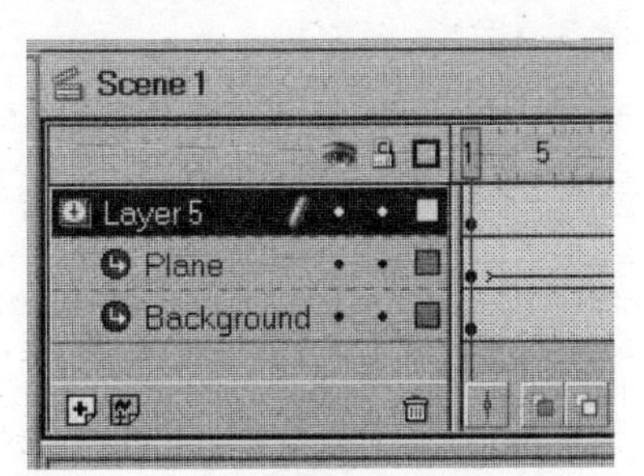

Fig.5.72 The masking layer set up in the Timeline

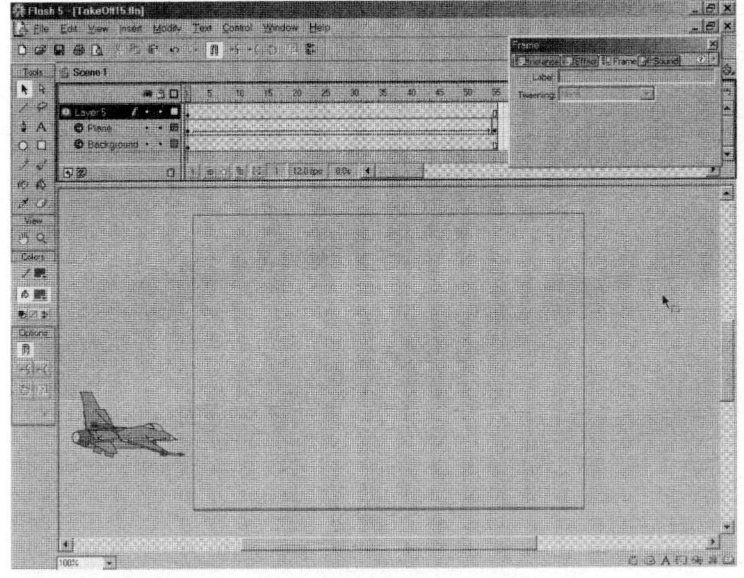

Fig.5.73 Things seem to have gone badly wrong!

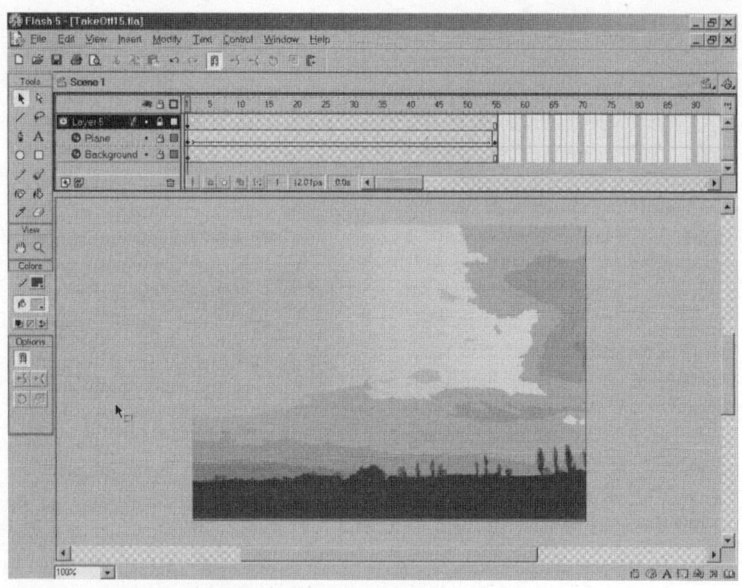

Fig.5.74 Locking all layers gives the desired effect

Any objects drawn on the masking layer will now act as masks, and anything in layers beneath them will be visible. Anything outside the masking objects is hidden from view. In this case only one masking object is needed, and this is a rectangle that just covers the background scene. It does not matter what fill colour is used for masking objects since neither the fill nor the outline will be visible in the movie. Having added the masking shape things seem to have gone totally wrong (Figure 5.73).

Fig.5.75 The plane enters from the left

Fig.5.76 The plane is correctly masked as it exits stage-right

The background is hidden behind the mask and the plane is still visible. For the masking effect to work within Flash it is necessary to lock all layers, and then things operate as expected (Figure 5.74).

The desired effect is obtained using the masking layer, as can be seen from Figures 5.75 and 5.76, which respectively show frames near the beginning and end of the movie. There are plenty more uses for masking. It can be used to produce a window with objects moving past the window. Objects on the masking layer can be animated using motion tweening or the frame by frame approach, offering more possibilities.

Symbols

Symbols are reusable graphics objects that can be called up from a library and used as and when necessary in a movie. Obviously it is not difficult to make copies of existing objects and use them elsewhere in a movie, but symbols and libraries offer a more versatile alternative. Also, simply copying graphics objects uses more memory and creates larger file sizes, because each occurrence of the object is a separate entity. A symbol only has to be stored once in memory or in a file, together with details of its location. This is a more efficient system, especially when a graphics object is used a large number of times.

Graphics programs often place limitations on the way in which symbols can be used, but Flash is reasonably accommodating in this respect. There are some restrictions, and symbols can not be shape tweened for example. A limited range of editing can be used though, such as rotation, scaling, and flipping.

Making symbols

If you have an existing object that could usefully be converted to a symbol it is quite easy to do so. Start by selecting all the elements in the object using the Arrow tool and (or) the Lasso tool. Next select the Convert to Symbol option from the Insert menu, which will produce the Symbol Properties dialogue box (Figure 5.77). A suitable name for the symbol is entered in the textbox, and the radio buttons are used to select the

Fig.5.77 The Symbol Properties window

type of symbol. Movie clips can be saved as symbols, as can buttons, which are covered in the next chapter. In this case it is a graphic object that is being saved as a symbol, so the Graphic button is operated. If you now try selecting part of the object that was saved as a symbol you will find that it is one object, and it is now a symbol rather than just a group.

To make a symbol "from scratch", select the New Symbol option from the Insert menu. This again produces the Symbol Properties dialogue box where a name for the symbol is entered and the appropriate type is selected using the radio buttons. A new drawing area appears when the OK button is operated, and it is blank apart from the registration mark at the centre. Above the Timeline it will show the name of the symbol you are creating. The symbol is now drawn up in the usual way.

You can even import a graphic and edit it. When you have finished, select Edit Movie from the Edit menu. This saves the symbol and returns the screen to normal.

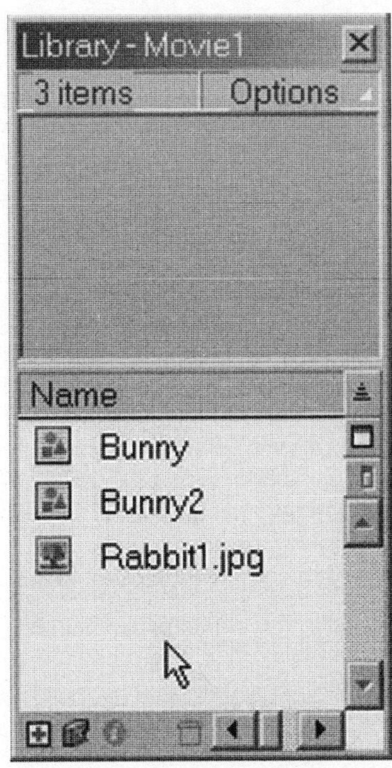

Fig.5.78 The Library window

Using symbols

In order to add a symbol to a movie the Library window is required. This is launched by selecting the Library option from the Window menu, and something like Figure 5.78 will then appear. The bottom part of the window shows a list of the symbols in the library for the current movie. Any imported files will be included along with any symbols you have created. Selecting one of the files produces a thumbnail image to appear in the upper part of the window. To add the symbol to the drawing area, drag its name or the thumbnail into place. A rectangle around the pointer indicates the area occupied by the symbol (Figure 5.79), and the symbol itself will be dropped into place on the drawing area when the mouse button is released (Figure 5.80). A blue rectangle appears around a symbol when it is selected, and there is also a small cross at the centre.

Symbol editing

A symbol can be edited in the usual way if it is selected and the Break Apart option of the Modify menu is used. However, it then ceases to be a symbol, and the advantages of using a symbol are lost. The basic symbol is easily edited, but all instances of that symbol will be affected by the changes made. Select any instance of the symbol and then choose Edit Selected from the Edit menu. This produces the same

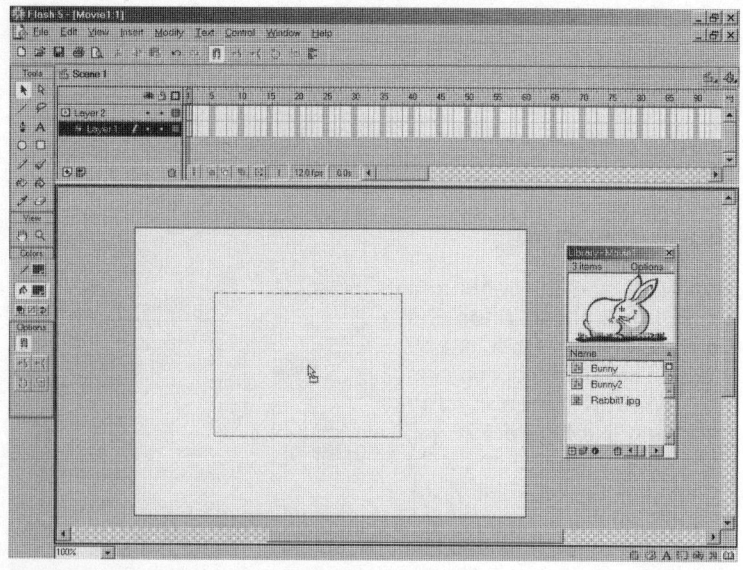

Fig.5.79 The rectangle represents the symbol

Fig.5.80 The symbol in position on the stage

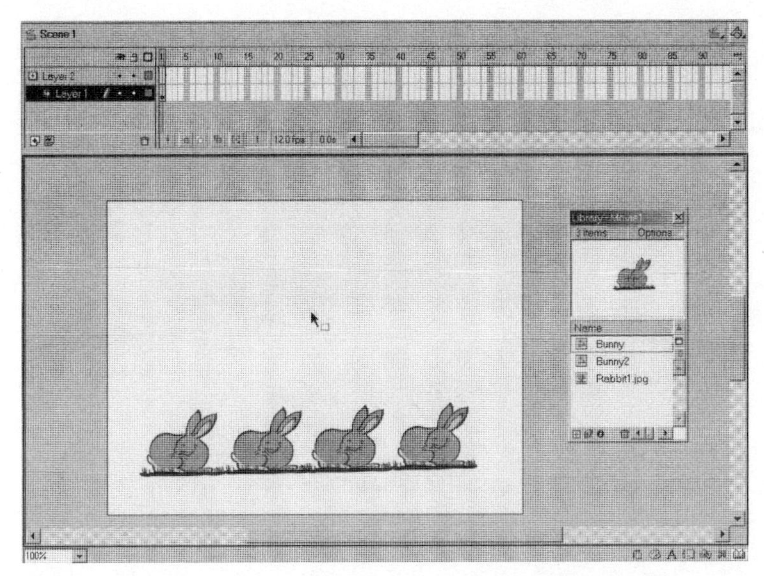

Fig.5.81 Editing a symbol changes all instances of that symbol

window that is used to create symbols, complete with the symbol ready for editing in the normal way. When the editing has been completed select Edit Movie from the Edit menu.

Back in the movie, all instances of the symbol will have changed to the new version. In Figure 5.81 for example, the rabbit image in the library window reflects the changes in scale and colour that have been made to the symbol, as do all four instances in the drawing area.

More editing

As pointed out previously, scaling, rotation, and flipping can be applied individually to any instance of a symbol. A few additional changes can be implemented by selecting the symbol and then choosing the Symbol option from the Modify menu. This brings up the Instance panel, which is shown

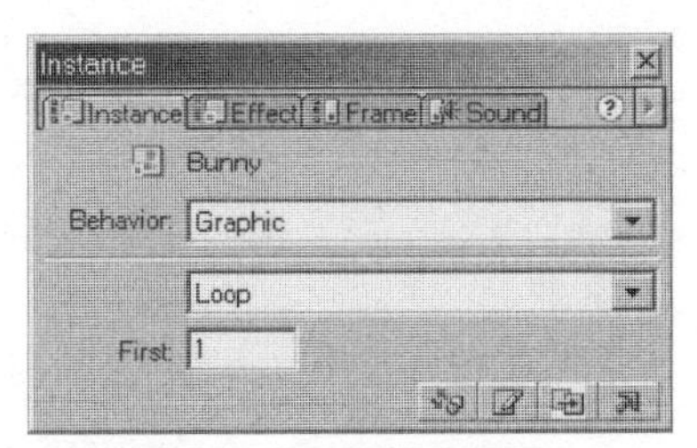

Fig.5.82 The Instance panel

Fig.5.83 Altering the tint changes the entire symbol to one colour

in Figure 5.82. Select the Effect tab to bring the Effect panel to the fore and then select one of the options from the menu.

The Tint option enables the colour of the object to be controlled in the usual way, but it does not give individual control over each colour in a multicoloured object. The entire object will be given the selected fill colour (Figure 5.83). Similarly, the brightness option (Figure 5.84) controls the brightness of the entire symbol, and the Alpha option controls the transparency of the whole symbol (Figure 5.85). Use the None option to return to the normal settings for the symbol.

Fig.5.84 Here the brightness of the symbol has been increased

Fig.5.85 The Alpha setting has been set at 28 percent

Points to remember

Layers are the computer equivalent to the traditional method of animation using sheets of transparent film and opaque inks or paints. Each major element in an animation normally has its own layer. This gives optimum versatility and makes the task of producing movies much easier, especially when numerous items must be moved in different directions.

Groups rather than different layers are used where you may wish to reposition objects, but will not need to animate them.

Layers can be switched off to make it easier to edit other layers. They can also be locked to prevent accidental changes, and set to outline mode.

The Onion Skin effect enables the movement of several frames, or even the whole movie, to be shown on a single frame.

The outline view gives a simplified version of tweened layers, but is not of much benefit with most modern computers which have the memory and computing power to handle the full version.

You are not restricted to using a single tween. Movies can, and usually are, built up from several sets of tweening running in parallel, one after the other, or a combination of the two. Shape tweening, motion tweening, and frame by frame sections can be freely mixed.

The frame rate is 12 per second by default, but can be changed. Very slow rates are useful for slideshows, where a series of still shots are being shown. Higher rates might not be achieved in practice due to hardware limitations in the viewing equipment. A high frame rate also gives larger files for a given duration.

Objects can be spun during a motion tween. Easing enables the rate of movement in motion tweens to be speeded up or slowed down as the movie progresses.

Objects in motion tweens can be made to follow a guideline, rather than simply going from point A to point B. This is a powerful feature that is used a great deal with motion tweens.

Shape tweening can make one object transform into another. It can also be used to make objects appear from nowhere, or disappear. It is often necessary to organise motion tweens on the basis of one object per layer in order to avoid unwanted effects.

Symbols provide an easy way of reusing graphics and reducing the file sizes of movies. However, relatively little editing is possible with symbols, and they can not be used in shape tweens.

6

Text and buttons

Flash or HTML

Flash is often used to produce fancy text for use in Web pages, such as large headings having a rollover effect. In other words, the text changes colour when (say) the pointer is placed over it. Flash can also be used for complete pages of text, and it has advantages over normal HTML coding of text. HTML is a very efficient way of coding text, but it has definite limitations. One of these is that the font you use may not be available on the computers of all users, and a substitute will then be used in its place. This may or may not give good results. The way an HTML page is displayed is to some extent dependent on the way it is interpreted by the browser program used, and pages are not always displayed with the intended layout.

Flash text does not rely on HTML, and a flash heading or a page of Flash text is a Flash movie much like the animations featured in previous chapters. This means that the text is only viewable if the browser is equipped with the Flash Player plug-in, but these days the vast majority of browsers can handle Flash elements without any problems. Results tend to be more consistent and precise because the text is being interpreted by the Flash Player rather than directly by the browser. Also, the Flash file can contain a more detailed description of the text, effectively including font details, which avoids a lot of the guesswork that can be involved with HTML.

One big advantage of Flash text is that it can use any compatible font installed on your computer, and another is that a full range of sizes is available. If you require text that is half the height of the screen, this is no problem when using Flash. Minute text is also possible, or any size in between. Last and certainly not least, Flash text can have rollover effects and do clever things.

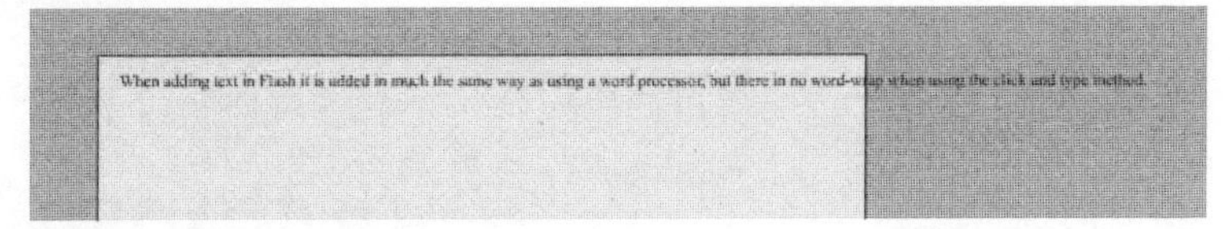

Fig.6.1 Left-clicking and typing text does not give word-wrapping

Adding text

If you have experience with other programs that can format text, you should have no difficulty mastering the basics of Flash text. To add text in the work area select the Text tool in the Tools palette and then left-click at the point where the text must start. When the using Text tool the pointer becomes a small cross with a letter A underneath to remind you that the Text tool is in use. A small rectangle with a flashing cursor appears at the selected point in the work area. Any text typed at the keyboard will then appear on the screen as you type, much like using a word processor. The rectangle expands to accommodate text as it is added. However, using this method of adding text there is no word-

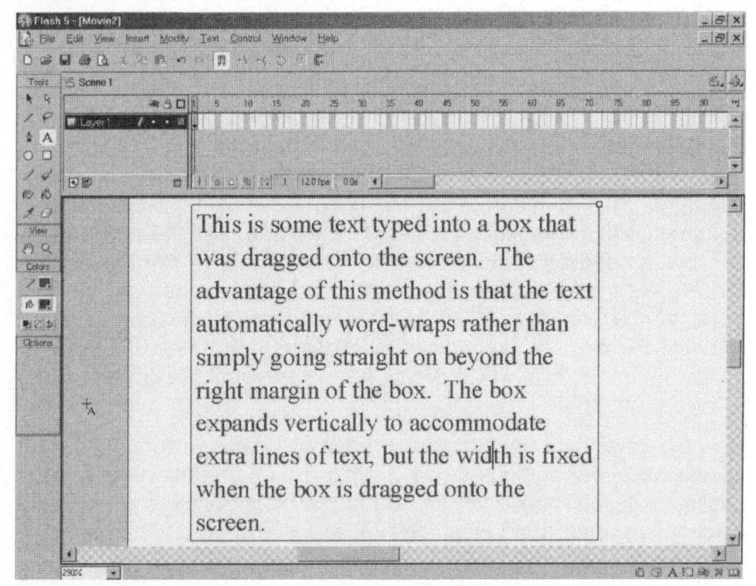

Fig.6.2 Drawing a text box and then adding text does give word-wrapping

wrap facility (Figure 6.1), because Flash has no way of knowing the positions of the margins.

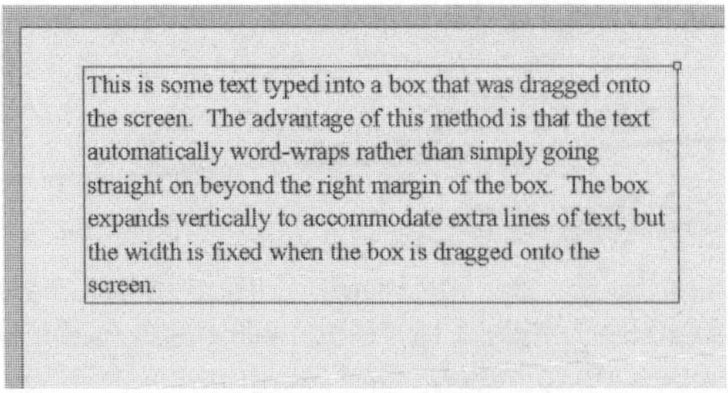

Fig.6.3 If the size of the box is changed, the text will be reformatted

The simple way around this is to drag a box onto the work area first using the text tool, left-click within the box, and then type the text. The text then word-wraps in normal word processor fashion, with the box expanding vertically to accept new lines of text (Figure 6.2). If the handle in the top right-hand corner of the box is dragged to produce a new width, the text will be automatically reformatted to suit and the height of the box will be adjusted to suit the change (Figure 6.3). With this handle it is not possible to resize the text, rotate it, or anything of this nature. The Text tool enables new text boxes to be added, existing text to be edited, and the width of text boxes to be altered. To edit existing text, left-click at the appropriate point in the text using

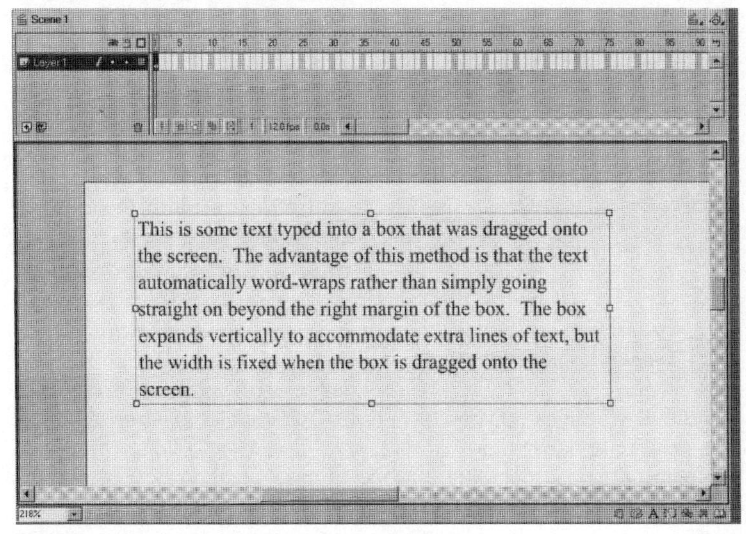

Fig.6.4 A block of text with scaling handles

the Text tool and then edit the material in the normal way. The cursor can of course be moved using the cursor keys once it has been placed within a block of text.

Scaling text

A block of text is effectively a group of objects, and left clicking on any character within a text block will result in the standard blue rectangle appearing to indicate that the group is selected. Operating the Rotate or Scale button in the Tools palette will then produce the usual complement of eight handles. Figure 6.4 shows a block of text with the scaling handles around the rectangle. The usual transformations can then be applied to the text, and the example of Figure 6.5 has been scaled up, stretched vertically, rotated, and skewed. Using the flip options of the Transform submenu it is also possible to produce upside-down text, or "mirror" text as in Figure 6.6.

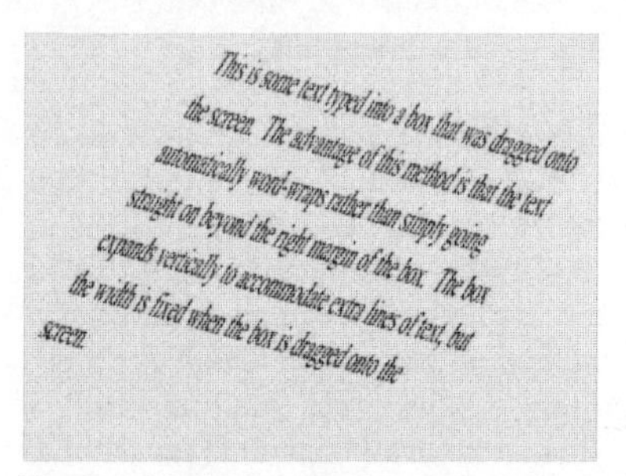

Fig.6.5 Various transformations have been applied to this text

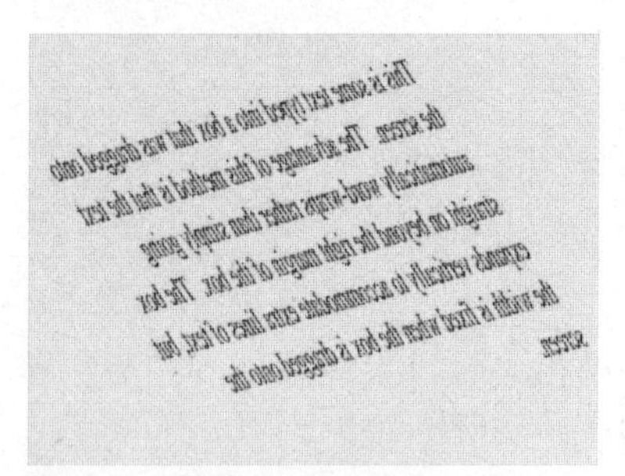

Fig.6.6 Here the text has been flipped horizontally

It is possible to produce really large headlines by starting with small text and then scaling and stretching it to the required size. The text of Figure 6.7 was scaled and stretched into the outsize headline of Figure 6.8.

This is not the only way of producing large text. The usual typographic facilities are available in Flash, including the ability to set a wide range of text sizes. Using these facilities you can have text of different fonts, sizes, colours, etc., within the same block of text. The Text menu offers a range of formatting options, including a range of preset text sizes (Figure 6.9). The current text size is indicated by a dot just to the left of the appropriate figure.

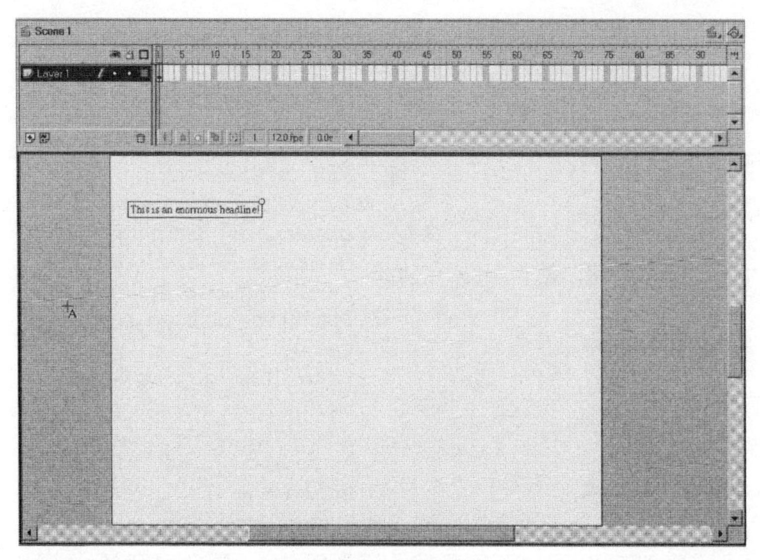

Fig.6.7 The original version of the headline

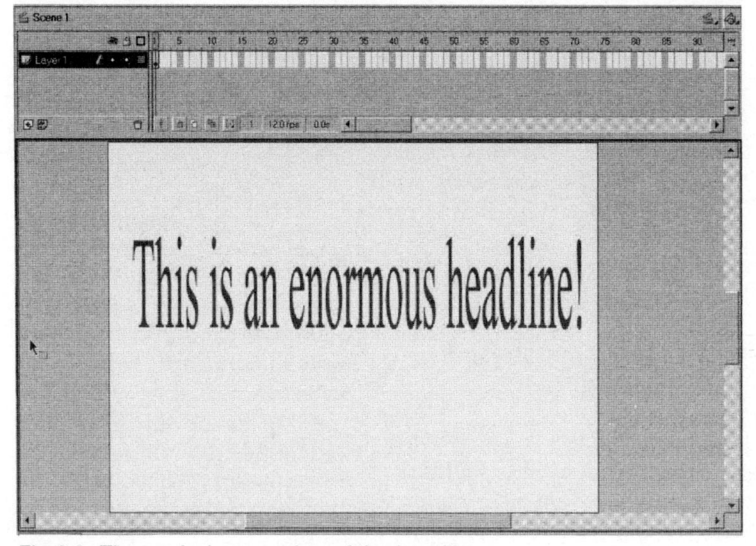

Fig.6.8 The scaled-up version of the headline

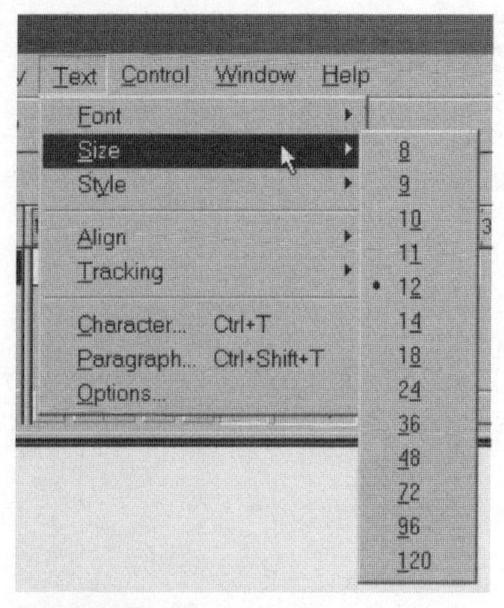

Fig.6.9 The Text menu

Further options are available from some of the panels, including the Character panel (Figure 6.10). In order to bring this one onto the screen select the Panels option from the Window menu, followed by the Character option from the submenu. A font height can be typed into the textbox just below the Font menu, or the usual slider control can be used to set a size between 8 and 96. Typing in a value has the advantage of permitting odd sizes to be selected, such as 11.5. The text sizes are normal point sizes incidentally.

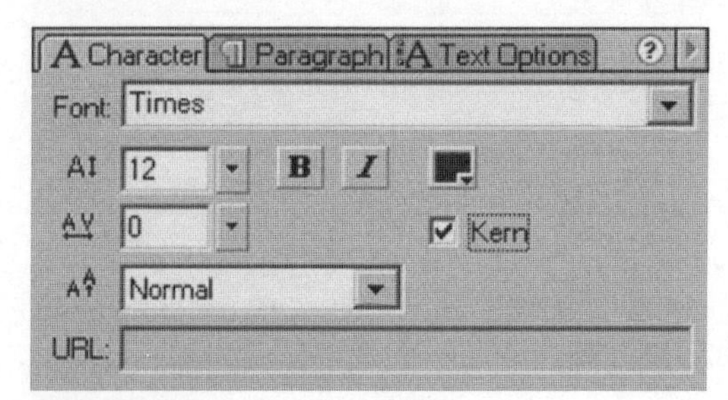

Fig.6.10 The Character panel

Tracking

The textbox beneath the height setting box is used to control the character spacing, or "tracking" as it is termed. Again a value can be typed into the box or adjustments can be made via a popup slider control. The number should be in the range –59 to +59, but in practice quite low values will normally have to be used. Figure 6.11 shows some text having normal spacing in the top row. The middle and bottom rows were respectively produced using the maximum and minimum spacing values.

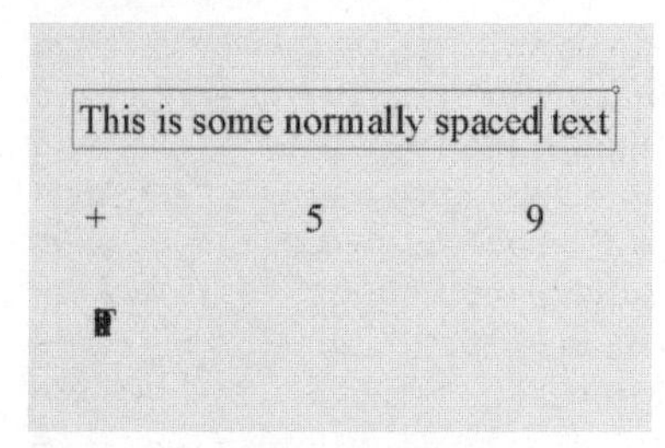

Fig.6.11 Normal, maximum, and minimum tracking

Using the minimum value the characters are not so much spaced as one on top of the other. In practice the spacing value will normally be between about –0.5 and +0.5, in the unlikely event that you need to change it at all. The Tracking submenu of the Text menu enables the tracking to be increased slightly, decreased slightly, or reset to its normal level. Larger changes can be obtained by repeatedly using the Increase or Decrease option until the required effect is obtained.

Styles

The menu beneath the two size boxes offers Normal lettering, Subscript, and Superscript. The buttons labelled B and I offer the usual bold and Italic styles. Figure 6.12 shows normal, subscript, and superscript text in the top row. The bottom row shows normal text, plus normal text with bold and Italic styles added. Note that bold and (or) Italic styles can be applied to subscript and superscript text if required. The third button enables the colour of the text to be changed using the standard colour chart or the colour mixer.

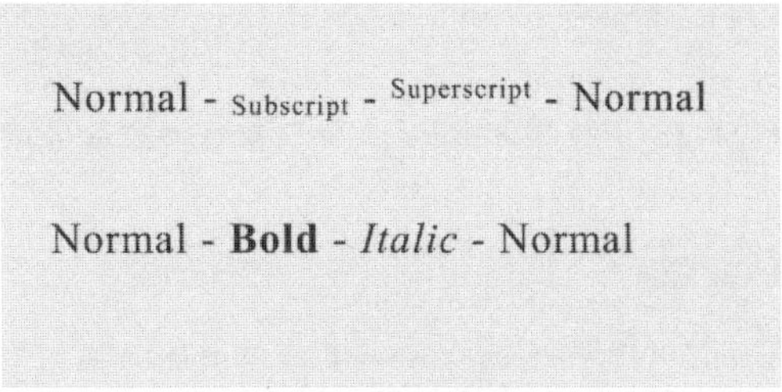

Normal - Subscript - Superscript - Normal

Normal - **Bold** - *Italic* - Normal

Fig.6.12 Text with various styles applied

Kerning

The Kern checkbox enables kerning to be switched off. Most fonts have proportional spacing, which means that wide letters such as "M" and "W" are given more space than narrow letters such as "I" and "j". Kerning takes things a stage further by reducing the spacing between certain combinations of letters. For example, the space between "L" and "W" is reduced, since it can otherwise look out of proportion to the rest of the letter spacing. This type of thing tends to be more noticeable with large lettering. Unless there is a good reason to do otherwise, leave the Kern checkbox ticked. A few fonts use monospacing incidentally. A monospaced font uses the same amount of space for each letter, like a traditional typewriter.

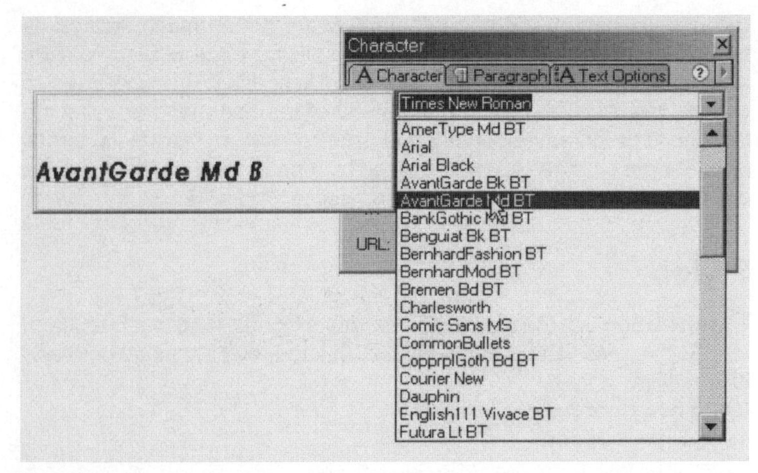

Fig.6.13 The Character panel enables fonts to be previewed

Fonts

The font menu gives access to all the fonts installed on your computer. The highlighted font is previewed in a box that appears to one side of the menu (Figure 6.13) so that you can see exactly what each one looks like without having to select it and add some text to the work area. If the text in the preview box is too small for you to accurately judge what fonts will look like in use, temporarily select a larger font size. The text is shown in the preview box at approximately the size it will be displayed with the zoom level at 100 percent.

Editing text

Changes made using the Text menu or the Character panel are applied to any text that is subsequently added to the work area. Both methods can also be used to edit the colour, font, etc., of existing text. First select the Text tool and then left-click somewhere within the block of text that is to be edited. Then drag the pointer over the part of the text that is to be changed. To select a single word, double-click on that word. The selected text will be highlighted using an inverse video effect (Figure 6.14). Where all the text has the same property, this property will be shown in the Character panel. Any settings made using the Character panel or the Text menu system will be applied immediately to the selected

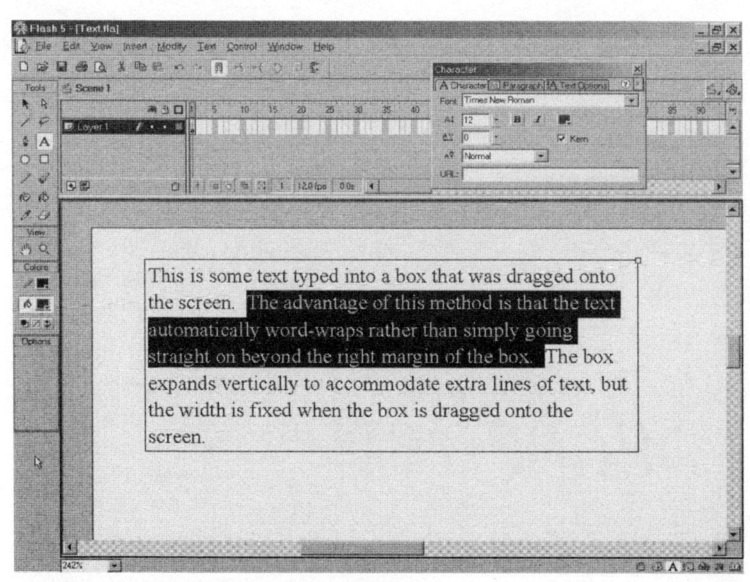

Fig.6.14 Selecting part of a paragraph

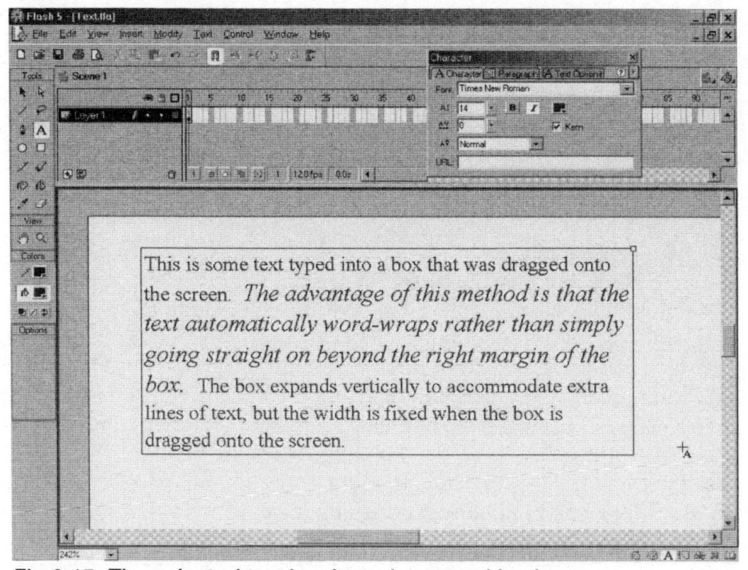

Fig.6.15 The selected text has been increased in size

text. Figure 6.15 shows the result of changing the selected text of Figure 6.14 from 12 to 14 points. The Italic style has also been applied.

Shape text

Text can be converted to ordinary graphics objects by selecting a block of text using the Arrow or Lasso tool and then choosing Break Apart from the Modify menu. The text in Figure 6.16 has received this treatment, and does not look any different to the original text. However, there is a big difference in that each character has been converted into a separate object that can be edited and animated just like any other graphic object. In Figure 6.17 some changes have been made to three characters by dragging their outlines using the Arrow tool.

Fig.6.16 Converted text does not look any different to the original

Fig.6.17 Shape text can be edited just like other objects

Apart from being able to edit and animate text like ordinary graphics objects there is another big advantage in turning text into shapes. Because it is in the form of graphics objects it does not rely on the viewer's computer having the right fonts installed. However unusual the font used, and even if you alter individual characters, it should always be displayed properly on users' computers.

There are also some drawbacks though. Not least of these is that breaking up text into shapes produces a large increase in the file size and a tenfold increase is by no means out of the question. This can greatly extend download times in Web applications. Also bear in mind that once text has been converted into shapes it can no longer be edited using the Text tool. Correcting even the most minor of spelling mistakes could be very difficult once text has been converted into shapes.

Paragraphs

There are some commands that govern the way paragraphs are formatted. Flash, in common with many programs, considers a paragraph to be any text between two carriage returns, or between a carriage return and the top or bottom of the document. The Paragraph panel is grouped with the Character panel, and can be selected by operating the appropriate tag if this group of panels is already on the screen. If not, selecting the Paragraph option from the Text menu will bring up this panel (Figure 6.18).

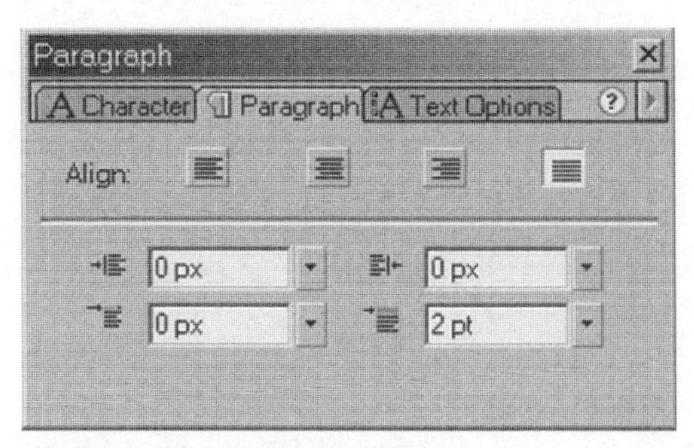

Fig.6.18 The Paragraph panel

The four buttons near the top of the panel give four types of alignment. Working from left to right these are left, centre, and right alignment, and justification. These options are also available from the Align submenu of the Text menu. Left alignment, which is also known as left justification, is the usual method with the text aligned on the left and ragged on the right. With Centre alignment the text grows out from the centre giving ragged left and right-hand edges, as in the top block of text in Figure 6.19. Centre alignment is used a great deal with headngs. Right aligned or right justified text has a neat right-hand edge and a ragged edge on the left, as in the middle paragraph in Figure 6.19. Justified text, or fully

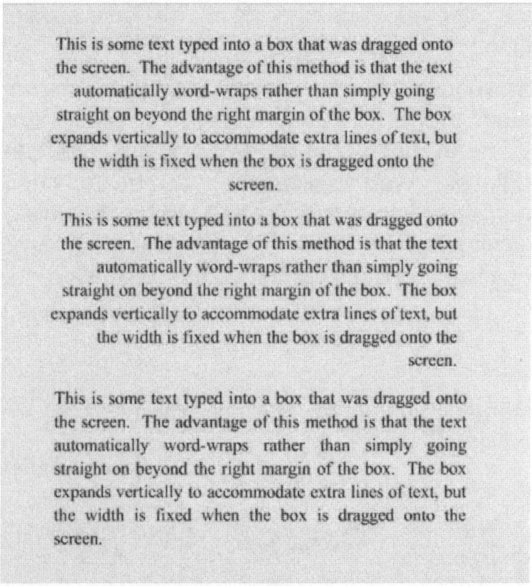

This is some text typed into a box that was dragged onto the screen. The advantage of this method is that the text automatically word-wraps rather than simply going straight on beyond the right margin of the box. The box expands vertically to accommodate extra lines of text, but the width is fixed when the box is dragged onto the screen.

This is some text typed into a box that was dragged onto the screen. The advantage of this method is that the text automatically word-wraps rather than simply going straight on beyond the right margin of the box. The box expands vertically to accommodate extra lines of text, but the width is fixed when the box is dragged onto the screen.

This is some text typed into a box that was dragged onto the screen. The advantage of this method is that the text automatically word-wraps rather than simply going straight on beyond the right margin of the box. The box expands vertically to accommodate extra lines of text, but the width is fixed when the box is dragged onto the screen.

Fig.6.19 The three alternative types of alignment

justified text as it is also known, has both the left and right edges neatly aligned, like the bottom paragraph of Figure 6.19.

The selected alignment option will be used as the default for any new paragraphs that are added. In order to change the alignment of an existing paragraph, place the text cursor anywhere within that paragraph and then select the new alignment option. It is not necessary to drag the text cursor to select the entire paragraph before selecting the new alignment option. However, this method will also work.

If you wish to change the alignment of more than one paragraph the dragging method can be used to select the paragraphs. Alternatively, place the text cursor at the beginning of the first paragraph, hold down the Shift key, and then left-click at the end of the last paragraph. This will select all the text from the previous position of the text cursor to its new position. The selected alignment option will then be applied to all the selected text. To change the alignment of an entire block of text, select the group using the Arrow or Lasso tool and then choose the new type of alignment from the Paragraph panel or the Align submenu.

Margins

The top two text boxes in the Paragraph panel select the widths of the left and right-hand margins. The figures are in screen pixels at the normal screen magnification. Figure 6.20 shows some text that has left and right-hand margins settings of 20 and 40 respectively. The bottom left-hand text box controls the amount of indentation used for the first line in each paragraph, and this value is again in screen pixels. The bottom right-hand textbox controls the line spacing, and the value used is in points. The text in Figure 6.21 has the indentation setting at 45 and the line spacing increased to 13 points. Note that all four textboxes can be adjusted by way of the usual popup slider controls, or new values can simply be typed into the boxes.

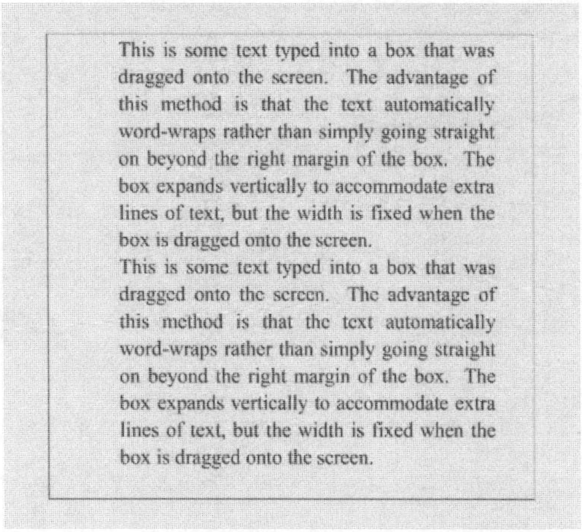

This is some text typed into a box that was dragged onto the screen. The advantage of this method is that the text automatically word-wraps rather than simply going straight on beyond the right margin of the box. The box expands vertically to accommodate extra lines of text, but the width is fixed when the box is dragged onto the screen.
This is some text typed into a box that was dragged onto the screen. The advantage of this method is that the text automatically word-wraps rather than simply going straight on beyond the right margin of the box. The box expands vertically to accommodate extra lines of text, but the width is fixed when the box is dragged onto the screen.

Fig.6.20 Left and right margins set at 20 and 40 respectively

This is some text typed into a box that was dragged onto the screen. The advantage of this method is that the text automatically word-wraps rather than simply going straight on beyond the right margin of the box. The box expands vertically to accommodate extra lines of text, but the width is fixed when the box is dragged onto the screen.

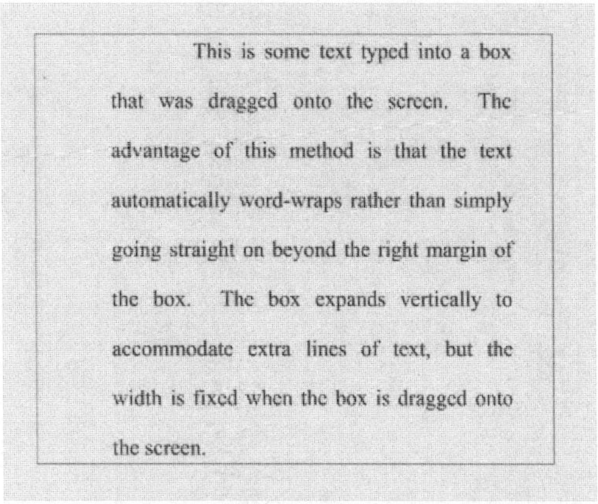

Fig.6.21 This paragraph has the indenting set at 45 and the line spacing at 13 points

Publishing

Movies and other material produced using Flash can be imported into an HTML editor such as Macromedia's Dreamweaver and used in HTML Web pages, or complete pages can be produced using Flash. The dummy page of Figure 6.22 contains some text and three images. In order to convert this into an HTML page it is merely necessary to select the Publish option from the File menu. Flash will then generate an HTML page plus a file having a swf extension that contains any flash text, graphics, or movies. The HTML page is largely empty, but it does contain one displayable item, which is the Flash file.

Fig.6.22 The example page

Fig.6.23 The example page being tested in Internet Explorer 5.5

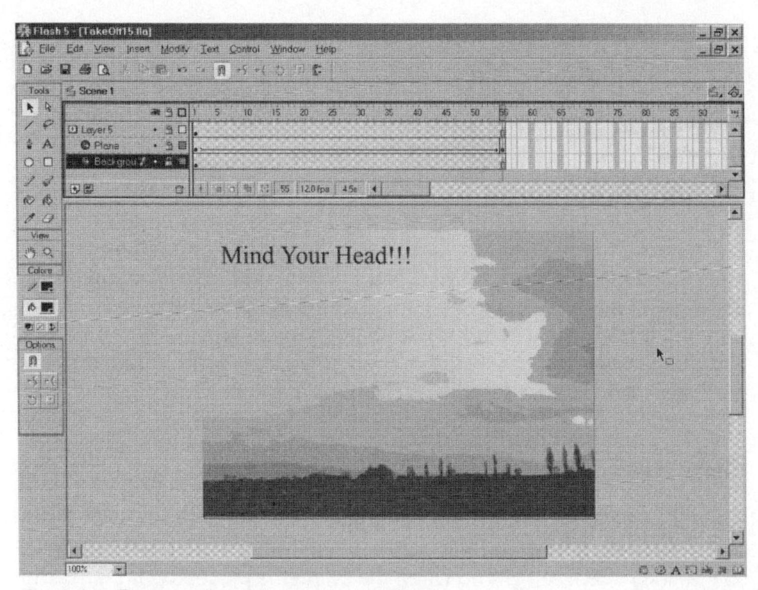

Fig.6.24 The movie as it appears in Flash

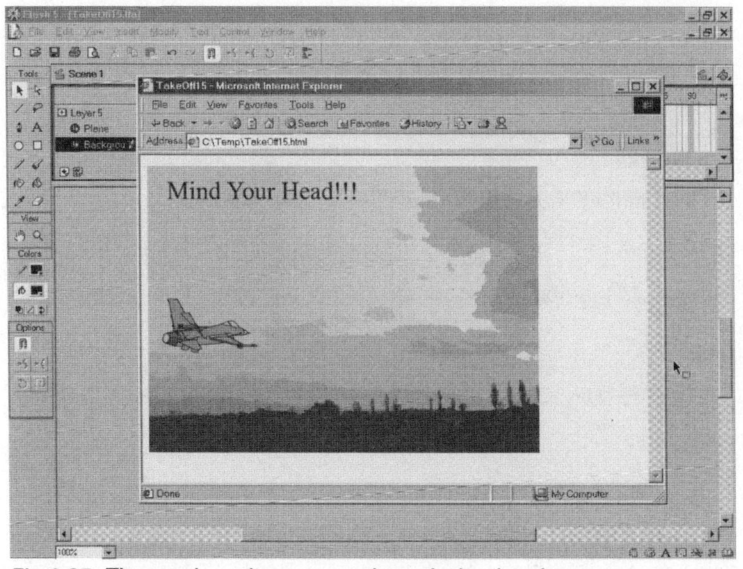

Fig.6.25 The movie as it appears when playing in a browser

You can check the page using a browser, or select Publish Preview from the File menu, and Default-(HTML) from the submenu. Alternatively, just operate the F12 function key. Either way the page will be shown in the default browser program. In Figure 6.23 the dummy page is previewed from within Flash using Internet Explorer 5.5.

In this example there are Flash graphics but no movie. However, the system works in exactly the same way if the page does contain a movie. In Figure 6.24 some text has been added to the background layer of an animation featured previously. This is the one where the jet plane flies in at the left of the screen and then flies out again on the other side. Apart from the added text it is the same as the original movie. When viewed using a browser the page is displayed correctly (Figure 6.25), and the animation loops indefinitely.

Buttons

Making buttons for Web pages is a popular use for Flash, and Flash buttons usually live up to their name. Flash buttons are often designed so that they seem to light up when the pointer is placed over them, and they get even brighter if the mouse is left-clicked. This is just one of many possibilities though. A common application for a Flash button is in a menu system on a Web page. Typically, it would then be linked to the appropriate page or URL using an HTML editor, but the linking can be done from within Flash. Left clicking on the button would cause the appropriate page to be displayed by the browser. Flash buttons can also be used to start and stop a movie, and there are many other possibilities.

In Flash terminology a button has these three states:

Up

In this state the pointer is not over the button.

Over

The pointer is over the button, but the left mouse button is not pressed.

Down

The pointer is over the button and the left mouse button is pressed.

As will be explained later, there is a fourth state, but there is no need to worry about this one at this stage.

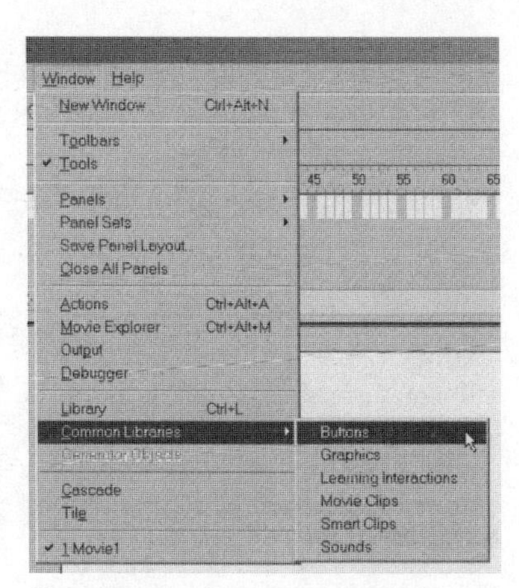

Fig.6.26 The Common Libraries submenu

It is not necessary for the button to have a different appearance in each of the three states. It could have one appearance for the Up and Over states, and a different appearance when it is left-clicked and it goes into the Down state. In a way this is more logical, because it is usually the Down state rather than the Over state that triggers an action. On the other hand, having a different appearance for the Over state can make a Web page more lively and attractive, and it also makes it clear to users that the buttons are active and will actually do something when operated. Note that buttons can actually have more than these three states, but these are the only ones that are needed for most purposes. The three basic states are the only ones we will consider here.

Button library

You can create buttons "from scratch" or use one of the buttons in the symbol library. We will consider the use of symbols from the library first. To gain access to the button library, select Common Libraries from the Window menu, and then Buttons from the submenu (Figure 6.26). A window like the one in Figure 6.27 will then appear. Many entries in this window are marked "Folder" in the Kind column, and this indicates that you must double-click on the entry in order to expand it and view the buttons in the Folder. The word "Button" in this

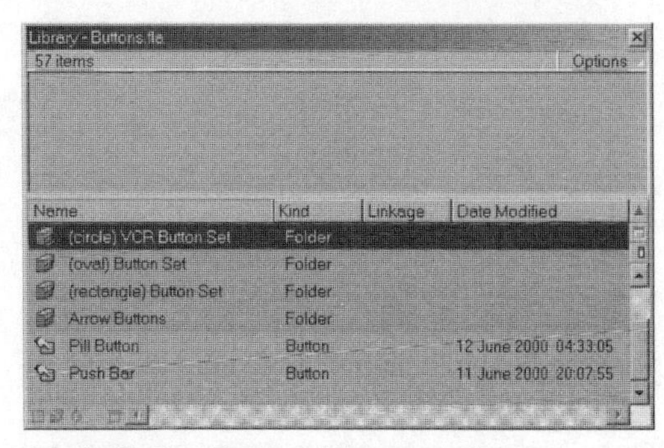

Fig.6.27 The Buttons Library window

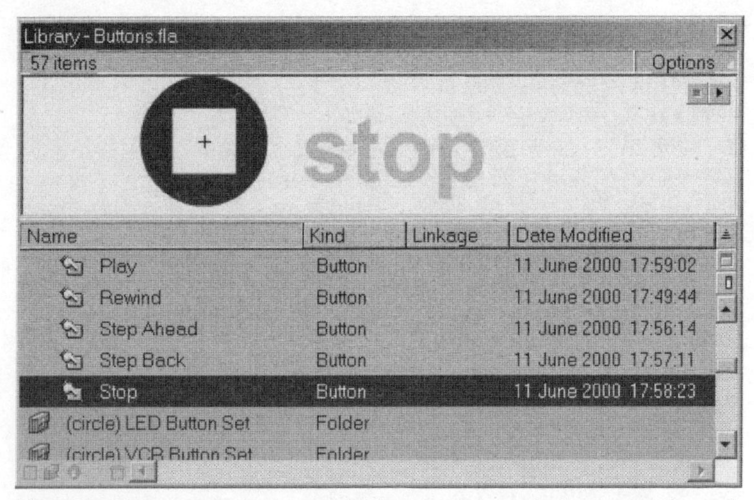

Fig.6.28 There are buttons and folders containing further selections of buttons. The selected button is previewed in the upper section of the window

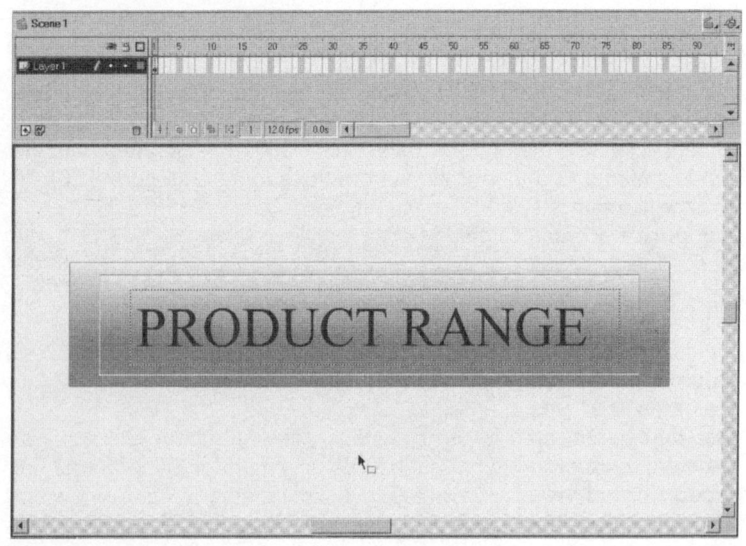

Fig.6.29 Text can be added on top of a button

column indicates that the entry is a button, and selecting it will give a preview of the button in the upper part of the window (Figure 6.28). Note that you must double-click on the icon at the extreme left-hand side in order to expand a folder's entry.

Take a look at some of the buttons in each folder. There is a good variety, including various tape recorder and VCR style buttons that have obvious applications in the control of Flash movies. The preview image can be cycled through its various states by operating the Play button, which is the one near the top right-hand corner of the window that is marked with an arrowhead.

To add a button onto the drawing area simply drag it out of the library window and into place. Once in place it can be scaled, rotated, and skewed just like any other symbol. The tint, brightness, etc., can also be edited using the Instance panel. In some cases icons can be used to indicate the function of a button, but it is often necessary to use text. Always make sure that users will find it easy to understand the functions of control buttons. Text can be added near to a button or on top of it if required (Figure 6.29).

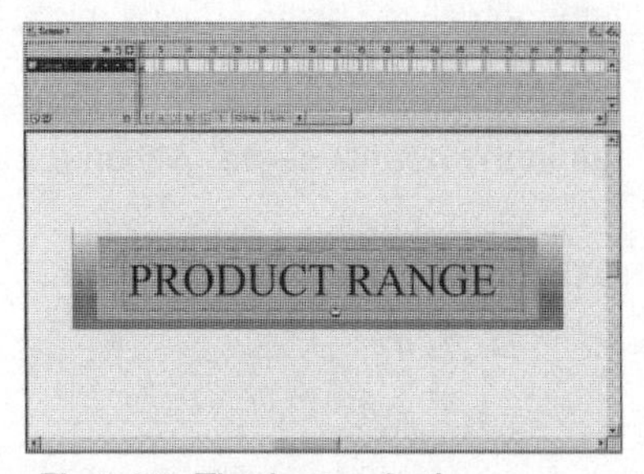

Fig.6.30 The button in the Down state

To test that a button is providing the correct changes in appearance it can be tested in a browser using the Publish Preview facility, or within Flash by selecting the Enable Simple Buttons option from the control menu. Figure 6.30 shows the button of Figure 6.29 being tested within Flash. The change in appearance with the button in the down state is clearly visible. Note that the rectangle around the text is not visible when the button is viewed using a browser.

Custom buttons

You are not restricted to using buttons from the library, and you can draw up your own buttons that can be as simple or elaborate as you like. A button is a form of symbol, so the first step in creating a new one is to go to the Insert menu and select the New Symbol option. This produces the Symbol Properties window (Figure 6.31) where the new symbol is given a name and the appropriate type of symbol is chosen

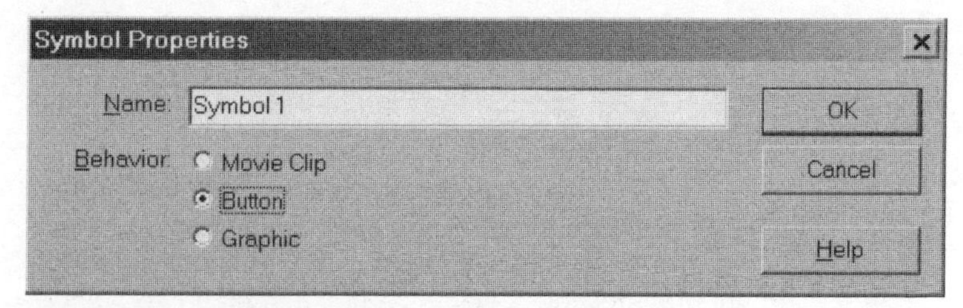

Fig.6.31 The Symbol Properties dialogue box

using the radio buttons. In this case it is clearly the Button option that should be selected. Left clicking the OK button takes the program into the symbol creation mode, with the registration mark at the centre of the drawing area (Figure 6.32).

Although at first glance things might look the same as when creating a graphics symbol, an important difference becomes evident if you look at the Timeline (Figure 6.33). A button is a form of movie, but it does not run in the normal sense. When a button movie is running, the button

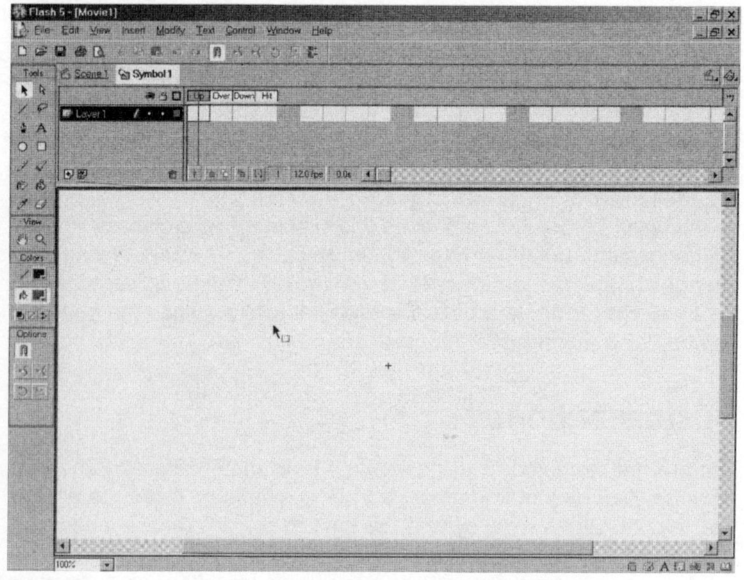

Fig.6.32 The screen obtained in the symbol creation mode

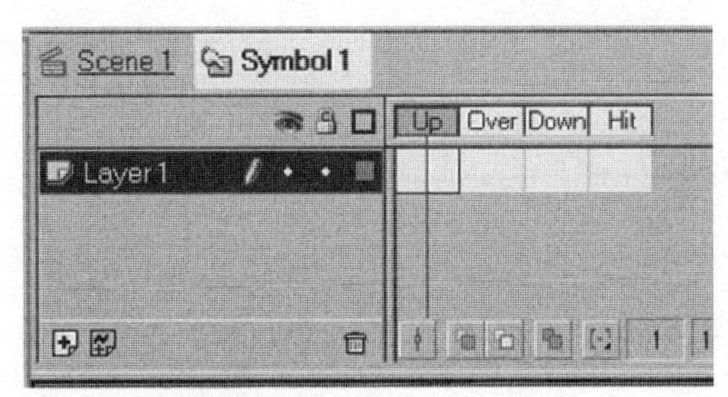

Fig.6.33 The Timeline in the symbol creation mode

responds to the pointer but it is otherwise static. There are four frames in the Timeline for a button, and it is in these that the three normal states (Up, Down, and Over) are defined. There is a fourth frame called Hit, and this is used to define the area that the pointer must be within in order to activate the button. In most cases this will be the same as the perimeter of the button, but it can be a larger or smaller area if preferred. If a button is a very elaborate shape it might be easier to use if the Hit area is a simple rectangle for example.

Initially the Up frame is selected, and this is the one that most people prefer to design first. Draw the button using any of the normal drawing

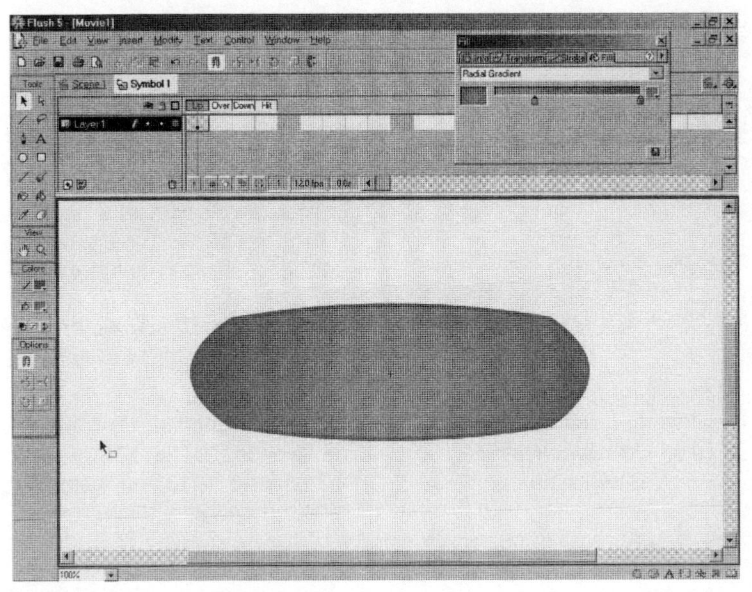

Fig.6.34 The completed button

and editing tools. For this type of thing it is often more than a little helpful to use the visible grid and the snap grid. Text can be added to the button, but you may prefer to add the text once the button has been added to a page. This enables the same button design to be used numerous times on a page, with different text being added to each instance. It text is included in the button design it will be necessary to have a separate button symbol for each occurrence on the page. Of course, if the text is to change from one state to another it must be incorporated into the button design.

Having drawn the button in its Up state you will have something like Figure 6.34, and it is time to move on to the button design for the Over state. Left-click on the Over box in the Timeline (not the box containing the word "Over", but the one beneath), and then select the Keyframe option from the Insert menu. This copies the original version of the button to the Over frame. If the button does not have to change in the Over state this is all you have to do for this frame. If changes are required, use the editing tools to make the necessary modifications to the design. The button can actually be completely different from one state to the next if preferred, but it is usually best not to get too carried away with this type of thing because it gets users confused. If you want to design the Over state "from scratch", choose the Blank Keyframe option instead of the Keyframe one.

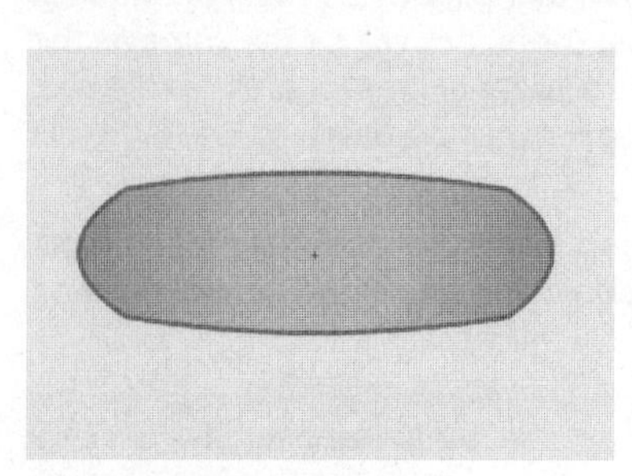

Fig.6.35 The button in the Over state

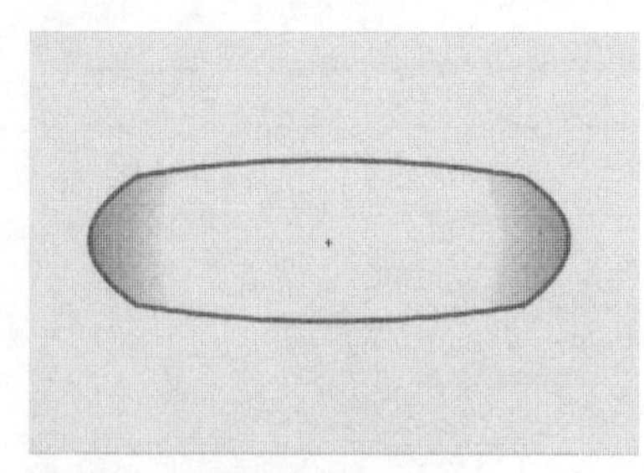

Fig.6.36 The button in the Down state

Having designed the Over button, move on to the Down frame, add a keyframe here, and make the required changes to the design. You then have all three versions of the button. Figures 6.35 and 6.36 show the Over and Down states of my demonstration button. It starts with middle tones for the fill and gets lighter in the Over and Down states.

It has been designed for use with black lettering, so it has been kept reasonably light in the Up state so that the lettering will be easy to read. A gradient radial fill has been used to give the effect of the button being lit up from within.

Hit frame

The final step is to select the Hit frame, add a keyframe, and then draw a shape to define the active area for the button. In most cases this just involves copying the shape of the button from the previous frame using the Keyframe option from the Insert menu. However, as explained previously, you can have a different shape here if preferred. In this example I have opted for a simple rectangle that is just large enough to fully cover the shape of the button (Figure 6.37). Note that the object in the Down frame will be used as the Hit shape if no shape is added to the Hit frame. When you have finished designing the button, select the Edit Movie option from the Edit menu.

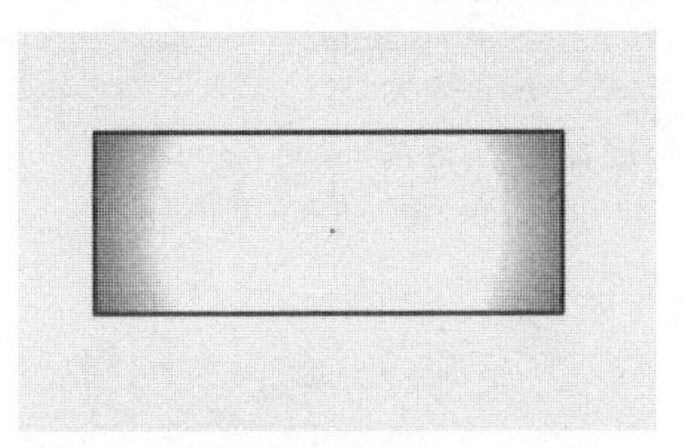

Fig.6.37 The Hit frame

Testing and editing

To test the button it must first be added to a page. Select the Library option from the Window menu and then drag the button onto the drawing area from the Library window. Go to the Control menu and choose the Enable Simple Buttons option and then test the button. Figure 6.38 shows a bank of three buttons using the demonstration design with the middle button in the Down state. As can be seen from Figure 6.39, the Hit area is larger than the buttons, with the Catalogue button going to the Over state with the pointer just outside the area

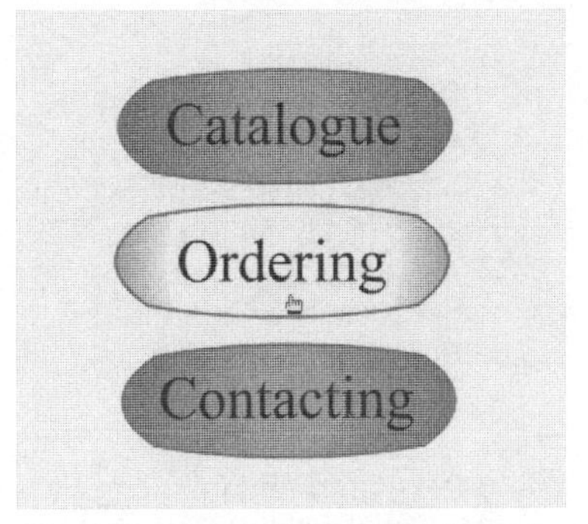

Fig.6.38 The bank of three buttons

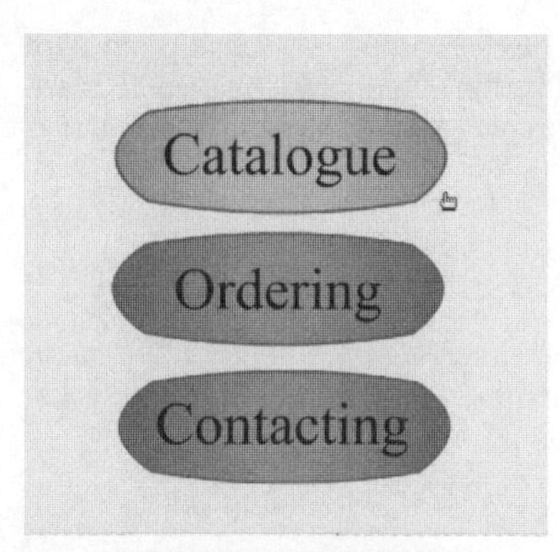

Fig.6.39 The Hit area can be larger than the button

occupied by the button. This shows that the rectangular Hit area is operating correctly.

It is quite likely that having tested a button you will wish to make some minor adjustments to it. In this case the button is slightly too dark in the Up state, so that the text is not quite as clear as it might be. A button can be edited by right clicking on its entry in the Library window and choosing Edit from the popup menu (Figure 6.40). Having made the required changes select the Edit Movie option from the Edit menu, and all instances of the button should then reflect the changes you have made (Figure 6.41).

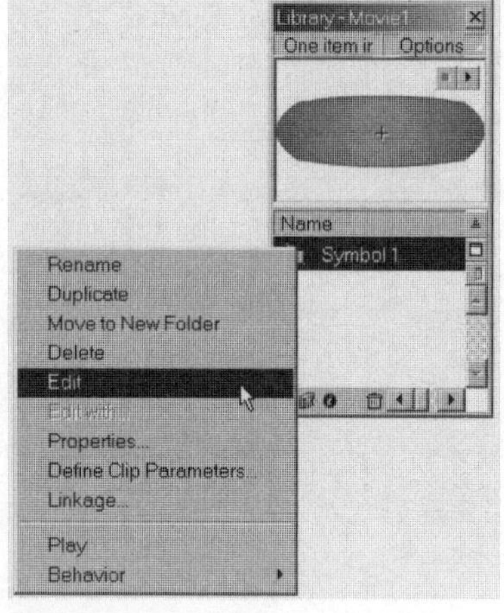

Fig.6.40 The popup menu

Flashy text

Flash is often used to produce text that alters when the pointer is placed over it. Usually this effect is reserved for large headlines, but it can be used with any block of text. Sometimes the text changes colour, in other cases the text itself changes. In either case the text is produced in the same way as a Flash button. In the headline of Figure 6.42 the text has been given a background, and both the text and background change colour when the pointer passes over the area occupied by the text (Figure 6.43). In the version of Figure 6.44 the rectangle is only used in the Hit frame, and in use it is never displayed on the screen. It defines the active area for the text, which duly changes colour when the pointer is placed within the rectangle.

There is a similar set-up in Figure 6.45, but there is also a change in the wording. However things are organised, the text is actually just an outsize Flash button.

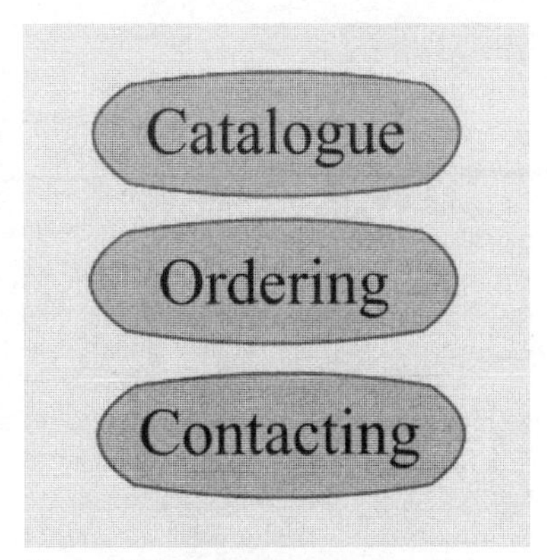

Fig.6.41 The edited version of the button

In control

Flash buttons can be used as links in Web pages, but they can also be used to control movies. Suppose that a long animation runs automatically when someone goes to the home page of your web site. This would typically be a "slideshow" with perhaps a dozen different frames being displayed for a few seconds each. This type of thing is easily achieved using Flash, and it is really a form of frame by frame animation with a totally different picture, etc., for each frame and a very low frame rate. This presentation might be

Fig.6.42 This headline has been given a coloured background

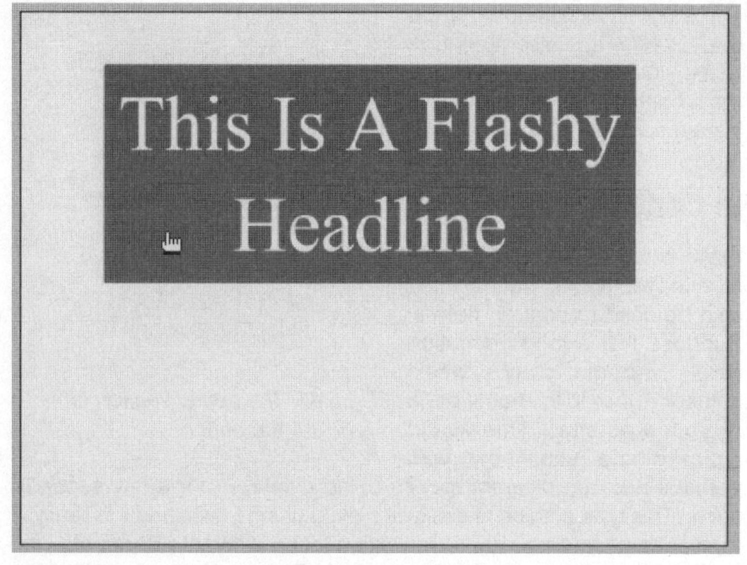

Fig.6.43 The text and background both respond to the pointer

fascinating the first time someone visits the site, but it might be a bit irksome on their 104th visit. Or would it just seem like their 104th visit? It would be useful to have a button that could be operated to make the movie skip straight to the last frame. Another possibility would be to only have the movie run if the visitor operated a Start button.

This type of thing is possible using Flash's Action Script programming language, but you do not have to learn to program using this language in order to add control buttons. You can program buttons using the menus, etc., and

Fig.6.44 The rectangle is only used to define the Hit area

Flash then writes the code for you. There are two stages to getting a button to perform the required task. First an event must be selected, and this is something like the mouse being left-clicked on the button. In other words the event is what the user has to do in order to trigger the appropriate action. The second stage is to define the action that occurs when the button is operated. This will be something like stopping or starting the movie.

Fig.6.45 The rolled-over version of Figure 6.44

As an initial experiment in programming buttons, add a button to the drawing area, select it using the Arrow tool, and then select the Instance option from the Modify menu. In the Instance panel, operate the Basic Actions button in the bottom right-hand corner of the window (Figure 6.46). This brings up the Object Actions window (Figure 6.47). Left-click on the Basic Actions icon to expand its entry in the list on the left, and then double-click on the On Mouse Event icon. The bottom section of the window will then change to look like Figure 6.48. The seven options detailed on the next page are available:

Fig.6.46 The Instance panel

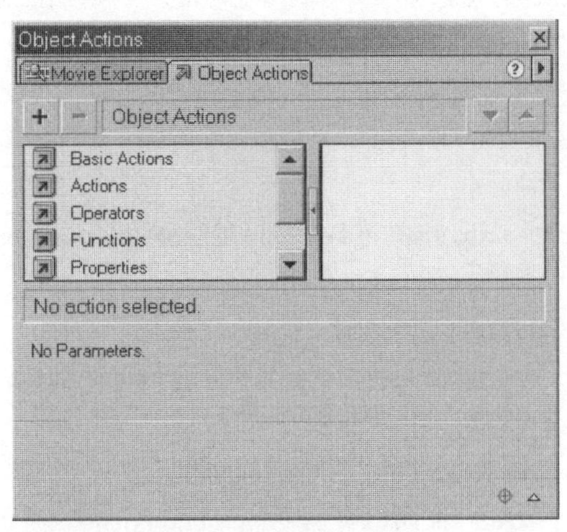

Fig.6.47 The Object Actions panel

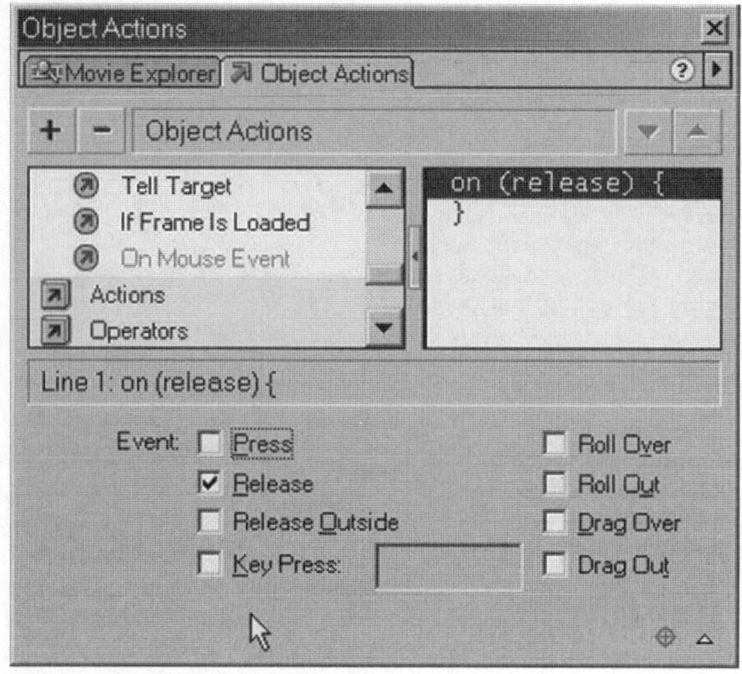

Fig.6.48 The Object Actions panel

Press

This is the event you are most likely to use. Clicking on a button creates this event.

Release

Similar to the Press event, but it does not occur until the mouse button is released.

Release Outside

Clicking within the Hit area, but not releasing the button until the pointer is outside this area generates this event.

Roll Over

Placing the pointer over the button generates this event. The mouse does not have to be clicked.

Roll Out

Similar to the Roll Over option, but this event is not generated until the pointer is moved off the button.

Drag Over

Dragging the pointer across the button generates this event.

Drag Out

To generate this event the mouse is clicked on the button with the pointer then being dragged off the button.

The Key Press option permits a key of the keyboard to be used to activate the button. To use this facility tick the Key Press checkbox and then press the key that will be used to trigger the button. The corresponding character will appear in the textbox. A key press is normally used in addition to one of the other options rather than instead of it.

Although there are seven options, practical applications for some of them are less than obvious. In most cases either Press or Release will be used when left clicking on the button must trigger the action. The Roll Over is used when simply placing the pointer over the button must trigger the action.

Actions

For the sake of this example select the Press option. Some highlighted text will appear in the right-hand section of the window, and this is the Action Script code that Flash has written for you. The button can now be triggered, and the next step is to assign an action to it. Return to the list of Basic Actions and choose the Stop option by double clicking on its icon. Some more code will then appear in the right-hand side of the window. The Stop action simply stops the movie, so the action of the button is to stop the movie when the button is clicked.

There are other actions available that control movies. The Play action starts a movie playing from the current frame. The bottom section of the window changes if the Go To option is selected (Figure 6.49). Operating the button causes the movie to jump to the frame number entered in the Frame textbox. With the Go To and Play checkbox ticked, having gone to the specified frame the movie is then played from that point. If this checkbox is not ticked, the movie jumps to the specified frame and stops.

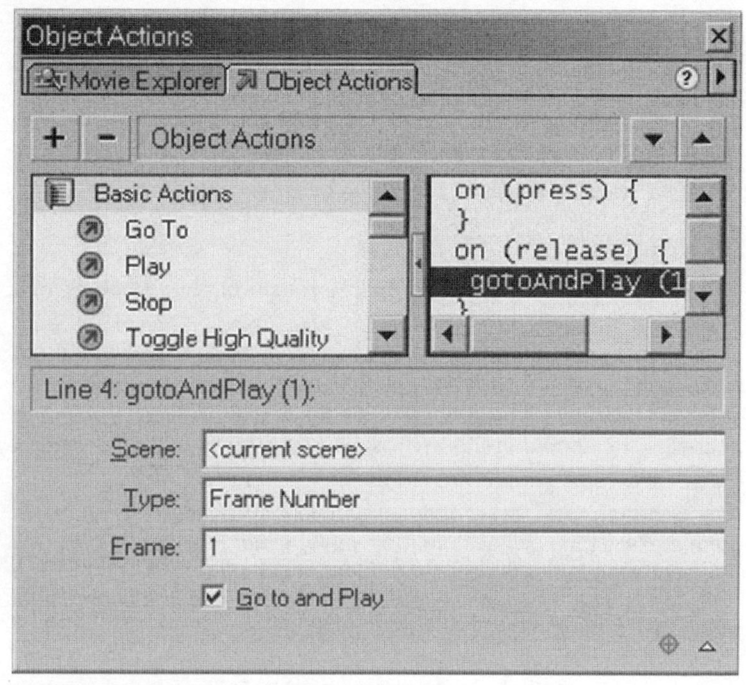

Fig.6.49 The panel with the Go To command selected

One way of using this button is to accept the defaults so that it acts as a replay button. Operating the button then takes the movie to frame 1 and plays it from there. It can also be used to simply take the movie to the first or last frame by using the appropriate frame number and not having the Go to and Play checkbox ticked.

Using these simple actions it is possible to provide users with full control over the playing of movies, providing them with VCR style pushbutton controls. Whether or not it is worth doing so depends on the size and nature of the movie, and exactly how it will be used. In most cases it is advisable to at least provide users with a Stop button.

Frame actions

Actions are not restricted to use with buttons and they can also be assigned to frames. If you try making a simple movie and then test it

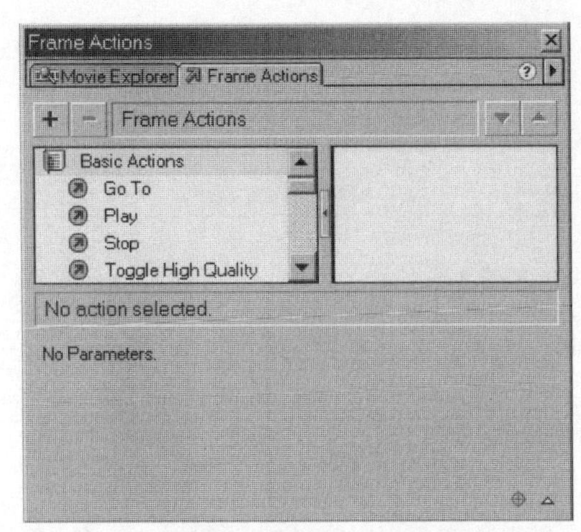

Fig.6.50 The Frame Actions window

using the Test Movie option of the Control menu, it will play over and over again. In order to make the movie play just once it is merely necessary to add a Stop action in the final frame. Select the final frame of the layer that contains the animation and then select the Actions option from the Windows menu. This brings up the Frame Actions panel (Figure 6.50), which is much the same as the Object Actions panel. Expand the Basic Actions section of the list on the left of the panel and then double click on the Stop entry. A small amount of code should then appear in the right-hand section of the window.

If you now try testing the movie it should run through once and then stop. Try adding a button and assigning a Go To frame 1 action to it. Make sure the Go to and Play checkbox is ticked. The movie will now play once, but operating the button will reset the movie to frame 1 and run it again. Now select frame 1 of the animated layer and add a Stop command here. Now when the movie is tested it will fail to run, but operating the button will result in it playing through once. Operating the button again will take the movie back to frame 1 but it will not run. The button action will try to run the movie, but this action will be counteracted by the stop command at frame 1.

Operating the button again will actually start the movie, as would a button assigned with a Play action. The button can be made to operate as a replay button if frame 2 rather than frame 1 is used in the Go To action. This misses out frame 1 when the movie is replayed, but this will not be noticeable with most movies. Obviously it will not give satisfactory results with something like a slideshow.

More than one action can be applied to a button or frame. In order to add an action left-click on the last action in the right-hand section of the

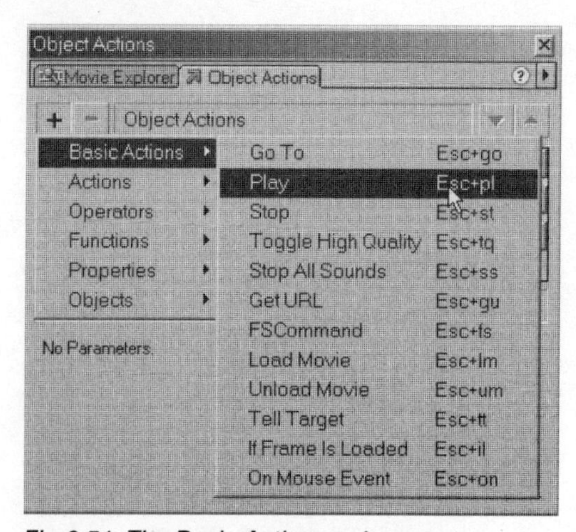

Fig.6.51 The Basic Actions submenu

Actions window to select it. Then operate the + button near the top left-hand corner of the window to produce a small menu. Select the Basic Actions option, which will produce a submenu (Figure 6.51). Select the required action from the submenu and it will be added to the code in the right-hand section of the window. To remove an action simply select it in the right-hand section of the window and then press the Delete key or operate the – button near the top left-hand corner of the window.

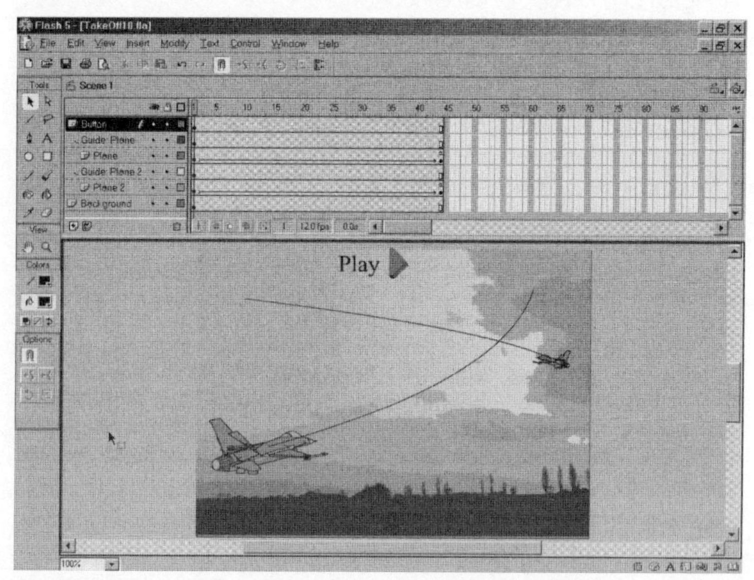

Fig.6.52 A Play button added to the twin jet plane animation

With simple animations for Web use it is generally advisable to keep the method of control as simple as possible. Usually something like the arrangement of Figure 6.52 will suffice. This is the animation featured previously where two planes fly across the screen guided by separate guidelines. A Stop action has been added in the final frame of the two layers that contain the motion tweens. Consequently, in use the movie plays through once and then stops. A new layer has been added in front of all the others, and this has been used for the Play button and its legend. The button is added in frame 1, and it produces a Play action when left clicked. If desired, the movie can therefore be played over and over again by repeatedly operating the play button.

URL

A button can be used to provide a link to a Web address (a URL), and the initial stages are the same as when using a button to control a movie. From the Basic Actions submenu or list in the right-hand section of the Actions panel choose the Get URL option. The bottom section of the panel changes (Figure 6.53), and the full URL of the linked Web page is then added in the URL textbox.

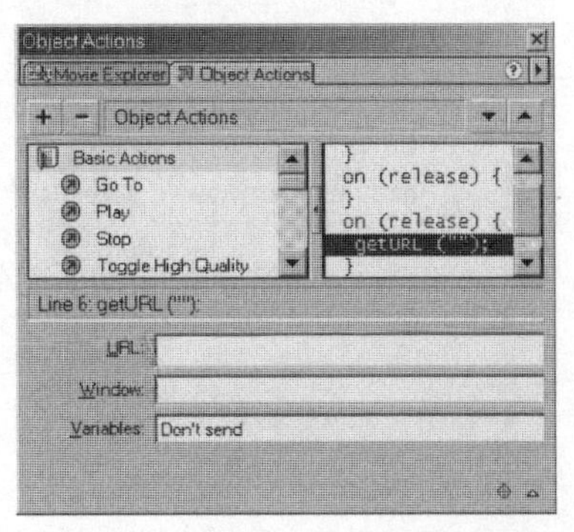

Fig.6.53 Linking a button to a URL

Adding sounds

Getting a complex soundtrack synchronised to a movie is not a straightforward affair, because movies can and do play at different rates on different PCs due to hardware limitations. It would be easy to produce a soundtrack that remained perfectly synchronised on your computer but was not even close when used with most others. Even playing the movie on your own computer but with the window resized could cause synchronisation to be lost. In general, the larger the window used for a movie, the greater the demands placed on the computer and its video system. Consequently, larger versions may play more slowly than small ones.

Fortunately, adding some basic sound effects to a movie is very straightforward indeed. Selecting Common Libraries from the Window

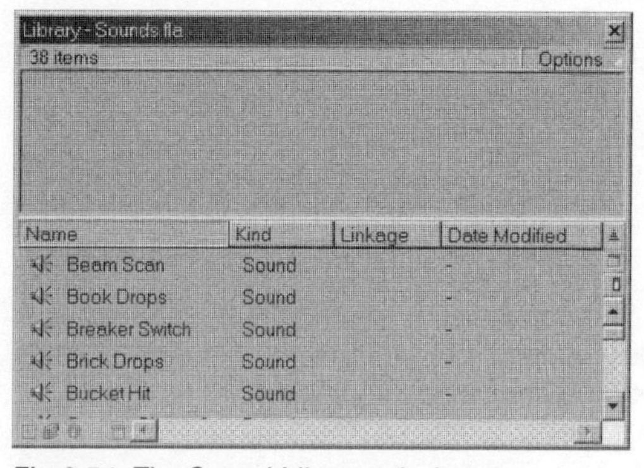

Fig.6.54 The Sound Library window

menu followed by Sounds from the submenu that appears, gives access the library of built-in sounds. This produces the window of Figure 6.54, and selecting a sound from the list in the bottom section of the window results in its waveform being displayed in the upper part of the window (Figure 6.55). Although usually referred to as a waveform display, the time axis is so compressed that it is really more of an envelope display. In other words, it shows how the volume of the sound varies over a period of time. Two waveforms are shown for stereo sounds, one for each channel (Figure 6.56). In order to hear the selected sound, operate the Play button near the top right-hand corner of the window.

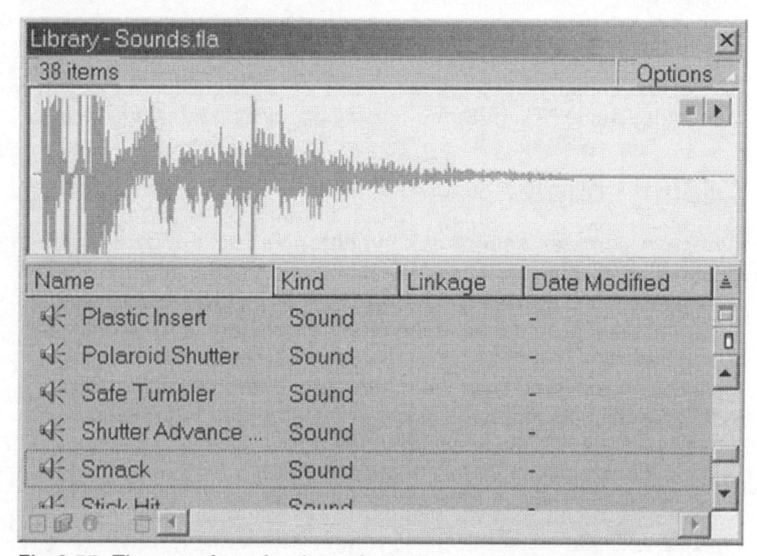

Fig.6.55 The waveform for the selected sound is displayed

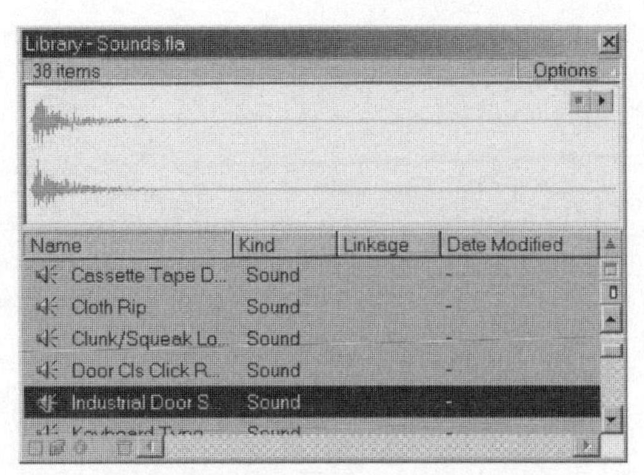

Fig.6.56 Both waveforms are shown for stereo sounds

Files in WAV and MP3 formats can be imported into a movie in the usual way. The Macintosh version can also import sound files in AIFF format. Select the Import option from the File menu and then use the file browser to locate and load the file. It then appears in the Library window along with any other symbols that are currently loaded. A sound is loaded into a keyframe much like any other symbol. First select the keyframe and then drag the icon for the required sound onto the stage. A small rectangle above the pointer represents the symbol (Figure 6.57), but there is no visual sign

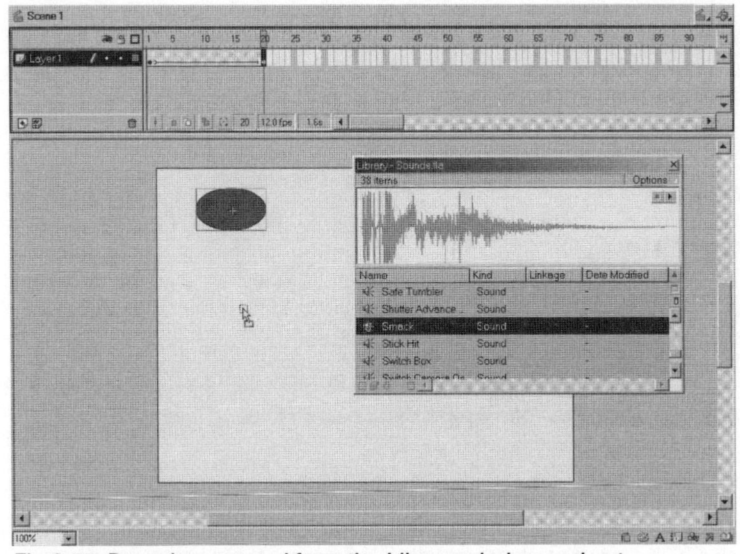

Fig.6.57 Dragging a sound from the Library window and onto the stage

of the symbol's presence when the mouse button is released. However, the Timeline does change to show the sound (Figure 6.58), confirming its presence.

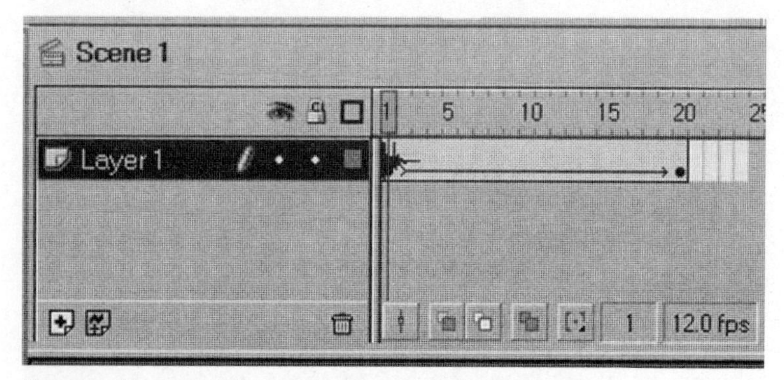

Fig.6.58 The sound's waveform appears in the Timeline

If more sounds are added into other keyframes they will all be shown in the Timeline. In the Timeline shown in Figure 6.59 there are two sounds loaded into keyframes. In order to try out sounds in a movie, first produce a simple animation like the one described previously where the ball bounces off the cube. Select frame 1 in the Sphere layer and then drag the Smack sound from Library window and onto the work area. Repeat

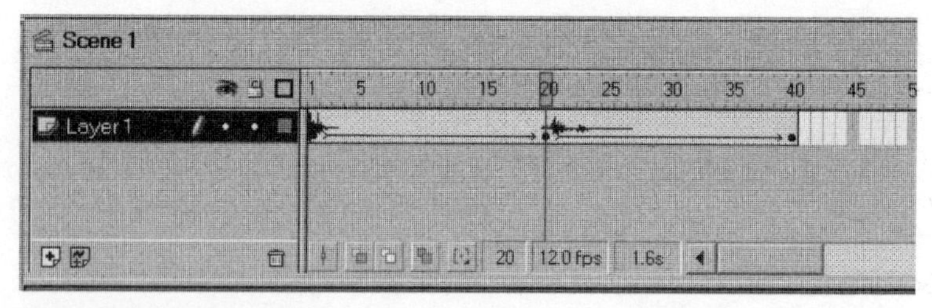

Fig.6.59 More than one sound can be used in each layer

this for the keyframe where the ball hits the cube, and again for the final frame where it stops. Add a few frames of motion tweening onto the end of the movie, but do not actually have anything move during these

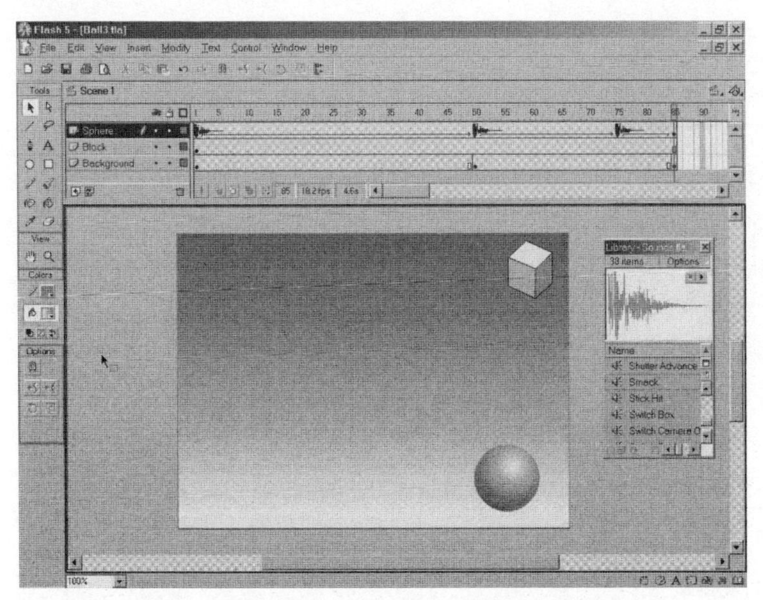

Fig.6.60 Adding sound to an earlier demonstration animation

frames. They are just somewhere for a final Smack sound to go. This is added to the final frame of the original version of the movie. You should then have something like Figure 6.60.

When the movie is run there is a Smack sound when the ball starts moving, another one when it bounces off the cube, and a third one when it stops. Synchronisation is not really a problem with simple sound effects of the type used here, because they are very short. The sound starts in the appropriate keyframe and soon fades away to nothing. Only the start of the sound has to be synchronised to the action and there is no need to worry about the exact point where it ends.

Sounds can be used in layers that contain graphics, but in practice it is generally more convenient if a separate layer is used for sounds. Since nothing on the sound layer will be displayed in the movie it does not matter where it is placed in the layer hierarchy. It will probably be most convenient if it is made the top or bottom layer.

Effects

These days computers are usually supplied complete with quite sophisticated sound systems, usually backed up by some sort of recording software so that you can record and edit you own sounds. Even so, it can be useful to provide some of the sound manipulation using Flash's sound editing facilities. Try producing a simple animation using tweening and then add a short sound in frame 1, preferably on its own layer. Select the frame that contains the sound and then launch the Sound panel. To do this choose Panels from the Window menu followed by Sound from the submenu that appears.

Fig.6.61 The Sound panel

The Sound panel (Figure 6.61) offers a limited but useful range of editing facilities. The Loop option enables a sound to be repeated a specified number of times, enabling a short sound to be stretched across as many

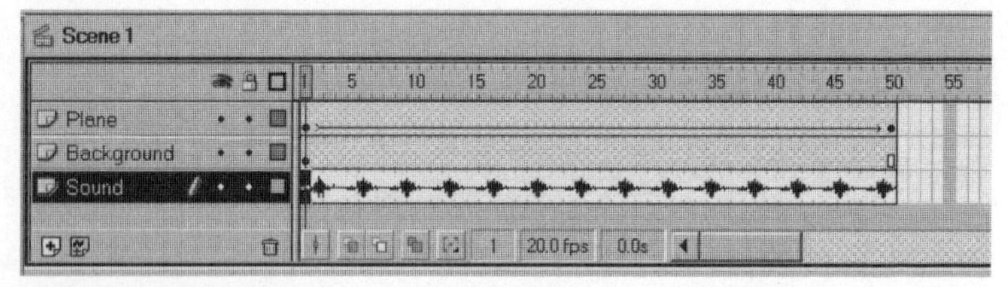

Fig.6.62 A looped sound in the sound layer of the Timeline

frames as required. However, bear in mind that repeating most sounds introduces a strong rhythmic effect, although this might be quite useful in some applications. If you add a number in the Loops textbox (about 10 or so should do) the Timeline should change to reflect the looping of the sound (Figure 6.62). Playing the movie will produce the looped

Fig.6.63 The first frame of the prop plane animation

Fig.6.64 The final frame of the animation

sound, and with a little trial and error it should be possible to adjust the number of loops so that the sound lasts more or less the same time as the movie.

Loop the loop

A little manipulation of the sound can often produce much more convincing results. Consider the animation shown in Figure 6.63 and 6.64, which are respectively the first and last frames. This is a variation on the earlier examples of a plane taking off, and in this case the plane is propeller driven. A sort burst of low frequency sound is looped in order to make the sound last until the end of the movie. A slight problem with this scheme of things is that the sound should fade out as the plane flies off into the distance, but with the looping technique there is no change in volume from one loop to the next. The Effect menu in the Sound panel offers various

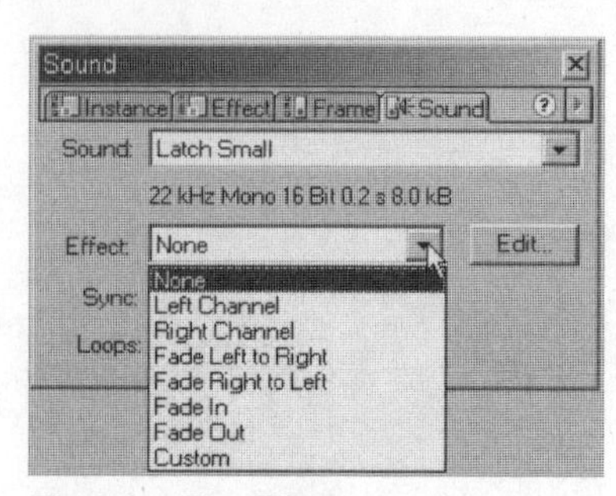

Fig.6.65 The Effect menu

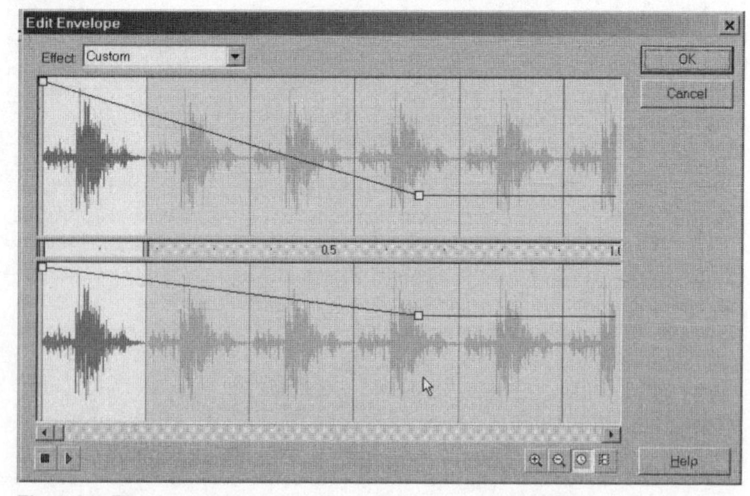

Fig.6.66 The envelopes of both channels can be edited

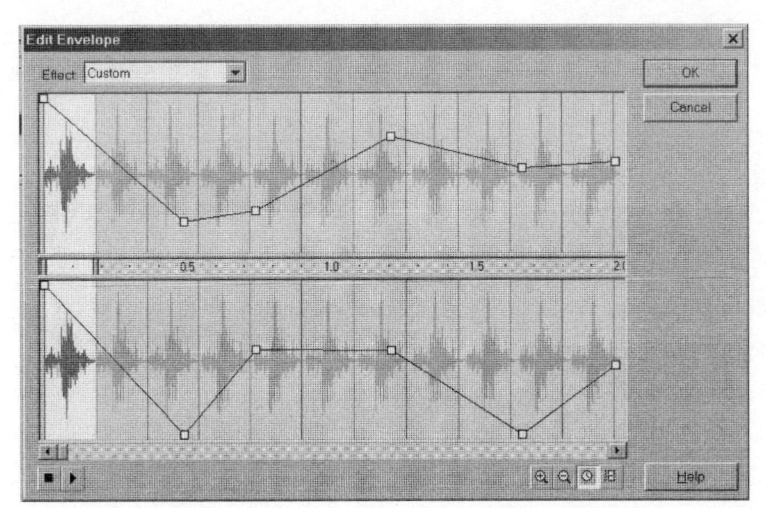

Fig.6.67 The display can be zoomed in, or zoomed out as in this example

options (Figure 6.65) governing the volume of sounds, including a Fade Out option. Unfortunately, this fades out the sound during each loop, and not over a number of loops.

The required action can be obtained by selecting the Custom option in the Effect menu, which brings up the Edit Envelope window (Figure 6.66). Monophonic sounds are normally played at equal volume in the left and right stereo channels. Here the signal is controlled separately in the two channels, with the top and bottom displays respectively representing the left and right channels. The two lines control the volume in each channel, and they can be used to produce quite elaborate changes if required. Left clicking on a line adds a node at that point in both channels, but different volume levels can be set in the two channels. The Stop and Play buttons in the bottom left-hand corner of the window enable changes to be tested easily. Using the + and – zoom buttons it is possible to zoom in on a short section of the sound, or zoom out to view a longer period (Figure 6.67).

Panning

Returning to the example of the plane taking off, the plane starts well over to the left of the screen so the left-hand channel should start at maximum volume with the right-hand channel set slightly lower. This places the apparent sound source over to the left of the sound stage. As the plane moves off into the distance it also moves across to the right. The sound should therefore be steadily reduced in volume in both channels, but it should be faded more in the left-hand channel. This gradually pans the apparent sound source across to the right and away from the listener. Some simple envelope shaping of this type can be very effective, and it is well worthwhile experimenting with this facility and some simple animations.

In the Event menu there is a Start option. There will probably be no apparent difference if this is chosen instead of the default Even setting. There is an important difference though, which is that the sound can not be triggered again if it is already running.

Stopping sounds

A sound can be prevented from continuing beyond the end of a movie by adding a Stop instruction in the final frame. Select the final frame in the sound layer and the choose the Blank Keyframe option from the Insert menu. Bring up the Sound panel by selecting the Panels option from the Window menu, and then Sound from the submenu that appears. Select the appropriate sound from the Sound menu, and then select Stop from the Sync menu. If the sound previously had a tendency to go on beyond the end of the movie, it should now switch off when the final frame is reached. Of course, sounds can be deliberately made slightly too long and then terminated in this fashion as a simple but effective means of synchronising the sound to the end of the movie.

Layer height

The default height of a layer used for sounds is 100 percent, which means that it is the same height as normal layers. It can be useful to increase the height to 200 or 300 percent so the waveform display can be seen more clearly. In order to do this, start by right clicking on the sound layer to produce a popup menu. Choose the Properties option from this menu, and the Layer Properties window will then appear (Figure 6.68). The menu at the bottom of the window offers the standard height plus 200 and 300 percent options. Figure 6.69 shows the sound layer with the height at 300 percent, and this gives a much improved waveform display.

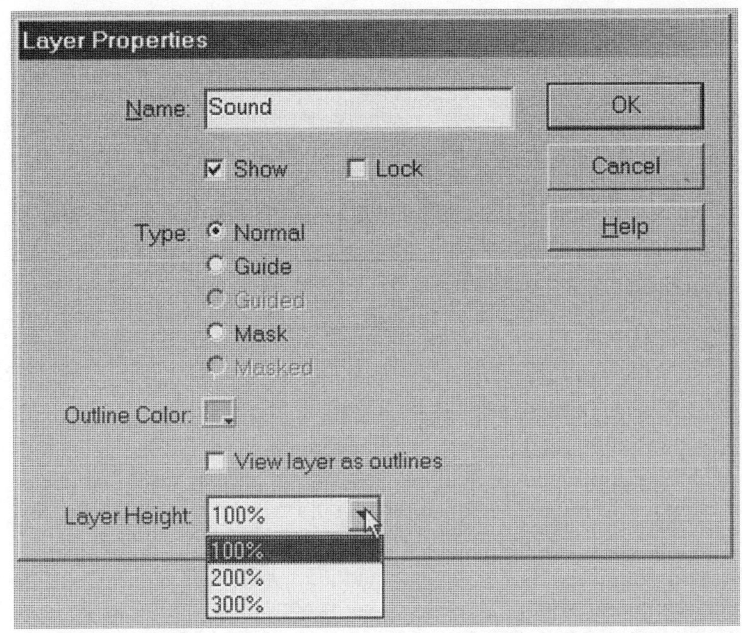

Fig.6.68 Altering the layer height using the Layer Properties window

Buttons and sound

Sounds are often used with buttons, and are generally used to add a simple "click" sound effect each time the button is operated. This makes it immediately clear to the user that the button has been operated successfully, a factor that is important if there is a delay between operating a button and anything happening as a result. The Flash sound library

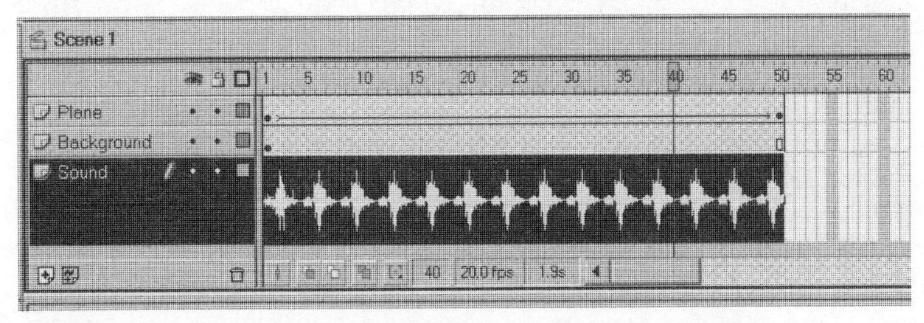

Fig.6.69 The Sound layer has the height set at 300 percent

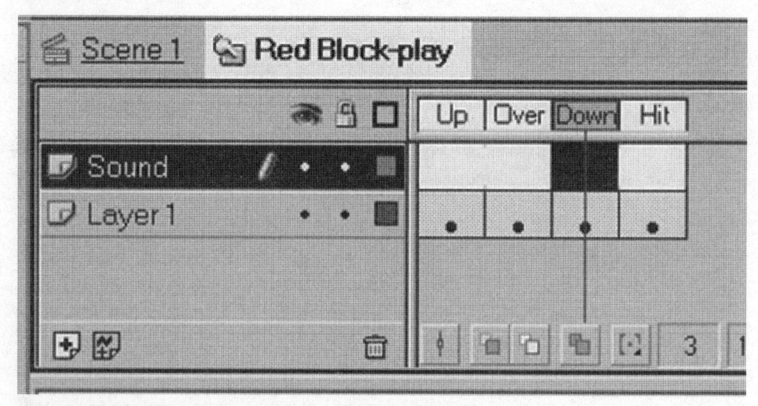

Fig.6.70 The Timeline prior to adding the sound

includes several sounds that are suitable for adding "click" effects to buttons. If you wish to use sound with buttons, start by setting up the animation and the buttons in the normal way.

To add sound to the first button, choose the Library option from the Window menu to bring up the Library window. Select the button you wish to add the sound to, and then left-click on the Options button near the top right-hand corner of the Library window. From the popup menu choose the Edit option, which takes the program into the symbol-editing mode. Add a new layer for the sound in the Timeline by left clicking the Timeline's Insert Layer button. Change the name of the layer to something appropriate such as Sound or Click.

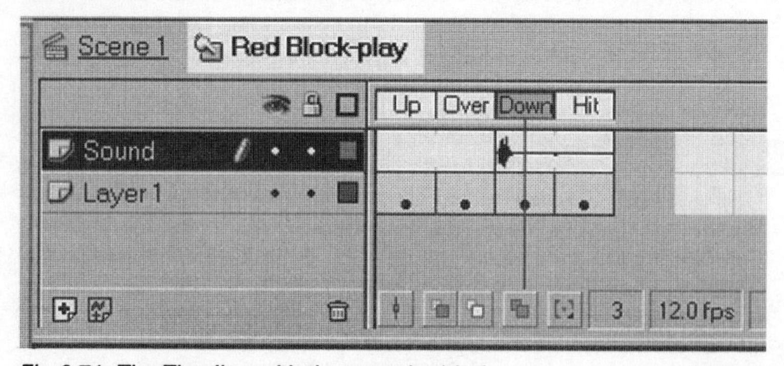

Fig.6.71 The Timeline with the sound added

Next select the Down frame in the new layer, or the Down and Over frames if you wish to add the sound to both states. Then select Blank Keyframe from the Insert menu. The Timeline should now look something like Figure 6.70. Finally, bring up the library window that contains the sound file for the button, and then drag the sound symbol into the work area. The waveform for the sound should then appear in the appropriate frame of the Timeline, as in Figure 6.71. Select the Edit Movie option from the Edit menu to return to the movie where the new sound effect can be tested. Repeat this process for any further buttons that are to be equipped with sound effects.

Interactive text

Flash has tremendous potential for adding interactivity via its Action Script programming language. Without learning a great deal about programming in this language, which is a subject that goes beyond the scope of this book, the possibilities are relatively limited. However, there are still some useful facilities that can be added without becoming an expert in Action Script. The basics of using buttons in movies were covered earlier in this chapter, and here things are taken a stage further by using a button to collect text from users and display it on the screen. In this exercise the user inputs some text via a textbox, and it is displayed in another textbox when the button is operated.

First a textbox is needed in order to take the text that will be provided by the user. Then another text box is needed to provide somewhere for the text to go when it is printed on the screen. Finally, we need the button that takes the text from the input textbox and prints it in the output textbox. There is actually a fourth stage to the process, and this is to write the short program that makes the button perform the required function. The program code can be produced using the normal popup menus, etc.

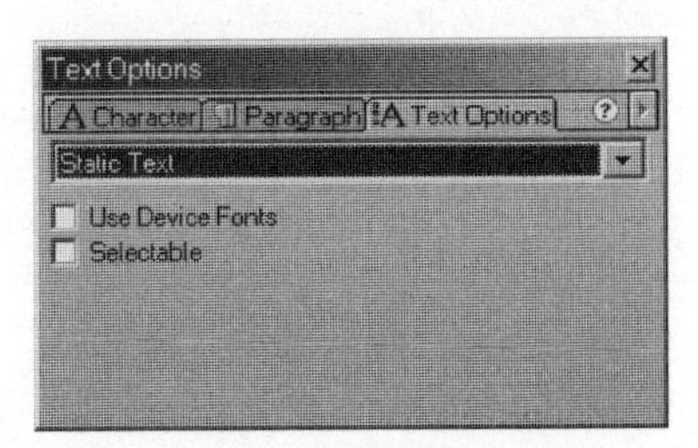

Fig.6.72 The Text Options panel

Start by using the Text tool to draw a box, which will act as the textbox that takes the text from the user. In this case only a name will be input, so this textbox does not have to be particularly large. One that will take about 20 or so characters should be more than adequate. With the box still present on

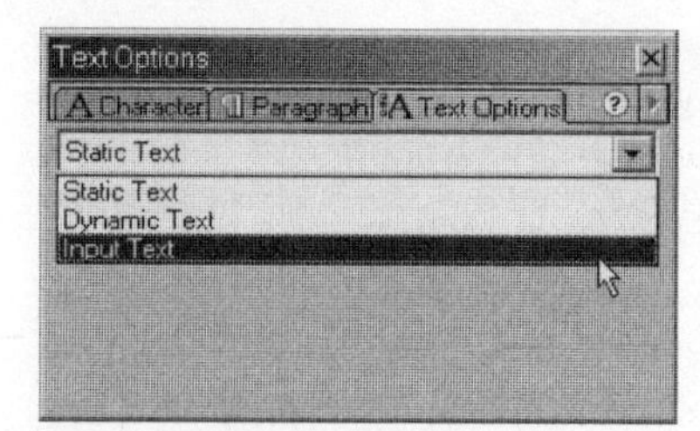

Fig.6.73 There are three options in the menu

the screen and effectively selected, choose the Panels option from the Window menu, and Text Options from the submenu. This will produce a panel like the one shown in Figure 6.72. The menu near the top of the panel offers three types of text (Figure 6.73), and as one would probably expect, it is the Input Text option that is required in this case. Several more options become available when Input Text is selected (Figure 6.74). The other menu offers single line text, multi-line text, and a password facility. In this example single line text will suffice, so leave it with the default setting.

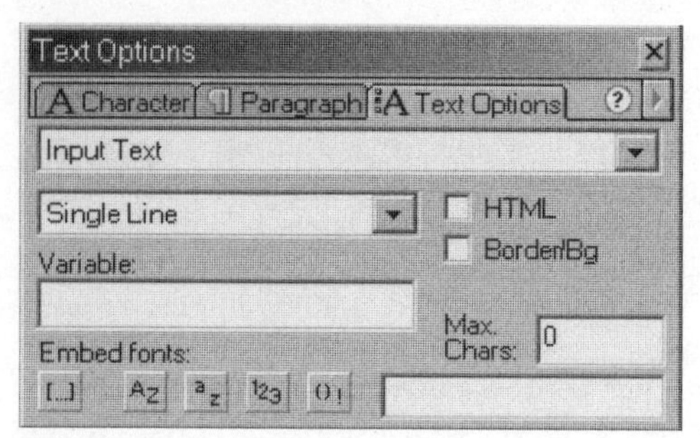

Fig.6.74 The Input Text options

Variables

The Variable textbox is used to enter a name for the text that will be entered into the box. If you have any experience at programming you will no doubt be familiar with variables, and they operate in Action Script in much the same way as with other programming languages. The text that is entered by the user is stored in the computer's memory, but it is difficult and inconvenient for programmers to deal directly with memory addresses. It is much easier to deal with a name such as "NameText" than to deal with an address such as "&H34AD65". With variables you give a piece of data a name, and then deal with it via that name. It is up to the programming language and the program it generates to keep track of memory addresses and make sure that the right data is always matched to each variable name.

The point of using a variable is that it makes it easy to deal with data that is not constant. In this example the user could enter any name, but it can always be called up and used by the program via the variable name.

The data is variable but the name is constant. Flash supplies default names for variables, but it is best to use more meaningful names of your own. Variable names in Flash can contain numbers and both upper and lower case letters. It is best to avoid spaces and other characters such as punctuation marks.

There are other options available from the Text Options panel, and a maximum number of characters can be set for the textbox for example. For this exercise just leave the default values for these. The BorderBg checkbox is an exception, and you may like to tick this one. A border will then be placed around the textbox.

The second textbox is produced in the same way as the first. Surprisingly perhaps, even though this textbox will be used to output text, the Input Text option is still selected from the menu. Data can be read from a variable, but it can also be changed by writing data to the variable. The Input Text option links the contents of a variable to a textbox, and that is what we require in both cases. Of course, the second variable must not be given the same name that was used for the first one.

Button code

Next the button is placed on the screen. One of the buttons in the Button library will do for this exercise. With the button selected, choose the Actions option from the Window menu, and the Object Actions panel will then appear. Left-click on the Basic Actions entry in the list on the left to expand it, and then double-click on the On Mouse Event entry. This will produce some code in the right-hand section of the window, and it will be in inverse video to indicate that it is selected. Change the event selected in the bottom section of the window if you wish. I used the Press option for this exercise. With the code still selected, left-click on the Actions entry to expand it and then double-click on the Set Variable entry. Some more code will then appear in the right-hand section of the window.

You should now have something like Figure 6.75, with some of the code highlighted in red to warn you that all is not well. The problem is simply that no name has yet been given for the variable that must be set, and we have not specified what it must be set to either. The variable assigned to the output text box is the one that must be set, and it must be set to the data contained in the input textbox's variable. Put the name of the output textbox's variable in the Variable field at the bottom of the Object Actions panel. Type the name of the variable assigned to the input textbox in the Value field beneath this.

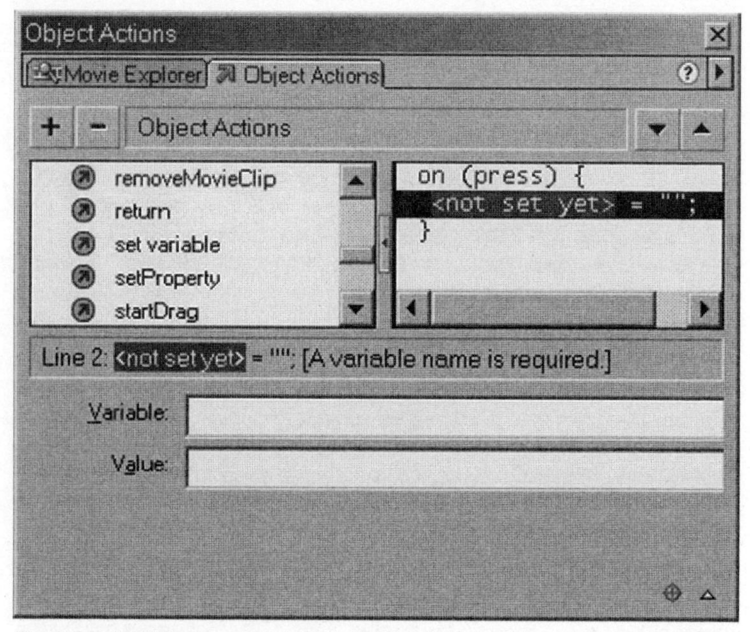

Fig.6.75 Adding the code in the Object Actions panel is accomplished via the icons or menus

Expressions

Even though it will not yet work properly, it is a good idea to use the Test Movie option of the Control menu to try out this version of the program. You should find that the program ignores the text entered into the input text box. Instead, when the button is operated the name of the input variable appears in the output text box. The problem is simply that the text entered in the Value field of the Object Actions window is being treated as the data to be written to the output textbox.

If you temporarily alter the text used in the Value field and try the program again, the new text will appear in the output textbox when the button is operated. This is a useful facility, enabling users to select the appropriate text by operating a button in a menu rather than having to type in the data. Obviously this method is not always applicable, but it is the best option to use where it is. It is clearly of little use with our name example, where it is necessary for the user to be able to enter any text.

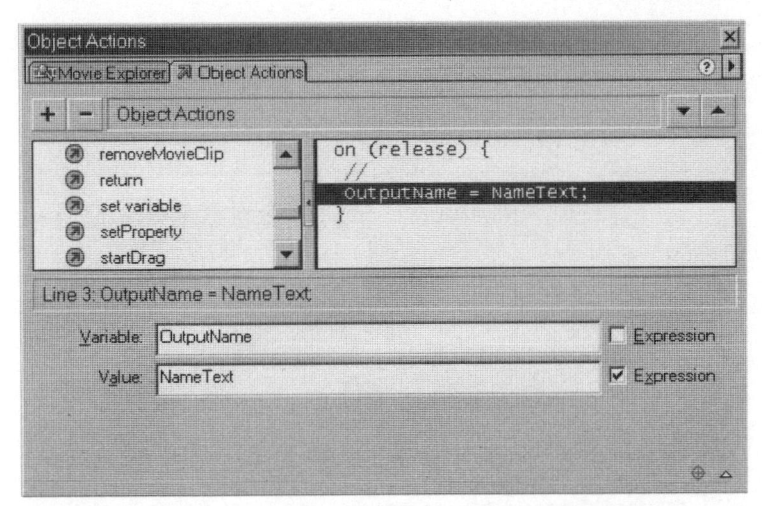

Fig.6.76 If necessary, widen the panel to reveal the checkboxes

The easy solution to the problem with the program is to tick the Expression checkbox next to the Value field. This may not be displayed by default, but can be brought into view by widening the Object Actions window (Figure 6.76). Ticking this box tells Flash that the text in the Value field is not to be taken literally and printed in the output textbox. It is a variable, a numeric value, or something of this nature. In this case the text matches the name of a variable, and that is the way that Flash will interpret it.

On running the program again you should find that it works properly. Figure 6.77 shows the program in operation. I have added some instructions at the top, which is definitely better than expecting users of the page to mind-read. My name has been added to the input textbox at the top, and in Figure 6.78 the button has been operated. This provides the required action and the input text has been transferred to the output textbox.

Expert mode

There is another way of altering the code so that Flash knows the text in the Value field is an expression. This is to manually alter the code, but this can not be done in the normal version of the Object Actions panel.

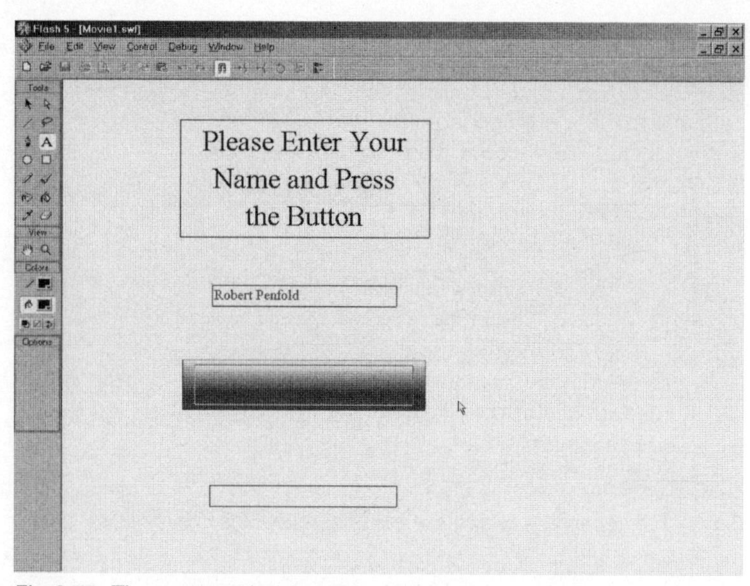

Fig.6.77 The program in operation, with my name entered

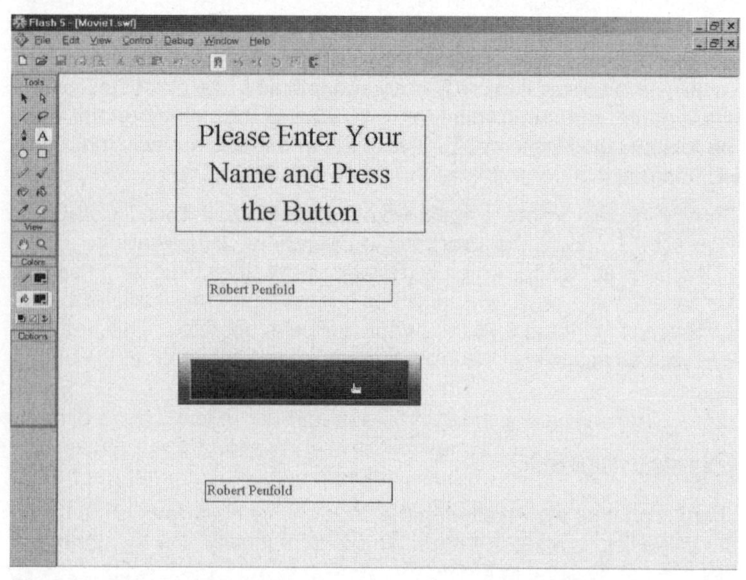

Fig.6.78 Pressing the button has completed the transfer

It has to be changed from Normal Mode to Expert Mode. This can be done by left clicking on the arrowhead near the top right-hand corner of the window. The popup menu of Figure 6.79 will appear, enabling the Expert Mode option to be selected. The Object Actions panel then looks something like Figure 6.80. In normal mode it is possible to select sections of code in the right-hand section of the window, but the code can not be edited other than erasing it. This restriction is removed in Expert Mode. The only alteration required is to remove the double quotation marks on either side of the input variable's name. Anything within quotation marks is used as data, but with these removed the name will be treated as an expression and the program should work.

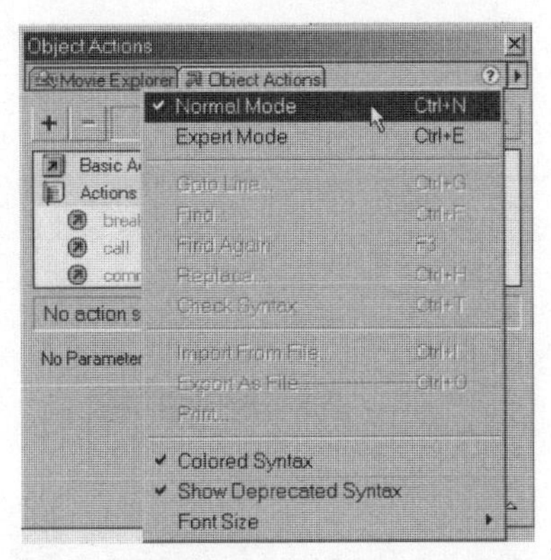

Fig.6.79 Switching to Expert Mode

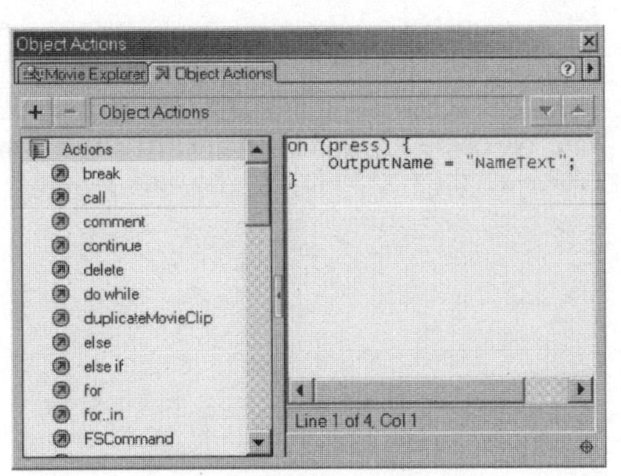

Fig.6.80 The Object Actions panel in Expert Mode

Moving text

Simply duplicating text entered by a user may not seem to be of much use, but remember that once text is in a variable it can be used in a variety of ways. Most of these require some programming expertise, while others are very straightforward. A typical use of text entered by the user is customised pages in a web site. For example, Instead of just saying welcome, a page can say welcome followed by the user's name. Text entered by the user can be used in animations.

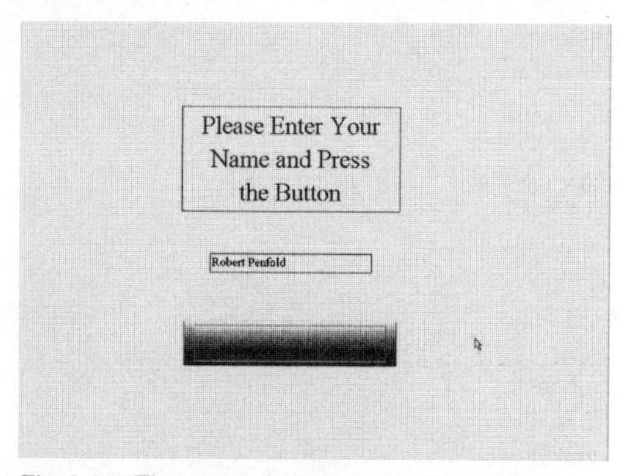

Fig.6.81 The name is entered in the textbox, as before

Figure 6.81 shows a modified version of the exercise featured previously. This is used as the first frame in a movie, so a Stop action has been added to this frame in order to halt the movie while the user enters their name. As before, operating the button assigns the text to a variable, but the textbox associated with this variable is not used in the first frame. The button also generates a Start action, moving things on to frame 2.

Frame 2 is shown in Figure 6.82, and here we have an image of a truck with "Welcome To" written on the side. There are three layers, and the truck is on the middle layer. The background is on the layer behind it,

Fig.6.82 In the next frame the name is placed on the side of a truck

and in this case just consists of a line to represent the road. Obviously a much more complicated background could be used if preferred. The output textbox containing the name input by the user is on the front layer. This is the textbox that was originally used in the first frame. Both the truck and this textbox are motion tweened so that they move across the screen together over the next 40 frames. Figures 6.83 and 6.84 respectively show frames 21 and 41. In this example the user's name has been placed on the side of a moving truck, but it could be used on a banner towed behind an aeroplane, or anything you like.

Fig.6.83 The truck, complete with name, on the move

Fig.6.84 The final frame of the truck movie

Running text

If you just require a simple running text display, this is easily achieved using Flash. Figure 6.85 shows the basic set-up needed to do this. The rectangle is a mask on a masking layer. The long line of text, which goes well outside the normal working area, is on a masked layer and is motion tweened. Figure 6.85 shows frame 1 of the tween, and Figure 6.86 shows the final frame. During the course of the tween the entire

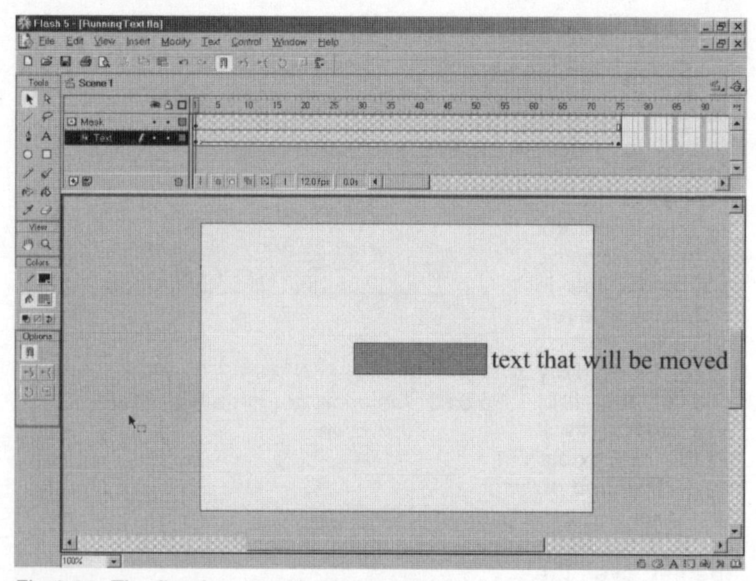

Fig.6.85 The first frame, with the beginning of the text masked

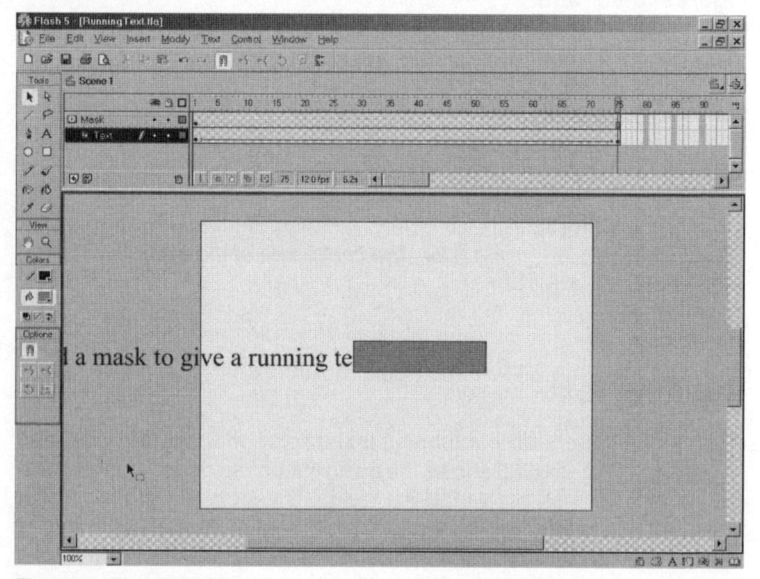

Fig.6.86 The final frame, with the end of the text masked

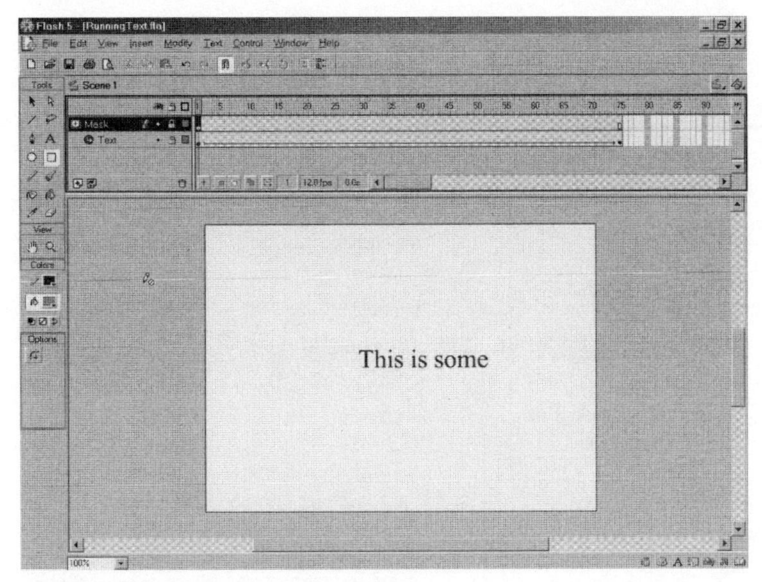

Fig.6.87 The first frame of the movie

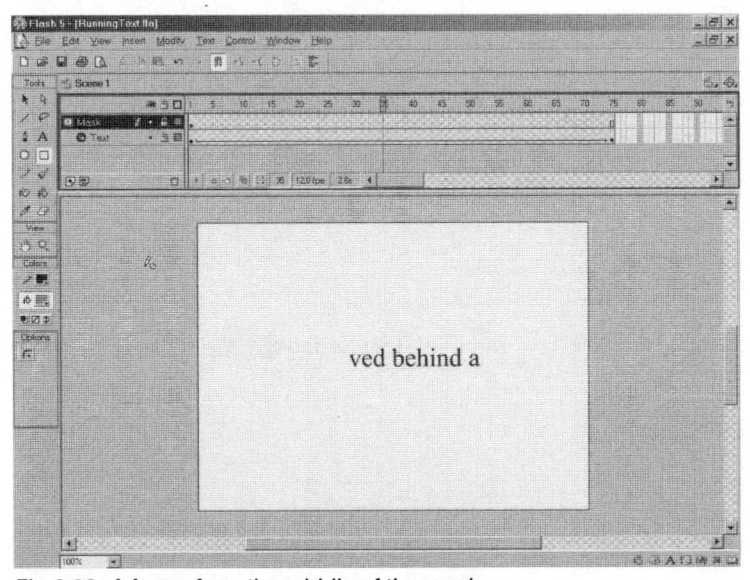

Fig.6.88 A frame from the middle of the movie

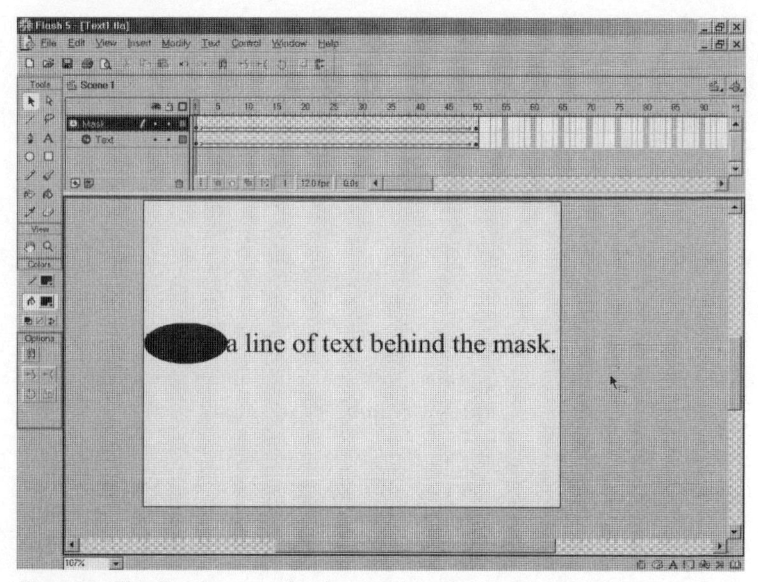

Fig.6.89 The first frame, with the mask at the start of the line

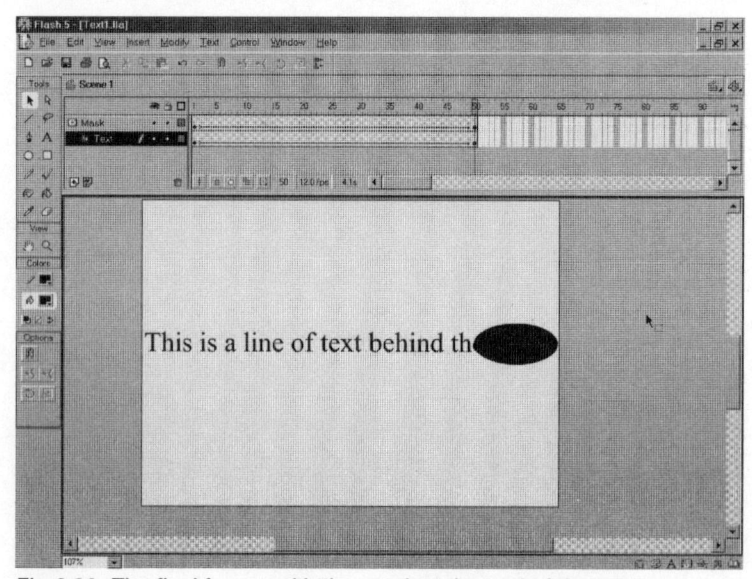

Fig.6.90 The final frame, with the mask at the end of the text

line of text is moved behind the mask, so that the text is readable from beginning to end during the movie. In Figure 6.87 the two layers have been locked so that the masking effect for frame 1 can be seen. A frame from the middle of the sequence is shown in Figure 6.88, and the required effect has been obtained, with the text moving behind the window provided by the mask. Of course, provided the page space is available, the mask can be the full width of the page, and with this type of thing it often is.

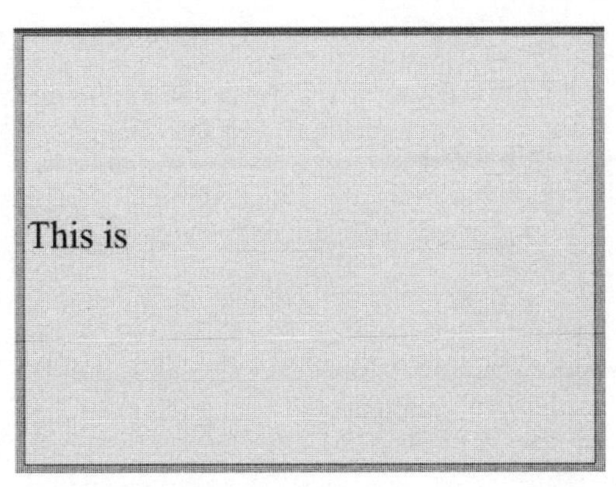

Fig.6.91 Frame 1 of the movie

Moving mask

The alternative method of using masking with text is to have a line of text across the page and a small mask that moves along the line, unmasking the text piece by piece. Figure 6.89 shows an arrangement of this type, with a line of text across the page and an elliptical mask at the beginning of the text. The mask is motion tweened so that it ends up at the other end of the text (Figure 6.90). Figure 6.91 shows frame 1 with the frames locked so that the masking effect is obtained. Figure 6.92 shows a later frame from the animation where the mask has moved further along the line of text. When doing this type of thing try to avoid having the

Fig.6.92 A frame from the middle of the movie

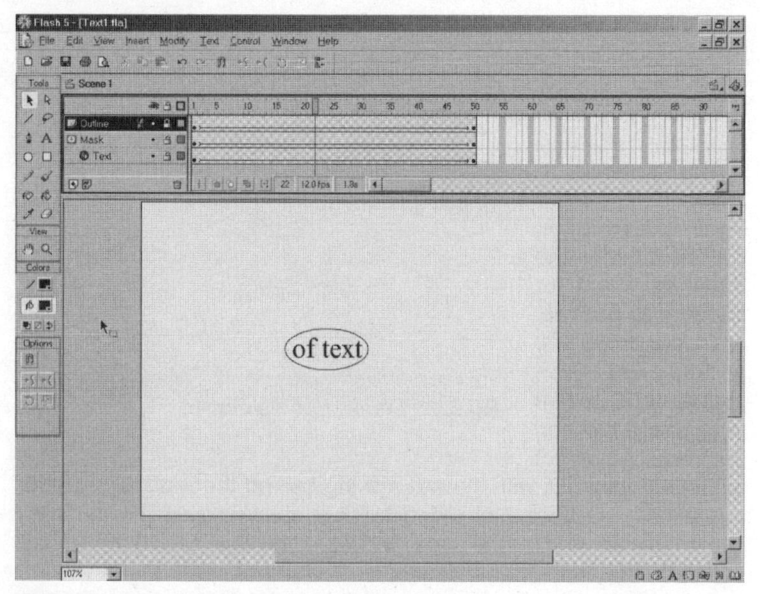

Fig.6.93 The border for the mask is actually on a separate layer

mask move too fast so that it is difficult to read the text. It is normal to have this type of thing repeat indefinitely so that users get more opportunities to read the text if they miss the beginning the first time around.

There are plenty of other possibilities with text and masks. In Figure 6.94 there is a similar set-up to the one used previously, with a line of text on one layer and a mask on another layer. The mask is again motion tweened. In this case the mask starts small and on the left, and gradually grows towards the right until it covers all the text (Figure 6.95). Of course, when the movie is run the opposite effect is obtained, with the text growing from the left side of the page until the entire line is revealed. Figure 6.96 shows the first frame of the movie, and Figure 6.97 shows a frame about half way through the sequence.

If you prefer to have a frame around the mask, this can be added on a third layer set in front of the other two. Copy the masking object from the masking layer to the new layer and then motion tween it to match the mask. This gives something like Figure 6.93, which shows a frame from the middle of the sequence.

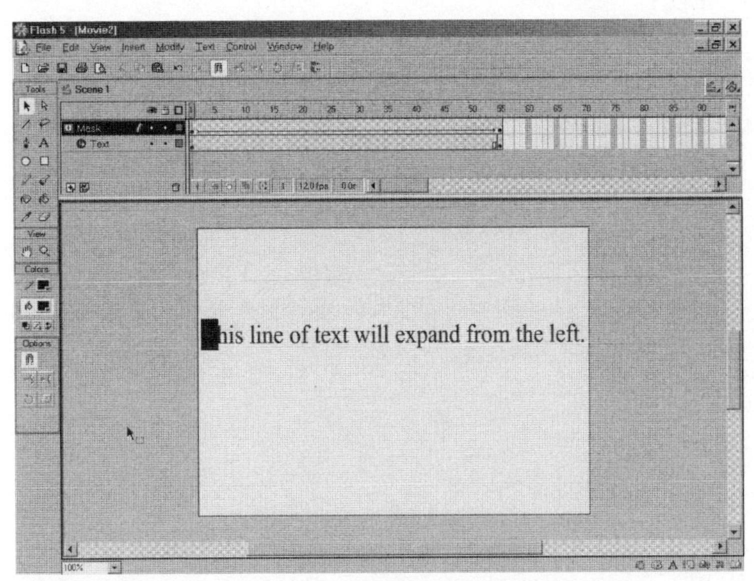

Fig.6.94 In frame 1 the mask is small and on the extreme left

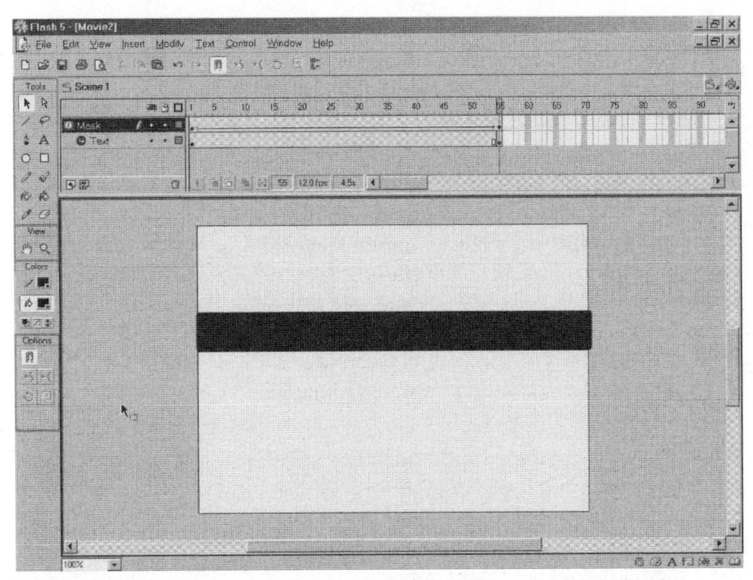

Fig.6.95 In the final frame the mask totally covers the line of text

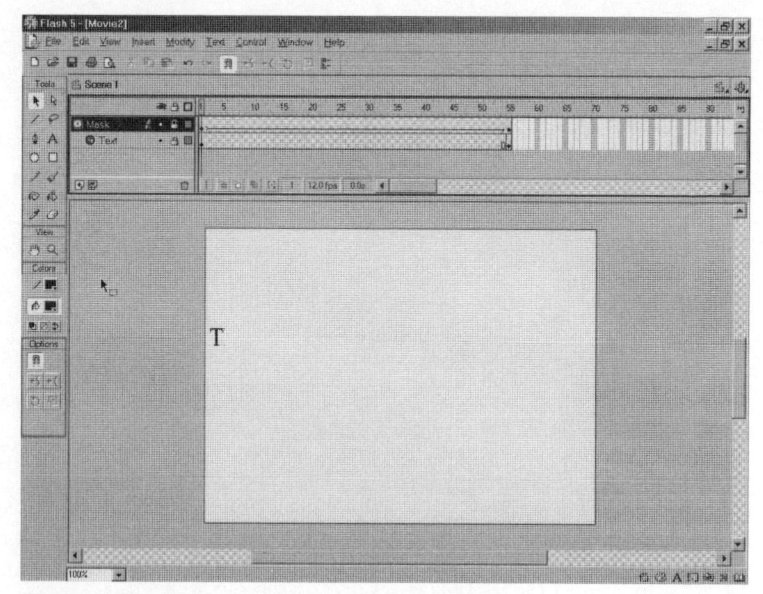

Fig.6.96 The first frame with both layers locked

Finally

In a book of this size it is impossible to cover all the capabilities of a program as complex as Flash. However, the main uses have been covered, such as simple Web animations with or without sound, buttons, and flashy text. Do not overlook Flash's abilities as a paint or illustration program. It is a vector graphics program, but it has many of the facilities and capabilities associated with paint programs, giving what could be regarded as the "best of both worlds". The Action Script programming gives tremendous scope for adding interactivity to Web pages, and it is something that is worthy of further study if you need to produce "clever" Web pages.

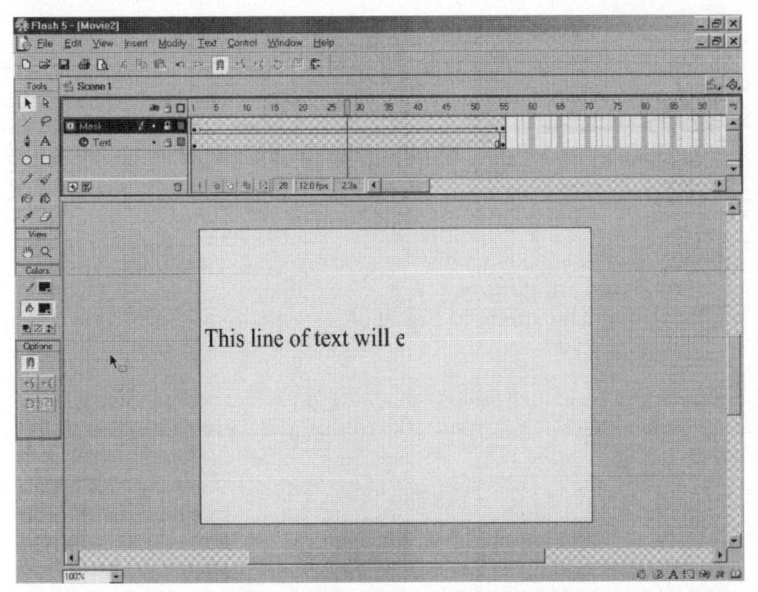

Fig.6.97 A frame near the middle of the sequence shows how the text seems to grow from the left-hand side of the stage

Points to remember

The usual typographic facilities are available when formatting text using Flash. Various text styles, fonts, and sizes are available, as are a full range of colours.

Indentation and various types of alignment (justification) are available for formatting paragraphs. Advanced features such as tracking adjustment and the ability to switch off kerning are also available.

Flash can be used to produce fancy headlines that can be used in Web pages using an HTML editor, or it can be used to produce complete HTML pages.

Flash text can be converted into graphics shapes, and it is then possible to safely use any font on your computer. The font will still be produced properly on users' computers, even if they do not have the correct font installed.

Using shape text you can even alter individual characters, since they can be edited like any other objects. Bear in mind that shape text uses far more memory than ordinary text, and that the normal text editing facilities are lost once text has been converted into shapes.

Buttons normally have three states, which are Up, Down, and Over. It is possible to have a totally different appearance in each of these states. The Hit state is used to define the active area of a button.

You can use buttons from the built-in library or designs downloaded from the Web. It is easy to make your own though.

Buttons can be used to provide links to Web pages, and to provide VCR style controls for Flash movies. This requires Action Script programs, but you do not have learn Action Script in order to undertake simple button programming. The programs can be produced via menus and panels.

Flash text can be made to respond to the mouse, permitting flashy headlines, etc., to be produced. This type of text is produced in the same way as buttons, and the pieces of text are effectively outsize buttons.

Buttons and textboxes can provide interactivity. For example, the user can enter text, and the text can then be used in animations.

The text entered by users is stored in variables, which are really memory locations in the computer. However, you just deal in the names assigned to the variables and the program takes care of the actual memory addresses.

Simple running text displays can be provided by motion tweening a long line of text behind a suitable mask on a masking layer.

Appendix

Useful Web addresses

http://www.macromedia.com

http://www.macromedia.com/support/dreamweaver/

http://www.macromedia.com/exchange/dreamweaver/

This is the web site of Macromedia Inc., the company that produces Flash. A fully working 30-day demonstration version of Flash can be downloaded from this site (Windows PC and Macintosh versions), and there are also demonstration versions of other Macromedia products available. The Dreamweaver and Fireworks programs are well worth trying. The second web address takes you direct to the Flash Support Centre. The third address is for the Flash Exchange, where various Flash extensions are available. These enable the capabilities of Flash to be increased. The extensions provided via this page are designed to be easy to install, but you do need to be reasonably expert with Flash.

http://www.extremeflash.com

This site provides tutorials for Flash users of all levels. There are also dozens of free Flash movies to try out.

http://www.flashplanet.com

Tutorials and articles are available from this site, as are further resources such as clipart, sounds, and the source code for some movies.

http://www.welcomesite.com

A site that makes extensive use of Flash, and also provides a number of Flash tutorials.

http://www.thesimpsons.com

This is the official web site of the popular cartoon family, and it makes extensive use of Flash. It shows what can be achieved using Flash if you have the time and ability.

http://www.macromedia.com/software/flash/gallery/collection

Part of the Macromedia site, use this page for a list of commercial sites that make use of Flash.

These web addresses have been checked, but note that web sites do sometimes change addresses. There are numerous sites devoted to Flash and related topics, so any search engine should provide a huge range of additional sites.

Index

A

B

C

D

O

P

R

S

W

Z

Notes

Notes